DIABETIC FOOD BIBLE

The Advanced Low-GI & Low-Carb Food Guide for Diabetics with a Step-by-Step Approach to Better Blood Sugar, Losing Weight, and Enjoying Flavorful Meals Without Sacrifice.

Julia Greenway

CONTENTS

The Science of Diabetes and Nutrition

Diabetes is one of the most pervasive health issues facing the world today. As a chronic disease, it affects millions of individuals, cutting across all demographics and regions. The global prevalence of diabetes has been rising at an alarming rate, transforming it into a significant public health challenge. According to the International Diabetes Federation, an estimated 537 million adults are living with diabetes, a number projected to increase to 643 million by 2030. This upward trend underscores the urgent need for effective strategies to manage and mitigate the impact of this disease.

Diabetes manifests primarily in three forms: Type 1, Type 2, and gestational diabetes, each with its unique characteristics and management needs. Type 1 diabetes is an autoimmune condition usually diagnosed in childhood, necessitating lifelong insulin therapy. Type 2 diabetes, the most common form, is closely linked to lifestyle factors and is characterized by insulin resistance and relative insulin deficiency. Gestational diabetes occurs during pregnancy and can have long-term health implications for both mother and child. Additionally, conditions like prediabetes signal an increased risk of developing Type 2 diabetes and cardiovascular diseases if left unmanaged.

The economic burden of diabetes is substantial. Direct medical costs, including hospital admissions, medications, and treatment for complications, combined with indirect costs such as lost productivity and disability, place a significant strain on both individuals and healthcare systems. In the United States alone, diabetes costs an estimated $327 billion annually. The human cost is equally, if not more, devastating, as diabetes can lead to severe complications such as heart disease, stroke, kidney failure, blindness, and lower limb amputations. These complications not only reduce the quality of life but also contribute to premature mortality.

Understanding the science behind diabetes and nutrition is crucial for several reasons. Firstly, it empowers individuals with the knowledge to make informed decisions about their health. Nutrition plays a pivotal role in managing blood glucose levels, which is central to diabetes care. By understanding how different foods impact blood sugar, individuals can tailor their diets to better control their condition and prevent complications.

Secondly, a comprehensive understanding of the interplay between diabetes and nutrition can guide healthcare providers in developing personalized treatment plans. With advancements in medical research, there is a growing recognition of the importance of individualized approaches to diabetes management. This includes not only pharmacological interventions but also lifestyle modifications centered around diet and exercise.

Lastly, public health strategies aimed at preventing diabetes can benefit significantly from insights into the relationship between diet and diabetes. By promoting healthier eating habits and increasing awareness about the risks associated with poor nutrition, we can potentially curb the rising tide of diabetes cases worldwide.

In this book, we delve into the intricate science of diabetes and nutrition, providing a thorough understanding of how these two domains intersect. We explore the different types of diabetes, the body's mechanisms for managing glucose, and the critical role of macronutrients and micronutrients. Additionally, we examine advanced nutritional knowledge, such as the impact of anti-inflammatory foods and the concept of food synergy, to offer a holistic approach to diabetes management.

TYPE 1 DIABETES

Type 1 diabetes is an autoimmune condition, typically diagnosed in children and young adults, but it can occur at any age. In this form of diabetes, the body's immune system mistakenly attacks and destroys insulin-producing beta cells in the pancreas. Insulin is a vital hormone that helps glucose, derived from the food we eat, enter cells to produce energy. The destruction of these cells leads to insulin deficiency, making external insulin administration essential for those with Type 1 diabetes.

The onset of Type 1 diabetes is usually sudden, presenting symptoms such as excessive thirst, frequent urination, hunger, weight loss, and fatigue. These symptoms arise because without insulin, glucose accumulates in the bloodstream instead of being utilized as energy by the body's cells. Managing Type 1 diabetes requires a careful regimen of insulin therapy, diet adjustments, and regular blood glucose monitoring to prevent acute complications like ketoacidosis and long-term complications, including damage to organs like the heart, kidneys, eyes, and nerves.

TYPE 2 DIABETES

Type 2 diabetes is the most common form of diabetes, affecting about 90% to 95% of those diagnosed with the disease. It typically develops in individuals over the age of 45, but in recent decades, it has increasingly been seen in younger ages, including adolescents and children. This type of diabetes is primarily characterized by insulin resistance, where the body's cells do not respond effectively to insulin, and eventually, the pancreas may not produce enough insulin to maintain normal glucose levels.

Risk factors for Type 2 diabetes include obesity, a sedentary lifestyle, genetics, and poor diet, with symptoms often developing gradually and being less marked than in Type 1. Some people might not even feel overt symptoms, which makes regular screening for those at risk significant. Management includes lifestyle interventions like diet and exercise improvements and, if necessary, medications to enhance insulin function and manage blood glucose levels. In some cases, insulin therapy may be required.

PREDIABETES

Prediabetes is a critical yet often overlooked condition that serves as a precursor to Type 2 diabetes. In prediabetes, blood sugar levels are higher than normal but not yet high enough to be classified as diabetes. It serves as a red flag for the risk of developing Type 2 diabetes and cardiovascular disease. Without intervention, many with prediabetes may progress to Type 2 diabetes within a few years.

Prediabetes often presents no clear symptoms, which underscores the importance of regular screening for those with risk factors similar to those for Type 2 diabetes. Lifestyle modifications such as enhancing diet quality, increasing physical activity, and achieving weight loss are proven strategies that can significantly delay or prevent the onset of Type 2 diabetes.

GESTATIONAL DIABETES

Gestational diabetes occurs during pregnancy and resembles Type 2 diabetes in that it involves insulin resistance. The hormones produced during pregnancy can make a woman's body more resistant to insulin. Gestational diabetes affects both the mother's and the baby's health. For the mother, it raises the risk of complications during pregnancy and delivery and increases the likelihood of developing Type 2 diabetes later in life. For the baby, it raises the risk of being born prematurely, at a high birth weight, and having low blood sugar levels.

Gestational diabetes is typically diagnosed through prenatal screening, rather than reported symptoms. Managing gestational diabetes involves monitoring blood glucose levels, adopting a healthy eating plan, performing regular physical activity, and, if necessary, insulin therapy.

Body's Glucose Management

The human body relies on a complex, finely tuned mechanism to manage glucose, which is a fundamental source of energy essential for cellular functions. This glucose management is primarily orchestrated by insulin, a hormone produced by the beta cells in the pancreas. Understanding how insulin facilitates glucose uptake and what goes awry in diabetes is crucial for grasping the challenges faced by individuals with this chronic condition.

INSULIN AND GLUCOSE UPTAKE

Under normal physiological conditions, the process begins when individuals consume food containing carbohydrates, which are broken down into simpler sugars such as glucose during digestion. This glucose enters the bloodstream, causing blood glucose levels to rise. In response, the beta cells of the pancreas secrete insulin.

Insulin serves as a key to unlocking cellular doors. Upon its release, insulin attaches to and signals insulin receptors on cell surfaces—particularly muscle, liver, and fat cells—initiating a cascade of reactions that lead to the cells' uptake of glucose. Here's how it happens:

Insulin interacts with insulin receptors, which activates a series of intracellular reactions. One of the pivotal outcomes of these reactions is the movement of glucose transporter type 4 (GLUT4) vesicles to the cell surface. GLUT4 is a protein that facilitates the transport of glucose across the cell membrane.

Once GLUT4 is embedded in the membrane, glucose can move from the bloodstream into the cell. This movement is driven by the concentration gradient—glucose levels are higher in the blood than in the cell, prompting its passage into the cell where it is lower.

Inside the cell, glucose is either used immediately to produce energy, through a process known as glycolysis, or stored for future use. In liver and muscle cells, excess glucose is stored as glycogen. This storage not only helps in regulating blood glucose levels but also provides a reserve of energy that can be mobilized during fasting or increased energy demands.

WHAT GOES WRONG IN DIABETES

In diabetes, this sophisticated system is disrupted, primarily in two ways, depending on the type of diabetes:

- In Type 1 diabetes, the immune system mistakenly attacks and destroys the beta cells of the pancreas, leading to little or no insulin production. Without insulin, GLUT4 transporters are not activated, which means glucose cannot enter most of the body's cells. As a result, despite the abundance of glucose in the bloodstream, cells are unable to access it for energy, leading to the classic symptoms of high blood sugar and cellular starvation.

- Type 2 diabetes involves a gradual decline in the body's response to insulin, known as insulin resistance, coupled eventually with an insulin secretion defect. Initially, the pancreas compensates for higher glucose levels by producing more insulin. However, as insulin receptors on cell surfaces become less responsive, more insulin is required to achieve the same effect, straining the pancreas and eventually leading to beta-cell dysfunction. Consequently, glucose accumulates in the bloodstream because it cannot be efficiently taken up by the cells.

CONSEQUENCES OF IMPAIRED GLUCOSE MANAGEMENT

The inability to effectively manage glucose levels has widespread consequences. Chronic high blood sugar can damage vessels that supply blood to vital organs, increasing the risk of heart disease and stroke, kidney disease, vision problems, and nerve problems. Elevated glucose levels can lead to increased production of free radicals and inflammatory cytokines, which further damage tissues and complicate insulin resistance. Despite high blood sugar levels, the inability of glucose to enter cells can lead to cell starvation, particularly impacting high-energy demanding organs like the brain and muscles.

Insulin Management and Innovations

People who have Type 1 diabetes or severe cases of Type 2 diabetes need to take insulin because their bodies either do not produce insulin or do not use it effectively.

Insulin management has seen significant advancements in recent years, offering individuals with diabetes more precise and convenient options to control their blood glucose levels. Traditional methods of insulin delivery, such as multiple daily injections, have been supplemented and, in some cases, replaced by innovative technologies that improve both the efficacy and ease of diabetes management.

One of the most notable advancements is the development of insulin pumps. These small, computerized devices deliver continuous subcutaneous insulin infusion throughout the day. By mimicking the body's natural insulin release, insulin pumps provide a more stable and controlled delivery, reducing the risk of blood sugar spikes and drops. Users can program their pumps to release insulin at variable rates to suit their personal needs, such as during meals or physical activity, allowing for more flexible and responsive diabetes management.

Smart insulin pens represent another leap forward in insulin delivery. These devices integrate with smartphone apps to track insulin doses, timing, and even the insulin temperature. This digital connectivity helps users avoid missed doses, reduces the risk of dosing errors, and provides valuable data for both the patient and healthcare provider to fine-tune insulin therapy. The convenience and intelligence of smart insulin pens empower users with greater control and insights into their diabetes management.

The advent of closed-loop systems, often referred to as artificial pancreas systems, marks a revolutionary shift in diabetes care. These systems combine continuous glucose monitors (CGMs) and insulin pumps to automate insulin delivery based on real-time glucose readings. The closed-loop system continuously adjusts insulin delivery to maintain optimal glucose levels, significantly reducing the burden of constant monitoring and manual adjustments. This technology not only enhances glucose control but also improves the quality of life for those living with diabetes by minimizing the frequency of hypoglycemic events and providing peace of mind.

In addition to advancements in insulin delivery methods, there has been progress in non-insulin medications that offer alternative or supplementary treatment options for managing diabetes. GLP-1 receptor agonists are a class of drugs that enhance the body's natural insulin secretion in response to meals. They also slow gastric emptying and promote satiety, which can aid in weight management—a critical aspect of diabetes care. GLP-1 receptor agonists can be particularly beneficial for individuals with Type 2 diabetes who struggle with obesity or have not achieved desired glucose control with insulin alone.

SGLT2 inhibitors are another group of non-insulin medications that have garnered attention for their effectiveness in diabetes management. These drugs work by blocking the reabsorption of glucose in the kidneys, leading to the excretion of excess glucose through urine. This mechanism helps lower blood glucose levels and offers additional benefits, such as reducing blood pressure and promoting weight loss. SGLT2 inhibitors have also been shown to confer cardiovascular and renal protection, making them a valuable option for many patients with Type 2 diabetes.

Other non-insulin medications, such as DPP-4 inhibitors and amylin analogs, further expand the arsenal of treatments available for diabetes management. DPP-4 inhibitors increase insulin release and decrease glucagon levels by enhancing the incretin system, providing another pathway to improve glycemic control. Amylin analogs, which mimic the hormone amylin co-secreted with insulin, slow gastric emptying and suppress glucagon secretion, thereby aiding in postprandial glucose management.

Nutritional Foundations: Carbohydrates, Proteins, and Fats

Macronutrients are the pillars of any diet, and understanding their roles and effects on the body is crucial, particularly for individuals managing diabetes. Carbohydrates, proteins, and fats each play unique roles in bodily functions and metabolic processes, and their management is key in controlling diabetes.

CARBOHYDRATES

Carbohydrates are the body's primary energy source. They are broken down into glucose, which enters the bloodstream and triggers the release of insulin, the hormone that helps glucose enter the body's cells to be used for energy. In diabetes, this process is impaired, which can lead to elevated blood glucose levels after eating carbohydrate-rich foods.

There are two main types of carbohydrates: simple and complex. Simple carbohydrates, found in foods like sugar, honey, and fruits, are quickly digested and can cause rapid spikes in blood sugar levels. Complex carbohydrates, found in whole grains, legumes, and vegetables, are digested more slowly and result in a more gradual increase in blood sugar levels. For individuals with diabetes, complex carbohydrates are preferable because they help maintain more stable blood glucose levels and provide sustained energy.

PROTEINS

Proteins are essential components of every cell in the body and are crucial for building and repairing tissues, making enzymes and hormones, and supporting immune function. Unlike carbohydrates, proteins do not cause a significant rise in blood glucose levels, making them a key component of a diabetic diet.

For people with diabetes, protein intake can help improve blood sugar control by providing energy without contributing to significant glucose fluctuations. Additionally, protein has a satiating effect, which can help reduce overall calorie intake and assist in weight management. However, it is important to choose lean protein sources, such as chicken, turkey, fish, and plant-based proteins like beans and lentils, to avoid excess intake of saturated fats, which can contribute to cardiovascular disease—a common complication in individuals with diabetes.

FATS

Fats are the most energy-dense macronutrient and play a vital role in supporting cell growth, protecting organs, and keeping the body warm. Fats also help the body absorb certain nutrients and produce important hormones. In the context of diabetes, the type of fat consumed is of paramount importance.

Monounsaturated and polyunsaturated fats, found in foods like nuts, seeds, avocados, and oily fish, can have beneficial effects on heart health. These fats can help reduce bad cholesterol levels and lower the risk of heart disease and stroke. This is particularly important for people with diabetes, who are at an increased risk for these conditions.

Conversely, saturated fats and trans fats should be limited. These fats, found in many fried foods, baked goods, and processed snacks, can increase cardiovascular risks by raising bad cholesterol levels and promoting inflammation. For diabetics, consuming high amounts of unhealthy fats can exacerbate heart health risks and interfere with the effective management of blood glucose levels.

The Role of Fiber and Fats in Enhancing Insulin Sensitivity

The management of diabetes involves not only monitoring carbohydrate intake but also understanding the significant roles that dietary fiber and fats play in maintaining insulin sensitivity and overall metabolic health. A nuanced approach that includes these nutrients can drastically improve blood glucose control and reduce the risk of diabetes complications.

THE MULTIFACETED FUNCTIONS OF DIETARY FIBER

Dietary fiber, found in various plant foods, is a crucial element for digestive health and blood sugar management. Fiber is categorized mainly into two types: soluble and insoluble. Soluble fiber dissolves in water to form a gel-like substance, which helps slow down the digestion and absorption of carbohydrates. This slower absorption helps prevent sudden spikes in blood glucose and insulin levels, which is crucial for managing diabetes. Sources of soluble fiber include oats, legumes, nuts, seeds, and some fruits and vegetables.

Insoluble fiber, on the other hand, does not dissolve in water and adds bulk to the diet, aiding in regular bowel movements and preventing constipation, which is often a concern for diabetic patients, especially those on medication. This type of fiber is abundant in whole grains, wheat bran, and vegetables.

The overall impact of fiber extends beyond digestion. It also influences the gut microbiota, a key player in metabolic health. High-fiber diets support a diverse and stable gut microbial community, which in turn helps regulate immune function, reduce inflammation, and enhance insulin sensitivity. The interaction between dietary fiber and gut bacteria also produces short-chain fatty acids (SCFAs) like acetate, propionate, and butyrate, which have been shown to possess anti-inflammatory properties and to improve insulin response.

HEALTHY FATS AND THEIR IMPACT ON INSULIN SENSITIVITY

While dietary fat once had a predominantly negative connotation in diabetes management, modern research highlights the importance of fat quality over quantity. Particularly, monounsaturated and polyunsaturated fats are shown to have beneficial effects on insulin sensitivity and overall cardiovascular health.

Monounsaturated fats (MUFAs) are particularly effective in managing blood lipid profiles and improving insulin sensitivity. They help reduce low-density lipoprotein (LDL) cholesterol levels while maintaining or increasing high-density lipoprotein (HDL) cholesterol levels. Regular intake of foods rich in MUFAs, such as olive oil, avocados, and certain nuts like almonds and peanuts, can thus be beneficial for people with diabetes.

Polyunsaturated fats (PUFAs), including omega-3 and omega-6 fatty acids, play critical roles in cellular function and maintain the fluidity of cell membranes, which helps insulin function more effectively. Omega-3 fatty acids, found in fatty fish like salmon, mackerel, and sardines, as well as in flaxseeds and walnuts, are particularly known for their anti-inflammatory effects. Reducing inflammation can help improve insulin resistance, which is a hallmark of type 2 diabetes.

DIETARY RECOMMENDATIONS FOR FIBER AND HEALTHY FATS

Given their significant health benefits, incorporating an adequate amount of fiber and healthy fats into the diet is crucial for individuals managing diabetes. The general dietary recommendations suggest that adults should consume a minimum of 25-30 grams of fiber per day. However, starting slowly and increasing fiber intake gradually along with adequate fluid can help prevent potential gastrointestinal discomfort.

For fats, the focus should be on replacing saturated and trans fats with monounsaturated and polyunsaturated fats. While no specific minimum intake exists for MUFAs and PUFAs, they should constitute the majority of dietary fat intake. The American Diabetes Association recommends that the total fat intake should not exceed 20-35% of the total daily calories, with less than 7% from saturated fat and minimal amounts from trans fats.

Practical implementations of these recommendations include choosing whole fruits over juices, integrating whole grains like quinoa and barley into meals, opting for lean proteins, and using oils rich in MUFAs and PUFAs for cooking and dressings. Nuts and seeds can be excellent snacks due to their fiber and healthy fat content.

Strategies for Blood Sugar Management

Achieving a balanced diet is crucial for everyone, but it takes on additional significance for individuals managing diabetes. A well-balanced diet can help maintain blood sugar levels within a normal range, reduce the risk of diabetic complications, and enhance overall well-being. Here, we delve into strategies to craft a diet that not only supports but enhances blood sugar management.

PORTION CONTROL

Portion control is a critical component of a balanced diet, particularly for those with diabetes. Eating excessive portions, even of healthy foods, can lead to weight gain and higher blood glucose levels. Using tools like measuring cups, scales, or even visual comparisons (for instance, a portion of meat should be the size of a deck of cards) can help manage portion sizes effectively.

Plate method is another helpful strategy for portion control and ensuring a balanced meal. This method involves filling half of the plate with non-starchy vegetables, one quarter with lean protein, and the remaining quarter with a complex carbohydrate source. This visual guide helps ensure that meals are balanced and portions are controlled.

MEAL TIMING AND FREQUENCY

The timing and frequency of meals can also affect blood sugar control. Eating regular meals and snacks can help prevent the highs and lows of blood sugar levels. It is generally recommended to eat every 3-5 hours to maintain a stable energy level and prevent overeating, which can lead to spikes in blood sugar.

Skipping meals, particularly breakfast, can lead to higher blood glucose levels later in the day. This is due to hormonal changes that increase blood glucose as part of the body's response to perceived starvation. Therefore, establishing a regular eating pattern can support better blood sugar management and overall metabolic health.

INCORPORATING DIETARY FIBER

Dietary fiber plays a significant role in a balanced diet for diabetes management. Fiber, particularly soluble fiber, can slow the absorption of sugar and help improve blood sugar levels. It can also help to lower cholesterol and promote a feeling of fullness, aiding in weight control which is beneficial for improving insulin sensitivity.

Foods rich in fiber such as fruits, vegetables, whole grains, and legumes should be included in daily meals. The aim should be to consume at least 25-30 grams of fiber per day. Gradually increasing fiber intake along with adequate fluid intake can help prevent digestive disturbances like gas and bloating, which can occur with sudden high fiber consumption.

LIMITING SUGARS AND REFINED CARBOHYDRATES

Managing intake of sugars and refined carbohydrates is critical for maintaining balanced blood sugar levels. These foods cause rapid spikes in glucose and insulin levels, which can be particularly problematic for people with diabetes. Avoiding sugary beverages, sweets, and refined carbohydrate-rich foods like white bread and pastries is essential.

Instead, focusing on natural sources of carbohydrates that are rich in fiber and have a lower glycemic index can be beneficial. Reading food labels carefully to identify hidden sugars and choosing whole or minimally processed foods can significantly aid in managing blood sugar.

MONITORING AND ADJUSTMENT

Finally, continuous monitoring and adjustment of dietary habits are necessary to maintain a balanced diet that supports diabetes management. Regularly checking blood glucose levels can help assess how well the diet is working and whether any adjustments are needed. Consulting with a healthcare provider or a dietitian can provide personalized advice and adjustments based on individual health needs, preferences, and lifestyle.

Glycemic Index, Glycemic Load, and Their Impact on Diabetes

The concepts of Glycemic Index (GI) and Glycemic Load (GL) are pivotal in managing diabetes and maintaining stable blood sugar levels. Both metrics are used to describe how different foods and meals impact blood glucose levels, allowing individuals with diabetes to make informed dietary choices.

GLYCEMIC INDEX: A MEASURE OF BLOOD SUGAR IMPACT

Glycemic Index is a scale that ranks carbohydrates on a scale from 0 to 100, based on how quickly and significantly they raise blood glucose levels after eating. Foods with a high GI are rapidly digested and absorbed, resulting in marked fluctuations in blood sugar levels. Conversely, foods with a low GI are digested and absorbed more slowly, producing a gradual, smaller rise in blood sugar and insulin levels.

For example, white bread has a high GI and can cause a swift increase in blood glucose. In contrast, whole-grain bread has a lower GI, leading to a more moderate and steady glucose response. This ranking helps individuals with diabetes choose foods that can maintain more stable blood glucose levels.

Foods are generally classified into three GI categories:

- Low GI: 55 or less
- Medium GI: 56 to 69
- High GI: 70 or higher

Low GI foods include legumes, non-starchy vegetables, some starchy vegetables like sweet potatoes, most fruit, and many whole grains such as barley and oats. Medium GI foods include some rices, whole wheat products, and rye bread. High GI foods typically include white bread, rice, and potatoes, but also some fruits like watermelons and dates, which despite their natural sugar content, spike blood glucose levels rapidly.

GLYCEMIC LOAD: A MORE PRACTICAL APPROACH

While the glycemic index provides valuable information about carbohydrate-containing foods, it does not account for the amount of carbohydrate typically eaten in a serving. Glycemic Load addresses this by combining the GI with the carbohydrate content in a typical serving to give a more comprehensive picture of a food's impact on blood sugar levels.

To calculate the GL of a food, you multiply its GI by the amount of carbohydrates in grams provided by a serving and then divide by 100. For instance, while carrots have a medium GI, they have a low GL because they contain very few carbohydrates per serving. This makes the glycemic load a more practical metric for everyday use.

For practical purposes, GL values are classified as:

- Low GL: 10 or less
- Medium GL: 11 to 19
- High GL: 20 or more

A food's GL can help individuals with diabetes understand how much a particular food will affect their blood sugar levels and thus manage their diet more effectively. For example, while watermelon has a high GI, its GL is relatively low, meaning it has a smaller impact on glucose levels than one might expect based on GI alone. This helps clarify dietary choices, enabling more precise control over glucose levels.

PRACTICAL APPLICATIONS IN DIET PLANNING

Understanding and utilizing the concepts of GI and GL can significantly enhance diet planning for individuals with diabetes. By focusing on low GI and low GL foods, they can ensure more stable blood glucose levels, which is crucial for long-term management of diabetes.

Incorporating low GI and low GL foods into meals also means that the body's insulin response is more controlled, avoiding the peaks and troughs that can occur with higher GI/GL diets. This can help in reducing cravings and energy dips, ultimately leading to better metabolic control.

Moreover, understanding these concepts empowers individuals to make smarter food choices. For instance, replacing a portion of mashed potatoes (high GI and GL) with a side of lentils (low GI and moderate GL) not only adds nutritional variety but also improves the meal's overall glycemic impact.

Micronutrients

Micronutrients are vitamins and minerals required by the body in small quantities to perform essential physiological functions. Despite their small required amounts, they play critical roles in maintaining health, particularly for individuals managing chronic conditions such as diabetes. Proper intake of essential micronutrients can significantly influence blood sugar control, insulin sensitivity, and overall metabolic health. Three key micronutrients that are particularly important in diabetes management are magnesium, chromium, and vitamin D.

MAGNESIUM

Magnesium is a crucial mineral involved in over 300 enzymatic reactions in the body, including those related to glucose metabolism and insulin action. It plays a pivotal role in maintaining normal muscle and nerve function, supporting a healthy immune system, and keeping bones strong. For individuals with diabetes, magnesium is particularly important because it helps regulate blood sugar levels by enhancing insulin's effectiveness. Studies have shown that magnesium deficiency is common in people with diabetes and can worsen insulin resistance. Dietary sources of magnesium include leafy green vegetables like spinach, nuts and seeds such as almonds and pumpkin seeds, whole grains like brown rice and oats, and legumes including black beans and lentils. Ensuring adequate magnesium intake can help improve insulin sensitivity and glycemic control.

CHROMIUM

Chromium is another essential mineral that plays a significant role in carbohydrate and lipid metabolism. It enhances the action of insulin, making it more efficient at helping glucose enter cells, thereby aiding in blood sugar regulation. Chromium is also involved in the metabolism of fats and proteins, contributing to overall metabolic health. Deficiency in chromium can lead to impaired glucose tolerance and increased insulin resistance, which are key challenges in managing diabetes. Good dietary sources of chromium include broccoli, whole grains such as barley and oats, nuts, and meat, particularly liver. Incorporating these foods into the diet can help maintain adequate chromium levels, supporting better blood sugar control and insulin function.

VITAMIN D

Vitamin D, often referred to as the "sunshine vitamin", is essential for bone health, immune function, and inflammation regulation. It also has a significant impact on insulin sensitivity and glucose metabolism. Research suggests that vitamin D deficiency is associated with an increased risk of developing Type 1 and Type 2 diabetes, as well as poorer glycemic control in those already diagnosed with the condition. Vitamin D helps regulate calcium and phosphorus levels in the blood, which are important for maintaining healthy bones and teeth. It also plays a role in modulating the immune system and reducing inflammation, both of which are critical in preventing the chronic inflammation associated with diabetes. Natural sources of vitamin D include fatty fish such as salmon and mackerel, fortified foods like milk and orange juice, and exposure to sunlight, which stimulates vitamin D production in the skin. For individuals who have limited sun exposure or dietary intake, vitamin D supplements may be necessary to achieve optimal levels.

B VITAMINS

B vitamins, including B1 (thiamine), B2 (riboflavin), and B6 (pyridoxine), are vital for energy metabolism and neural function. Thiamine (B1) is crucial for the conversion of carbohydrates into energy, which is particularly important for glucose metabolism. Thiamine also plays a role in nerve function and can help prevent diabetic neuropathy, a common complication of diabetes. Good sources of thiamine include whole grains, legumes, nuts, and seeds, as well as pork and fortified cereals.

Riboflavin (B2) is essential for cellular energy production and the metabolism of fats, drugs, and steroids. It also helps maintain healthy skin and eyes, which are areas often affected by diabetes-related complications. Riboflavin can be found in dairy products, eggs, green leafy vegetables, lean meats, and fortified cereals. Ensuring an adequate intake of riboflavin can support overall metabolic health and help manage the physical stresses associated with diabetes.

Pyridoxine (B6) is involved in more than 100 enzyme reactions in the body, many of which relate to protein metabolism. B6 is also crucial for cognitive development, immune function, and the production of neurotransmitters. It helps in the conversion of stored glycogen to glucose, which is essential for maintaining stable blood sugar levels. Sources of pyridoxine include poultry, fish, potatoes, chickpeas, bananas, and fortified cereals. Adequate intake of B6 is particularly important for preventing nerve damage and supporting mental health in people with diabetes.

ZINC

Zinc is a trace mineral that plays a pivotal role in insulin synthesis, storage, and release. It also contributes to immune function, wound healing, and DNA synthesis. Zinc deficiency can impair insulin production and exacerbate the symptoms of diabetes. Furthermore, zinc has antioxidant properties that help protect cells from oxidative stress, a common issue in diabetes. Rich dietary sources of zinc include meat, shellfish, legumes, seeds, nuts, dairy products, and whole grains. Ensuring sufficient zinc intake is crucial for maintaining effective insulin action and overall metabolic health.

POTASSIUM

Potassium is an essential mineral that helps regulate fluid balance, nerve signals, and muscle contractions. It plays a critical role in maintaining normal heart and kidney function, which are often compromised in individuals with diabetes. Potassium also helps balance the effects of sodium and maintains healthy blood pressure levels. Good sources of potassium include fruits like bananas, oranges, and avocados, vegetables such as spinach and sweet potatoes, and legumes like beans and lentils. Adequate potassium intake can help manage hypertension, a common comorbidity in diabetes, and support cardiovascular health.

VITAMIN C

Vitamin C, also known as ascorbic acid, is a powerful antioxidant that helps protect cells from damage caused by free radicals. It also supports the immune system, aids in the absorption of iron from plant-based foods, and promotes healthy skin and blood vessels. For people with diabetes, vitamin C can help reduce the risk of developing cardiovascular disease by preventing oxidative stress and inflammation. Additionally, it may improve endothelial function, which is often impaired in diabetic individuals. Excellent sources of vitamin C include citrus fruits, berries, kiwifruit, bell peppers, tomatoes, and leafy greens. Regular consumption of vitamin C-rich foods can help mitigate oxidative stress and support overall health in diabetes management.

Advanced Nutritional Knowledge for Diabetes Management

Effective diabetes management extends beyond basic blood sugar monitoring and macronutrient balance. Advanced nutritional strategies, such as incorporating anti-inflammatory foods and understanding food synergy, can significantly enhance glycemic control and overall health. These approaches focus on reducing insulin resistance and optimizing the body's metabolic response to food.

Insulin resistance is a condition where the body's cells become less responsive to the hormone insulin, which is crucial for regulating blood glucose levels. This resistance forces the pancreas to produce more insulin to maintain normal glucose levels, which can eventually lead to beta-cell exhaustion and Type 2 diabetes. Chronic inflammation is a key contributor to insulin resistance, disrupting normal cellular function and exacerbating metabolic disorders.

Anti-inflammatory foods can play a vital role in reducing insulin resistance and improving glycemic control. These foods contain compounds that help mitigate inflammation and improve the body's response to insulin.

Omega-3 fatty acids, found in fatty fish like salmon, mackerel, and sardines, as well as in flaxseeds and walnuts, are among the most potent anti-inflammatory nutrients. These essential fats help reduce the production of inflammatory molecules such as cytokines and eicosanoids. Regular consumption of omega-3 fatty acids has been shown to improve insulin sensitivity, lower triglyceride levels, and reduce the risk of cardiovascular disease, which is a common complication of diabetes.

Turmeric, a bright yellow spice commonly used in Indian cuisine, contains curcumin, a powerful anti-inflammatory and antioxidant compound. Curcumin has been extensively studied for its potential to improve insulin sensitivity and lower blood sugar levels. It works by inhibiting inflammatory pathways and reducing oxidative stress, thereby protecting pancreatic beta cells from damage. Incorporating turmeric into the diet, through curries, soups, or supplements, can offer significant benefits for diabetes management.

Leafy greens, such as spinach, kale, and Swiss chard, are rich in vitamins, minerals, and antioxidants that combat inflammation. These vegetables are high in fiber, which helps slow the absorption of glucose into the bloodstream, leading to more stable blood sugar levels. Additionally, leafy greens provide essential nutrients like magnesium and vitamin K, which are important for metabolic health. Including a variety of leafy greens in daily meals can support better glycemic control and reduce inflammation.

Beyond individual anti-inflammatory foods, the concept of food synergy emphasizes the combined effects of different foods and nutrients, which can enhance their overall health benefits. Food synergy involves strategically pairing foods to optimize their nutritional impact and improve glycemic control.

For example, combining carbohydrate-rich foods with proteins or healthy fats can slow the digestion and absorption of glucose, leading to more stable blood sugar levels. An example of this is eating an apple with a handful of almonds. The fiber in the apple and the protein and healthy fats in the almonds work together to moderate the release of glucose into the bloodstream, preventing spikes in blood sugar.

Another example of food synergy is pairing high-fiber foods with foods rich in antioxidants. For instance, a salad made with leafy greens, colorful vegetables, and a sprinkle of nuts or seeds provides a diverse array of nutrients that work together to reduce inflammation, improve insulin sensitivity, and support overall metabolic health.

Incorporating these advanced nutritional strategies into daily life requires mindful meal planning and an understanding of how different foods interact. By focusing on anti-inflammatory foods and leveraging the principles of food synergy, individuals with diabetes can achieve better blood glucose control, reduce insulin resistance, and improve their overall health.

Foods for Diabetes:
What to Eat and What to Avoid

Diabetes management is critically dependent on dietary choices. The right selection of foods can significantly stabilize blood glucose levels and improve overall health, while poor choices can lead to severe complications.

The connection between diet and diabetes is strong, with different types of foods having varied effects on blood sugar levels. Complex carbohydrates from whole grains and vegetables, for instance, help maintain stable glucose levels due to their slow digestion and absorption. In contrast, simple carbohydrates found in sugary snacks can cause rapid blood sugar spikes.

Choosing whole, unprocessed foods over highly processed options is vital as the latter often contain harmful sugars and fats. Balancing macronutrients—carbohydrates, proteins, and fats—is also essential to manage blood glucose effectively. Foods rich in fiber, omega-3 fatty acids, and antioxidants can enhance insulin sensitivity and reduce the risk of long-term diabetes complications.

Ultimately, making informed food choices is not about strict restrictions but about integrating knowledge of how different foods interact with the body's metabolic processes.

Foods to Include in Your Diet

Building on our understanding of how diet influences diabetes management, this section identifies specific foods that are particularly beneficial for those aiming to stabilize blood glucose levels and enhance overall health. Whole grains like quinoa, barley, and whole wheat are foundational. These grains provide complex carbohydrates, which are crucial for maintaining stable glucose levels through slow digestion and prolonged satiety.

Fruits also play an essential role in a balanced diabetic diet, especially those with a low glycemic index such as berries, apples, and pears. These fruits not only deliver vital vitamins and minerals but also help maintain blood sugar stability due to their high fiber content.

Protein is equally important. Lean animal sources like chicken, turkey, and fish, along with plant-based options such as beans, lentils, and tofu, are excellent choices. They support tissue repair and muscle maintenance with minimal impact on blood sugar levels.

Healthy fats, sourced from avocados, nuts, seeds, and olive oil, enhance cardiovascular health and provide steady energy. These fats are essential for overall well-being and support the absorption of fat-soluble vitamins.

Non-starchy vegetables like leafy greens, broccoli, and peppers are indispensable. They add a wealth of nutrients and fiber while contributing minimal calories, making them an excellent choice for diabetes management.

Although starchy vegetables and dairy products are richer in carbohydrates, they still play a vital role in a balanced diet when consumed in moderation. Foods like sweet potatoes, peas, and low-fat dairy provide necessary nutrients without excessive sugar intake. For those following vegan or lactose-intolerant diets, this chapter also explores plant-based alternatives to ensure that everyone has access to nutritious options that suit their dietary restrictions.

Throughout this chapter, we not only discuss the nutritional benefits of these foods but also offer practical advice on incorporating them into daily meals. This ensures that you can apply this knowledge effectively, creating enjoyable, healthful dishes that support your diabetes management goals.

WHOLE GRAINS

Whole grains are fundamental to managing diabetes effectively, as they are rich in complex carbohydrates that break down slowly in the body. This slow release of glucose into the bloodstream helps maintain stable blood sugar levels, avoiding the spikes that are particularly detrimental for those with diabetes.

Unlike their refined counterparts, whole grains retain their bran and germ during processing, ensuring that all the natural fibers, vitamins, and minerals are preserved. These nutrients not only aid in blood sugar control but also contribute to overall health by improving insulin sensitivity and reducing the risk of cardiovascular diseases.

Fiber is a key component of whole grains and offers multiple benefits. It not only assists with digestion but also helps control blood sugar by slowing the breakdown of carbohydrates. This means that the body's insulin response is more gradual and controlled. Additionally, the satiating quality of fiber-rich foods can help in weight management by curbing unnecessary snacking and overeating, which is vital for preventing obesity-related diabetes complications.

Incorporating whole grains into the diet is both beneficial and versatile. They can serve as the foundation for a range of dishes—from hearty breakfasts and nutritious salads to main dishes and snacks. Cooking whole grains typically involves boiling them until they're tender, but each variety may have slightly different cooking times and methods. These grains not only enhance the nutritional profile of meals but also add delightful textures and flavors, making every meal more enjoyable and health-supportive.

Quinoa

Quinoa, often referred to as a "super grain", is actually a seed from the Chenopodium quinoa plant. It is cherished for its nutritional richness and is a staple in health-conscious diets worldwide. Originating from the Andean region of South America, it has been a significant source of nutrition in local diets for thousands of years. Unlike many grains, quinoa is gluten-free and boasts a high protein content, along with a host of essential amino acids, making it a complete protein source—rare among plant foods.

NUTRITIONAL INFORMATION PER 100 GRAMS OF UNCOOKED QUINOA
Total Calories: 368 kcal
Protein: 14.1 g
Total Fat: 6.1 g
Saturated Fat: 0.7 g
Unsaturated Fat: 5.0 g
Total Carbohydrates: 64.2 g
Dietary Fiber: 7.0 g
Sugars: 4.9 g
Sodium: 5 mg
Vitamins and Minerals: High in magnesium, phosphorus, manganese, and folate. It also contains significant amounts of thiamin, riboflavin, vitamin B6, and zinc.
Glycemic Index[1] (GI): 53

The nutritional makeup of quinoa makes it a formidable choice for those managing their diet. Its low GI and moderate GL values indicate that it impacts blood sugar levels gently, which is crucial for preventing spikes and maintaining energy stability. The high fiber content not only aids digestive health but also contributes to a feeling of fullness, helping in weight management. The protein in quinoa is complete, meaning it supplies all nine essential amino acids necessary for human health, a feature especially important for vegetarians and vegans who may struggle to obtain complete proteins through diet alone. Furthermore, the unsaturated fats found in quinoa, including a notable amount of heart-healthy omega-3 fatty acids, contribute to cardiovascular health.

COOKING IDEAS WITH QUINOA

Quinoa's versatility in cooking is as impressive as its nutritional content. Its mild, nutty flavor and unique texture make it an excellent substitute for rice or couscous. For a simple preparation, quinoa can be cooked similarly to rice—simmered in water or broth until it becomes fluffy and the germ forms a visible spiral. It makes a fantastic base for a colorful quinoa salad tossed with cherry tomatoes, cucumbers, red onions, parsley, and a lemon vinaigrette dressing.

Quinoa can also serve as a robust addition to breakfast, cooked with almond or cow's milk and topped with berries, nuts, and a drizzle of honey for a nutritious porridge. Moreover, it can be incorporated into baked goods such as muffins and bread, enhancing

---

[1] The Glycemic Index (GI) indicates how quickly a food raises blood glucose levels. While it typically doesn't depend on the quantity consumed (100 grams), it's included here for

convenience and to provide a more comprehensive overview of each food item's impact on blood sugar levels.

their protein and fiber content. For a savory lunch or dinner, stuffed quinoa peppers are a wholesome option, filling bell peppers with a mixture of quinoa, black beans, corn, tomatoes, and spices, topped with a sprinkle of cheese and baked until tender.

Bulgur

Bulgur, a whole grain made from cracked wheat, has been a staple in Middle Eastern cuisine for centuries. It is produced by parboiling wheat, drying it, and then coarsely grinding or cracking it. Its robust nutty flavor and quick preparation time make it a popular choice for busy cooks looking to incorporate healthy grains into their meals. Not only is bulgur a traditional component of many cultural dishes such as tabbouleh and kibbeh, but it also offers impressive nutritional benefits, making it a favored ingredient in a health-conscious diet.

NUTRITIONAL INFORMATION PER 100 GRAMS OF UNCOOKED BULGUR
Total Calories: 342 kcal
Protein: 12 g
Total Fat: 1.33 g
Saturated Fat: 0.232 g
Unsaturated Fat: 0.884 g
Total Carbohydrates: 75.87 g
Dietary Fiber: 18.3 g
Sugars: 0.41 g
Sodium: 17 mg
Vitamins and Minerals: High in magnesium, iron, and B-vitamins. It also contains phosphorus, zinc, and selenium.
Glycemic Index (GI): 48

Bulgur stands out for its high fiber content, which is beneficial for digestive health and helps in maintaining long-lasting satiety, crucial for weight management. The low GI and GL values make it an excellent grain choice for maintaining stable blood sugar levels, particularly important for individuals managing diabetes or metabolic syndrome. The protein content in bulgur, though not as high as in some other grains like quinoa, still contributes significantly to dietary protein needs, especially in plant-based diets. Furthermore, the minimal fat content, primarily unsaturated, aligns well with a heart-healthy diet. The presence of iron and B-vitamins helps in energy production and maintaining healthy blood cells, making bulgur not just nutritious but also a functional addition to any meal.

COOKING IDEAS WITH BULGUR

Bulgur's versatility in the kitchen is vast. For a simple and quick preparation, it can be boiled in water or broth until tender, which usually takes about 10-15 minutes. Once cooked, it has a texture similar to couscous but slightly chewier, making it a fantastic base for salads and pilafs. One of the most renowned dishes featuring bulgur is tabbouleh, a refreshing herb and tomato salad that pairs perfectly with grilled meats or as part of a mezze platter.

Bulgur can also be used as a hearty breakfast cereal, cooked with milk or water, and sweetened with honey or fruits for a warm, satisfying start to the day. Its ability to absorb flavors makes it an excellent component in stuffed vegetables, such as bell peppers or tomatoes, mixed with aromatics, spices, and other grains or proteins. Additionally, bulgur can be incorporated into soups and stews to add texture and nutritional density. For a creative twist, it can be used as a substitute for rice in risotto recipes, providing a nuttier flavor and a more substantial bite.

Barley

Barley is one of the oldest known cereal grains, revered since ancient times for its versatility and nutritional benefits. Originally cultivated in Eurasia, it serves not only as a staple food but also as a traditional ingredient in beer brewing. This grain is cherished for its chewy texture and nutty flavor, which make it a popular choice in various culinary traditions around the world.

NUTRITIONAL INFORMATION PER 100 GRAMS OF UNCOOKED BARLEY
Total Calories: 354 kcal
Protein: 12.48 g
Total Fat: 2.3 g
Saturated Fat: 0.482 g
Unsaturated Fat: 1.2 g
Total Carbohydrates: 73.48 g
Dietary Fiber: 17.3 g
Sugars: 0.8 g
Sodium: 12 mg
Vitamins and Minerals: High in magnesium, phosphorus, and manganese. Contains substantial amounts of selenium, iron, and B-vitamins, particularly niacin and thiamin.
Glycemic Index (GI): 30

Barley is low in glycemic index and high in dietary fiber, particularly beta-glucan, which has been shown to reduce cholesterol and improve heart health. The substantial fiber content promotes good digestive health and helps maintain a feeling of fullness, aiding in weight management. Rich in essential minerals and B-vitamins, barley supports overall metabolic functions and energy production, making it a nutritious choice for a balanced diet.

COOKING IDEAS WITH BARLEY

Barley's robust flavor and hearty texture make it ideal for a variety of dishes beyond the traditional soups and stews. When making barley risotto, known as "orzotto," the grain is simmered slowly with broth and wine, stirred frequently until it reaches a creamy consistency, then finished with a sprinkle of Parmesan and fresh herbs. This method showcases barley's ability to absorb flavors and offer a satisfying, creamy texture.

For a refreshing take, consider a barley salad tossed with roasted vegetables, fresh herbs, and a zesty vinaigrette, perfect for serving warm or cold. Its ability to maintain a pleasant chewiness adds a delightful contrast to the crisp vegetables.

Barley also makes an excellent addition to breakfast routines. Cooked similarly to oatmeal, it can be served with a mix of cinnamon, nuts, and fresh fruit, providing a fiber-rich start to the day that keeps you full well into lunchtime.

Incorporating barley into baked goods such as bread and muffins can enhance their nutritional profile. Using barley flour introduces a nutty flavor and boosts the fiber content, making everyday recipes healthier and more satisfying.

Whole Oat Groats

Whole oat groats are the purest form of oats you can consume. They are whole oat kernels that have had their hard outer hulls removed, offering a robust texture and a nutty flavor. As one of the least processed forms of oats available, groats retain all of their bran, germ, and endosperm, making them a powerhouse of nutrition. They are celebrated not just for their hearty, chewy texture but also for their impressive health benefits, including enhancing heart health and aiding in digestion.

NUTRITIONAL INFORMATION PER 100 GRAMS OF UNCOOKED WHOLE OAT GROATS	
Total Calories: 379 kcal	
Protein: 13.15 g	
Total Fat: 6.52 g	
Saturated Fat: 1.217 g	
Unsaturated Fat: 3.98 g	
Total Carbohydrates: 67.7 g	
Dietary Fiber: 9.1 g	
Sugars: 0.99 g	
Sodium: 2 mg	
Vitamins and Minerals: Rich in phosphorus, magnesium, and manganese. Contains significant amounts of zinc, iron, and B vitamins, especially thiamin and folate.	
Glycemic Index (GI): 55	

Whole oat groats stand out due to their high fiber content, particularly beta-glucan, a type of soluble fiber known for its ability to lower cholesterol levels and stabilize blood glucose levels. The moderate glycemic index makes them suitable for a steady energy release, which is critical for managing blood sugar levels, especially beneficial for those with diabetes. The protein in groats, coupled with their high fiber content, provides a feeling of fullness that can aid in weight management. Their rich mineral profile supports bone health and metabolic functions, making them an excellent choice for a nutrient-dense diet.

COOKING IDEAS

Cooking with whole oat groats offers a variety of culinary uses beyond the typical breakfast cereal. When prepared, they require a longer cooking time than other forms of oats due to their minimal processing, usually simmering for 30-40 minutes or until tender. This quality makes them an excellent candidate for slow-cooked dishes.

A traditional way to enjoy oat groats is in a hot breakfast porridge. Simmered slowly with water or milk and topped with fruits, nuts, and a drizzle of honey, they provide a warm, satisfying start to the day. Their chewy texture and nutty flavor make them a robust base for pilafs or grain bowls, combined with sautéed vegetables, legumes, and a flavorful dressing.

Groats can also be used in stews and soups, where they absorb flavors and contribute to a hearty, thick consistency. For a creative twist, toasted groats can be ground into flour and used for baking healthier breads or muffins, offering a richer, more textured alternative to regular oat flour.

Farro

Farro is a term that encompasses three types of heirloom grains: spelt, emmer, and einkorn. Originating in the Fertile Crescent, this ancient grain has been a staple in Mediterranean and Near Eastern cuisines for thousands of years. Renowned for its nutty flavor and chewy texture, farro is a robust grain that stands out not only for its taste but also for its substantial nutritional profile, making it a favorite among health enthusiasts and culinary professionals alike.

NUTRITIONAL INFORMATION PER 100 GRAMS OF UNCOOKED FARRO
Total Calories: 338 kcal
Protein: 14.57 g
Total Fat: 2.39 g
Saturated Fat: 0.51 g
Unsaturated Fat: 1.61 g
Total Carbohydrates: 63.51 g
Dietary Fiber: 11.3 g
Sugars: 1.9 g
Sodium: 12 mg
Vitamins and Minerals: High in magnesium, phosphorus, and zinc. Contains significant amounts of niacin, iron, and B-vitamins.
Glycemic Index (GI): 40

Farro is celebrated for its high fiber content, which promotes digestive health and helps in maintaining a feeling of fullness, aiding in weight management and appetite control. Its low glycemic index makes it an excellent choice for those monitoring their blood sugar levels, including individuals with diabetes. The rich protein content makes farro a valuable plant-based protein source, especially beneficial for vegetarians and vegans. Additionally, its wealth of vitamins and minerals supports overall wellness, enhancing everything from metabolic functions to immune system health.

COOKING IDEAS WITH FARRO

Farro's hearty texture and rich, nutty flavor make it versatile in the kitchen, suitable for a variety of culinary applications beyond simple side dishes. To prepare farro, it can be boiled until the grains are tender but still chewy—about 30 minutes—and then drained.

One popular way to enjoy farro is in a warm salad. Cooked farro can be tossed with roasted vegetables, fresh herbs, a squeeze of lemon, and a drizzle of olive oil for a satisfying lunch or dinner. It also makes an excellent base for grain bowls, topped with a protein source such as grilled chicken or chickpeas, and a dollop of yogurt or tahini sauce.

For a comforting meal, farro can be used to make risotto-style dishes. Cooked slowly with broth and stirred frequently, farro absorbs flavors beautifully, resulting in a creamy, flavorful dish that is perfect for a cozy evening. Additionally, incorporating farro into soups adds texture and nutritional value, making classic recipes more filling.

Brown Rice

Brown rice, distinguished from its refined counterpart, white rice, retains its bran and germ layers, which are rich in nutrients. This whole grain has been a dietary staple in various cultures worldwide due to its nutritional benefits and versatility in cooking. Brown rice offers a mildly nutty flavor and a chewier texture compared to white rice, making it a favored choice for those seeking a healthier, more fiber-rich diet.

NUTRITIONAL INFORMATION PER 100 GRAMS OF UNCOOKED BROWN RICE
Total Calories: 370 kcal
Protein: 7.5 g
Total Fat: 2.68 g
Saturated Fat: 0.5 g
Unsaturated Fat: 2.18 g
Total Carbohydrates: 77.24 g
Dietary Fiber: 3.5 g
Sugars: 0.85 g
Sodium: 5 mg
Vitamins and Minerals: Good source of magnesium, phosphorus, selenium, thiamin, niacin, and vitamin B6.
Glycemic Index (GI): 50

The moderate glycemic index and higher fiber content of brown rice make it beneficial for stabilizing blood sugar levels, which is crucial for diabetes management and preventing spikes in blood sugar. The fiber also aids in digestion and can help in maintaining a healthy weight by promoting a feeling of fullness. Rich in essential minerals like magnesium and selenium, brown rice supports heart health and boosts antioxidant defenses. The presence of B vitamins enhances metabolic functions and plays a key role in energy production.

COOKING IDEAS WITH BROWN RICE

The hearty texture and rich flavor of brown rice make it suitable for a wide range of dishes beyond the typical side dish. To cook brown rice, it generally requires about 45 minutes of simmering in water, resulting in grains that are tender yet firm.

One delightful way to use brown rice is in stir-fries, where its chewy texture complements a variety of vegetables and proteins like tofu, chicken, or shrimp. Toss the ingredients together in a savory sauce for a quick and nutritious meal.

Brown rice also serves as an excellent base for pilafs, where it can be sautéed with onions, garlic, and spices before being cooked in a flavorful broth. Add dried fruits, nuts, or fresh herbs to create a colorful and aromatic dish that can stand as a meal on its own or accompany other dishes.

For a creative twist, use brown rice to make rice salads. Cooked and cooled rice is mixed with ingredients such as chopped vegetables, beans, and a tangy vinaigrette, making for a refreshing and filling meal perfect for hot days or as a substantial side dish.

Another hearty option is using brown rice in soups and stews. Its robust texture holds up well during longer cooking times and adds a satisfying depth to these dishes. Whether it's a vegetable soup or a chunky stew, brown rice enhances the nutritional profile and fiber content.

Millet

Millet is not just one grain but a family of highly variable small-seeded grasses widely cultivated around the world as cereal crops or grains for fodder and human food. Millets are important crops in the semiarid tropics of Asia and Africa, particularly in India, Mali, Nigeria, and Niger, with 97% of millet production occurring in developing countries. This ancient grain is gluten-free, rich in nutrients, and offers a sweet, nut-like flavor, making it a popular alternative to more common grains like wheat and rice.

NUTRITIONAL INFORMATION PER 100 GRAMS OF UNCOOKED MILLET
Total Calories: 378 kcal
Protein: 11 g
Total Fat: 4.22 g
Saturated Fat: 0.72 g
Unsaturated Fat: 3.5 g
Total Carbohydrates: 72.85 g
Dietary Fiber: 8.5 g
Sugars: 0.5 g
Sodium: 5 mg
Vitamins and Minerals: Rich in magnesium, phosphorus, and manganese. Contains iron, B-vitamins, especially niacin, B6, and folic acid.
Glycemic Index (GI): 70

While millet has a higher glycemic index, which means it can raise blood sugar levels more quickly, its impact on blood glucose can be moderated by portion control and pairing it with other foods that lower the overall glycemic load of a meal. Its high fiber content helps in this regard, slowing the absorption of sugar into the bloodstream. Millet is also praised for its high magnesium content, which can aid in improving insulin response and lowering blood sugar. The presence of significant amounts of phosphorus supports body repair and maintenance, while B-vitamins enhance energy production and overall metabolism.

COOKING IDEAS WITH MILLET

Millet's mild flavor and light texture make it incredibly versatile in the kitchen. It can be cooked fluffy like rice or creamy like mashed potatoes, depending on the amount of water used and the cooking time.

For a basic preparation, simmer millet in water for about 15-20 minutes until the grains are tender but still burst slightly to the bite. This method is perfect for creating pilafs or for adding to salads. You can toast the grains in a dry skillet beforehand to enhance their nutty flavor.

Millet makes an excellent base for a hearty breakfast porridge. Cook it in milk or a milk alternative and top with fresh fruits, nuts, and a drizzle of honey or maple syrup for a nutritious start to the day.

Incorporate cooked millet into vegetable burgers for a delightful texture and nutritional boost. Mix millet with mashed beans, spices, and a bit of flour to bind, then form into patties and pan-fry or bake until crisp on the outside.

Another creative use of millet is in stuffed peppers or tomatoes, where it can be mixed with a variety of vegetables, herbs, spices, and a protein source like cheese or ground meat, offering a satisfying and complete meal that is both nutritious and flavorful.

Wild Rice

Wild rice, often considered a gourmet grain due to its unique flavor and texture, is not actually rice but a species of grass that produces edible seeds resembling traditional rice. Originating from the shallow waters of North America, particularly from the Great Lakes region, wild rice is cherished for its robust, nutty flavor and impressive nutritional profile. It is a traditional staple of Native American cuisine and has gained popularity worldwide for its health benefits and culinary versatility.

NUTRITIONAL INFORMATION PER 100 GRAMS OF UNCOOKED WILD RICE	
Total Calories: 357 kcal	
Protein: 14.73 g	
Total Fat: 1.08 g	
Saturated Fat: 0.144 g	
Unsaturated Fat: 0.936 g	
Total Carbohydrates: 74.9 g	
Dietary Fiber: 6.2 g	
Sugars: 2.5 g	
Sodium: 7 mg	
Vitamins and Minerals: High in magnesium, phosphorus, and manganese. Contains significant amounts of zinc, vitamin B6, and niacin.	
Glycemic Index (GI): 45	

Wild rice is noted for its high protein content, which is considerably greater than that of most other whole grains. This makes it an excellent choice for vegetarians and those looking to boost their protein intake. The low glycemic index of wild rice makes it suitable for those managing diabetes, as it helps maintain stable blood sugar levels. The fiber content aids in digestion and promotes satiety, helping with weight management. Additionally, the rich array of minerals and B-vitamins supports energy metabolism and overall cellular health.

COOKING IDEAS WITH WILD RICE

Wild rice's chewy texture and hearty flavor make it a standout ingredient in a variety of dishes. To prepare, it typically requires boiling in water for about 45 minutes until the grains are tender and begin to burst open, revealing their white interior.

One classic way to enjoy wild rice is in a pilaf, sautéed with finely chopped onions, garlic, and mushrooms, then simmered in a rich broth until fluffy. This dish can be enhanced with herbs such as thyme and parsley for added flavor.

Wild rice also makes an excellent base for salads. Combine cooked wild rice with dried cranberries, sliced almonds, chopped green onions, and a citrus dressing for a refreshing and nutritious side dish that pairs well with grilled meats or can be enjoyed on its own.

For a comforting meal, add wild rice to soups or stews. Its robust texture holds up well during the cooking process and adds a nutty flavor that complements a variety of ingredients, from chicken and vegetables to creamy mushroom bases.

Another delightful use for wild rice is as a stuffing for vegetables such as bell peppers, squash, or tomatoes. Mix it with a combination of sautéed vegetables, nuts, and perhaps some crumbled cheese, then bake until the vegetables are tender and the filling is heated through.

Rye

Rye is a hearty grain known for its deep, earthy flavor and impressive nutritional profile. Originating in Turkey and surrounding areas over 2000 years ago, it has since become a staple grain in many parts of Eastern, Central, and Northern Europe. Rye is often considered a superior choice for bread-making, especially for producing dense, dark breads that are rich in flavor. It is also appreciated for its ability to thrive in poorer soils where other grains might fail.

NUTRITIONAL INFORMATION PER 100 GRAMS OF UNCOOKED RYE	
Total Calories: 335 kcal	
Protein: 14.8 g	
Total Fat: 2.5 g	
Saturated Fat: 0.245 g	
Unsaturated Fat: 2.255 g	
Total Carbohydrates: 69.76 g	
Dietary Fiber: 14.6 g	
Sugars: 0.9 g	
Sodium: 2 mg	
Vitamins and Minerals: Excellent source of manganese, and a good source of phosphorus, magnesium, and zinc. Contains B-vitamins including niacin, thiamin, and vitamin B6.	
Glycemic Index (GI): 34	

Rye's notably low glycemic index makes it an ideal grain for those managing diabetes or aiming to maintain stable blood sugar levels. The high fiber content not only aids in digestion but also contributes to prolonged satiety, which can help in weight management. Its rich mineral and vitamin content supports overall cellular health and energy metabolism. Furthermore, the lignans found in rye have been linked to heart health and reducing the risk of chronic diseases.

COOKING IDEAS WITH RYE

Rye's distinct flavor makes it a versatile grain in the kitchen, suitable for both traditional recipes and innovative culinary experiments. Here are a few ways to incorporate rye into your cooking:

Rye berries, the whole form of the rye grain, can be cooked similarly to wheat berries or barley. Boil them in water until they become tender yet chewy, which usually takes about an hour. These can then be used as a base for hearty salads, mixed with roasted vegetables, nuts, and a tangy vinaigrette.

Rye flour is perhaps the most common use of rye, particularly for baking. It is excellent for making rye bread, which is known for its dense, moist texture and slightly sour flavor, characteristic of traditional Eastern European breads. Mix rye flour with a sourdough starter to create authentic sourdough rye bread.

For a simple yet satisfying breakfast, rye flakes can be used in place of oatmeal. Cook them in milk or water and top with fresh fruits, a sprinkle of cinnamon, and a drizzle of honey for a nutritious start to the day.

Incorporate ground rye into pancakes or waffles for a rustic and flavorful twist. The nutty taste of rye pairs beautifully with maple syrup and butter, providing a more nutritious alternative to standard white flour recipes.

Whole Grain Bread

Whole grain bread is a fundamental element of many diets worldwide, prized not only for its robust flavor and satisfying texture but also for its nutritional benefits. Unlike white bread, which is made from heavily processed wheat that strips away the nutrient-rich germ and fiber-dense bran, whole grain bread includes every part of the grain kernel. This includes the bran, germ, and endosperm, ensuring that all the nutrients and fiber are retained.

NUTRITIONAL INFORMATION PER 100 GRAMS OF WHOLE GRAIN BREAD	
Total Calories: 247 kcal	
Protein: 13 g	
Total Fat: 3.6 g	
Saturated Fat: 0.8 g	
Unsaturated Fat: 2.0 g	
Total Carbohydrates: 41 g	
Dietary Fiber: 7 g	
Sugars: 6 g	
Sodium: 474 mg	
Vitamins and Minerals: High in B vitamins, iron, magnesium, and selenium	
Glycemic Index (GI): 51	

Whole grain bread is a highly beneficial component of any diet, especially for those managing blood sugar levels such as diabetics. The fiber in whole grain bread helps slow the absorption of glucose into the bloodstream, providing more stable energy levels and reducing spikes in blood sugar. It's also packed with B vitamins which are essential for energy metabolism, and

minerals like iron and magnesium that support overall health. Its moderate glycemic index makes it a preferable choice over white bread, which often spikes blood glucose levels rapidly.

COOKING IDEAS

Whole grain bread is incredibly versatile and can be used in a variety of diabetes-friendly recipes. One simple yet delicious use is to create a hearty sandwich with lean proteins such as turkey or chicken breast, lots of fresh vegetables like lettuce and tomatoes, and a slice of low-fat cheese for a well-rounded meal that balances carbs with protein and fiber.

Another creative way to use whole grain bread is in breakfast dishes. Try an avocado toast; mash avocado with a pinch of salt, pepper, and lemon juice, then spread it on toasted whole grain bread and top with a sprinkle of sesame seeds or chili flakes for a nutritious start to the day.

For a warm, comforting option, use whole grain bread as the base for a healthy French toast. Dip slices of bread in a mixture of egg, milk, cinnamon, and vanilla extract, then cook on a non-stick skillet until golden brown. Serve with a dollop of yogurt and fresh berries for added antioxidants without excess sugar.

Additionally, whole grain bread crumbs can be made by pulsing toasted bread in a food processor. Use these breadcrumbs as a topping for baked casseroles or as a binder for meatballs, combining with herbs and minced garlic for flavor. This not only adds texture and substance but also incorporates more fiber into your meals.

Lastly, a simple snack or side dish can involve brushing whole grain bread slices with olive oil and garlic, then broiling them until crisp to make homemade garlic bread, a perfect accompaniment to salads and soups.

Whole Grain Pasta

Pasta is a beloved staple in many diets around the world, but for those managing diabetes, choosing the right type of pasta is crucial. The main difference between regular pasta and whole grain pasta lies in the processing. Regular pasta is typically made from refined flour, which has been stripped of the bran and germ, reducing its fiber, vitamin, and mineral content. Whole grain pasta, on the other hand, is made from the entire grain kernel, which includes the bran, germ, and endosperm. This difference in processing results in a significant variance in nutritional benefits and impacts on blood sugar levels.

NUTRITIONAL INFORMATION PER 100 GRAMS OF WHOLE GRAIN PASTA	
Total Calories: 350 kcal	
Protein: 13 g	
Total Fat: 2.5 grams	
Saturated Fat: 0.5 g	
Unsaturated Fat: 2.0 g	
Total Carbohydrates: 71 g	
Dietary Fiber: 12 g	
Sugars: 3 g	
Sodium: 5 mg	
Vitamins and Minerals: Whole grain pasta is a good source of B vitamins (including thiamin, riboflavin, niacin, and folate), as well as minerals such as iron, magnesium, and zinc.	
Glycemic Index (GI): 45	

COOKING IDEAS

When preparing pasta for a diabetic diet, the objective is to craft dishes that are well-balanced, fo-cusing on minimizing blood sugar spikes while maximizing nutritional value. Here's how you can in-corporate whole grain pasta into your meals effectively and deliciously.

Begin with a vibrant, vegetable-loaded pasta salad. Cook the whole grain pasta and toss it with a colorful assortment of fiber-rich vegetables, such as cherry tomatoes, spinach, and bell peppers. Add a protein source like grilled chicken or chickpeas, enhancing the nutritional profile. For dressing, whisk together olive oil and vinegar to create a light vinaigrette that keeps the salad fresh and entic-ing.

Alternatively, you might opt for a robust dish of whole grain pasta served with lean protein and a fla-vorful homemade tomato sauce, seasoned liberally with herbs. Incorporate proteins such as ground turkey or tofu, which not only enrich the dish but also help moderate the glycemic impact, thereby stabilizing blood sugar levels.

For a creative twist, stir-fry cooked whole grain pasta with an array of vegetables and a choice of protein like shrimp or lean beef. Season this mix with low-sodium soy sauce, garlic, and a hint of sesame oil to bring an Asian-inspired zest to your meal.

Whole grain pasta is also an excellent addition to soups. It promotes a healthier pasta-to-vegetable ratio, boosting fiber content while reducing carb density. A comforting option could be a hearty min-estrone filled with kidney beans and a medley of vegetables, provid-ing both nourishment and warmth.

Consider crafting a baked pasta dish as well. Com-bine whole grain pasta with a ricotta and spinach mix-ture, top with a bit of mozzarella, and bake until the cheese is bubbly and golden. This method not only deepens the flavors but also maintains the low glyce-mic qualities of the pasta, essential for blood sugar management.

It's beneficial to cook whole grain pasta to an 'al dente' texture. Firmer pasta has a lower glycemic index than its softer counterpart, ensuring a slower release of glucose into the bloodstream, which aids in better blood sugar control. By integrating these culinary strategies into your diet, whole grain pasta can become a delicious and integral part of managing diabetes.

LOW GLYCEMIC FRUITS

Low glycemic fruits are essential in a diabetes man-agement plan because they have a minimal impact on blood sugar levels. Fruits such as berries, apples, and pears fall into this category and are prized not just for their low sugar content but also for their high fiber and nutrient density. These characteristics make them ideal for satisfying sweet cravings without causing rapid spikes in glucose levels, which are particularly harmful for those managing diabetes.

The fiber in low glycemic fruits slows the absorp-tion of sugar, helping to control blood sugar spikes af-ter meals. This slower absorption rate is crucial for maintaining stable energy levels throughout the day. Additionally, the antioxidants and vitamins present in these fruits support overall health by reducing oxida-tive stress and enhancing immune function, which can be compromised in individuals with chronic conditions like diabetes.

Incorporating these fruits into the diet offers a way to enhance flavor and nutritional value without com-promising glycemic control. They can be enjoyed fresh as a snack, blended into smoothies, or used as natural sweeteners in dishes that benefit from a touch of sweet-ness. Moreover, their versatility makes them easy to include in meals across all times of the day—from a fresh fruit topping on morning oatmeal to a vibrant, tangy salad for lunch, or a light and healthy dessert op-tion.

Embracing a variety of low glycemic fruits can also help broaden the nutritional diversity of a diabetic diet, providing not only essential vitamins and minerals but also introducing different textures and flavors to daily meals.

Cherries

Cherries are a beloved fruit known for their vibrant color and sweet, tangy flavor. Available in numerous varieties, including sweet cherries like Bing and tart or sour cherries like Montmorency, cherries are not only a delightful treat but also boast a profile rich in nutrients and health benefits. Cherries have been a part of human diets for centuries, cherished for their culinary versatility and their use in traditional remedies.

NUTRITIONAL INFORMATION PER 100 GRAMS OF CHERRIES	
Total Calories: 63 kcal	
Protein: 1.06 g	
Total Fat: 0.2 g	
Saturated Fat: 0.04 g	
Unsaturated Fat: 0.05 g	
Total Carbohydrates: 16 g	
Dietary Fiber: 2 g	
Sugars: 12.82 g	
Sodium: 0 mg	
Vitamins and Minerals: Rich in Vitamin C, potassium, and antioxidants	
Glycemic Index (GI): Low to medium (20-25 for tart cherries, 30-35 for sweet cherries)	

Cherries are particularly notable for their deep red color, which comes from the antioxidant anthocyanin. These compounds not only give cherries their eye-catching appearance but are also linked to a variety of health benefits. Regular consumption of cherries can help reduce inflammation, manage symptoms of arthritis, and support heart health. The fiber in cherries aids digestion and helps maintain stable blood sugar levels, making them a great choice for people with diabetes. Their low to medium glycemic index ensures that they have a gentle impact on blood sugar.

COOKING IDEAS WITH CHERRIES

Cherries can be incorporated into a diabetic diet in creative and delicious ways. Start by using cherries to craft a nutritious smoothie; blend pitted cherries with plain Greek yogurt and a splash of almond milk for a creamy, luscious drink. Add a touch of cinnamon or vanilla for extra flavor without sugar.

Create a vibrant cherry salsa by combining chopped cherries, fresh basil, a little onion, and a squeeze of lime juice. This salsa pairs wonderfully with grilled chicken or fish, adding a burst of flavor and color to your plate.

For a wholesome dessert, pit fresh cherries and mix them with other low-GI fruits like berries and peaches for a baked fruit crumble. Top the fruits with a mixture of rolled oats, chopped nuts, and a bit of butter or coconut oil, then bake until the topping is golden and the fruits are bubbling.

Another excellent way to enjoy cherries is to poach them in a little water and a dash of cinnamon or nutmeg, creating a warm, syrupy topping that can be spooned over pancakes made from almond or coconut flour.

Lastly, for an easy and healthful snack, simply freeze pitted cherries and enjoy them as a frosty treat or blend them into homemade ice pops with coconut water for a refreshing, hydrating snack on a hot day.

Plums

Plums are a stone fruit, belonging to the same family as cherries and peaches. Known for their juicy texture and sweet yet slightly tart flavor, plums come in a variety of sizes and colors, including red, purple, and yellow. This versatile fruit is not only delicious but also packed with health-promoting nutrients and compounds.

Plums are an excellent source of vitamin C, an antioxidant that helps protect the body against free radicals and supports the immune system. They also provide vitamin K, which is essential for bone health, and potassium, which helps manage blood pressure levels. The low glycemic index of plums makes them an ideal fruit for managing blood sugar levels, and their fiber content aids in digestion and prolongs satiety.

NUTRITIONAL INFORMATION PER 100 GRAMS OF PLUMS	
Total Calories: 46 kcal	
Protein: 0.7 g	
Total Fat: 0.28 g	
Saturated Fat: 0.02 g	
Unsaturated Fat: 0.17 g	
Total Carbohydrates: 11.42 g	
Dietary Fiber: 1.4 g	
Sugars: 9.92 g	
Sodium: 0 mg	
Vitamins and Minerals: High in Vitamin C, Vitamin K, and potassium	
Glycemic Index (GI): 40	

COOKING IDEAS WITH PLUMS

Plums can be used in a variety of dishes to add natural sweetness and moisture. Begin by slicing plums and adding them to a mixed greens salad along with nuts and a vinaigrette for a refreshing summer salad. Their tart-sweet flavor balances well with the savory elements of the salad.

For a warm dish, halve plums and grill them until they are slightly charred. Serve these alongside grilled pork or chicken as a fruity, tangy accompaniment that enhances the savory flavors of the meat.

Plums also make a fantastic compote; simmer sliced plums with a touch of cinnamon and vanilla until they break down into a thick sauce. This compote can be served over whole grain pancakes or stirred into plain yogurt for a touch of sweetness.

Incorporate plums into breakfast by chopping them and adding them to oatmeal or whole grain cereal. The natural sweetness of plums enriches the meal, reducing the need for added sugars.

Finally, for a simple dessert, bake halved plums with a sprinkle of nutmeg or ginger until tender. Enjoy them with a dollop of whipped coconut cream for a decadent yet healthy treat that beautifully showcases the rich flavor and juiciness of plums.

Grapefruit

Grapefruit, a citrus fruit known for its vibrant color and a unique blend of sweetness and tartness, stands out for its nutritional richness and health benefits. Originating from Barbados as an accidental cross between the orange and the pomelo, it comes in varieties ranging from white and pink to ruby red. Each variety offers a slightly different flavor profile and array of nutrients, making grapefruit a versatile choice for health-conscious eaters.

NUTRITIONAL INFORMATION PER 100 GRAMS OF GRAPEFRUIT
Total Calories: 42 kcal
Protein: 0.77 g
Total Fat: 0.14 g
Saturated Fat: 0.02 g
Unsaturated Fat: 0.03 g
Total Carbohydrates: 10.66 g
Dietary Fiber: 1.6 g
Sugars: 6.89 g
Sodium: 0 mg
Vitamins and Minerals: Rich in Vitamin C, Vitamin A, and potassium
Glycemic Index (GI): 26

Grapefruit is lauded for its high vitamin C content, which enhances immune function and skin health through its antioxidant properties. It also provides a good amount of dietary fiber, which aids in digestion and helps maintain blood sugar levels, making it particularly beneficial for diabetes management. Additionally, the pink and red varieties contain lycopene, an antioxidant known to help reduce the risk of certain types of cancers.

COOKING IDEAS WITH GRAPEFRUIT

Grapefruit can be enjoyed in numerous ways that cater to a diabetes-friendly diet. Start by including fresh grapefruit segments in a morning smoothie, combining them with other low-GI fruits and unsweetened almond milk for a refreshing and filling start to the day.

Create a vibrant salad by mixing grapefruit segments with avocado slices, mixed greens, and a sprinkle of chopped nuts. Dress this salad with a light vinaigrette made from olive oil and lemon juice for a nutrient-rich lunch or dinner that balances healthy fats, proteins, and carbohydrates.

Grapefruit also lends itself well to savory dishes. Add grapefruit juice to marinades for chicken or fish to impart a citrusy brightness that enhances the flavors of the protein. Grill the marinated meats and serve with a side of steamed vegetables for a complete meal.

For a simple yet elegant dessert, broil grapefruit halves topped with a sprinkle of cinnamon and a drizzle of honey until caramelized. This method enhances the fruit's natural flavors and adds a touch of indulgence without significantly raising the sugar content.

Lastly, grapefruit can be used in homemade salsas. Combine finely chopped grapefruit with diced tomatoes, onions, cilantro, and a squeeze of lime juice for a tangy salsa that goes well with grilled fish tacos or as a refreshing dip for vegetable crudites.

Pears

Pears are a beloved fruit known for their sweet, juicy flavor and soft, buttery texture. Originating thousands of years ago in Eastern Europe and Asia Minor, pears come in over a thousand different varieties, each with its own distinct taste and texture. This versatile fruit is not only delicious but also packed with nutritional benefits, making it a valuable addition to a balanced diet.

NUTRITIONAL INFORMATION PER 100 GRAMS OF PEARS
Total Calories: 57 kcal
Protein: 0.36 g
Total Fat: 0.14 g
Saturated Fat: 0.02 g
Unsaturated Fat: 0.09 g
Total Carbohydrates: 15.23 g
Dietary Fiber: 3.1 g
Sugars: 9.75 g
Sodium: 1 mg
Vitamins and Minerals: High in Vitamin C, Vitamin K, and copper
Glycemic Index (GI): 30

Pears are celebrated for their high content of dietary fiber, which aids in digestion and helps maintain stable blood sugar levels, a boon for individuals managing diabetes. They are also a good source of vitamin C and K, essential for immune function and bone health, respectively. The low glycemic index of pears allows for a slower release of glucose into the bloodstream, which aids in managing post-meal blood sugar spikes.

COOKING IDEAS WITH PEARS

Incorporate pears into your diet by starting with a simple breakfast of chopped pears mixed into low-fat Greek yogurt. Add a sprinkle of chia seeds for extra fiber and omega-3 fatty acids, making a well-rounded meal that keeps you full throughout the morning.

For a savory lunch option, slice pears and add them to a salad with mixed greens, walnuts, and a slice of grilled chicken. Dress the salad lightly with balsamic vinegar and olive oil to enhance the flavors without adding excess calories.

Pears also make a wonderful addition to entrees. Try baking pears with a sprinkle of cinnamon and nutmeg as a side dish to accompany pork or chicken. The natural sweetness of pears complements the savory flavors of the meat, adding complexity to the dish.

For a quick and healthy snack, poach pear slices in a little water with cinnamon and cloves until tender. Serve this warm or cold for a satisfying treat that curbs sweet cravings without spiking your blood sugar.

Finally, consider making a pear compote by simmering diced pears with a touch of vanilla and lemon zest. This can be served over whole grain pancakes or mixed into oatmeal, providing a delicious way to enjoy the natural sweetness of pears without needing added sugars.

Oranges

Oranges, the fruit of the Citrus sinensis tree, are one of the most popular fruits around the world. Known for their vibrant color and refreshing taste, oranges are a staple in many diets. They originated thousands of years ago in Asia, and today, they are grown in warm climates worldwide, celebrated not only for their flavor but also for their impressive health benefits.

Oranges are renowned for their high vitamin C content, a powerful antioxidant that boosts the immune system and skin health. The fiber in oranges helps regulate blood sugar levels and promotes digestive health, making it particularly beneficial for individuals with diabetes. The moderate glycemic index of oranges allows for a more gradual increase in blood sugar,

making them a safer choice for those needing to manage their glucose intake.

NUTRITIONAL INFORMATION PER 100 GRAMS OF ORANGES	
Total Calories: 47 kcal	
Protein: 0.94 g	
Total Fat: 0.12 g	
Saturated Fat: 0.015 g	
Unsaturated Fat: 0.023 g	
Total Carbohydrates: 11.75 g	
Dietary Fiber: 2.4 g	
Sugars: 9.35 g	
Sodium: 0 mg	
Vitamins and Minerals: High in Vitamin C and also provides potassium, thiamine, and folate	
Glycemic Index (GI): 35	

COOKING IDEAS WITH ORANGES

Start your day with a refreshing orange smoothie by blending fresh orange segments with unsweetened yogurt and a dash of vanilla extract. This combination provides a creamy texture and a rich source of protein and fiber.

Create a colorful salad by combining orange slices with mixed greens, sliced almonds, and red onion. Dress lightly with olive oil and white wine vinegar for a zesty and nutritious meal that balances sweetness and acidity perfectly.

Oranges also add a delightful twist to savory dishes. Add orange segments or freshly squeezed orange juice to marinades for chicken or fish to infuse the meat with a citrusy flavor that enhances the dish without overwhelming it.

For a simple, diabetic-friendly dessert, caramelized orange slices make a great option. Lightly grill orange slices until they are just charred, then sprinkle with a touch of cinnamon. This method brings out the natural sweetness without adding sugar.

Lastly, incorporate orange zest into whole grain muffin or bread recipes to add flavor and fragrance. This not only enhances the taste but also increases the nutritional value of your baked goods, making them a welcome treat in any diabetic-friendly diet.

Peaches

Peaches, scientifically known as Prunus persica, are juicy fruits cherished for their lush flavor and velvety texture. Originating from China over 8,000 years ago, peaches have become a symbol of longevity and a popular ingredient in cuisines worldwide. With their sweet aroma and a wealth of health-promoting properties, peaches hold a special place in both culinary arts and nutrition.

NUTRITIONAL INFORMATION PER 100 GRAMS OF PEACHES	
Total Calories: 39 kcal	
Protein: 0.91 g	
Total Fat: 0.25 g	
Saturated Fat: 0.019 g	
Unsaturated Fat: 0.068 g	
Total Carbohydrates: 9.54 g	
Dietary Fiber: 1.5 g	
Sugars: 8.39 g	
Sodium: 0 mg	
Vitamins and Minerals: Rich in Vitamin C, Vitamin A, potassium, and contains notable amounts of niacin and vitamin E	
Glycemic Index (GI): 35	

Peaches are a low-calorie fruit packed with vitamins and minerals essential for overall health. The high vitamin C content acts as a potent antioxidant, while vitamin A supports skin health and vision. The low glycemic index of peaches makes them an excellent choice for individuals managing diabetes, as they help maintain stable blood sugar levels. Additionally, the fiber in peaches aids digestion and helps provide a feeling of fullness, which can assist in weight management efforts.

COOKING IDEAS WITH PEACHES

Enjoy peaches in your breakfast by slicing them into fresh Greek yogurt. Top with a sprinkle of flax seeds for a meal rich in protein, fiber, and healthy fats, providing a balanced start to your day.

Grill peach halves and serve them with a dollop of ricotta cheese or drizzle them with a bit of honey for a decadent yet healthy dessert. The grilling process intensifies the natural sugars in the peaches, making them an excellent treat.

Create a refreshing peach salsa by chopping peaches and mixing them with cucumber, jalapeño, red onion, and cilantro. Serve this salsa over grilled fish or chicken for a burst of sweetness and spice that enhances the flavors of your protein.

Incorporate peaches into salads by adding thin slices to a bed of arugula, walnuts, and feta cheese, dressed lightly with balsamic vinaigrette. This salad offers a delightful mixture of sweet, nutty, and savory flavors, making it a nutritious and satisfying meal.

Lastly, make a simple peach compote by simmering sliced peaches with a touch of cinnamon and lemon juice until the fruits are soft and the flavors meld. Serve warm over whole grain pancakes or stir into oatmeal for a naturally sweet addition to your breakfast or dessert.

Apricots

Apricots are small, golden-orange fruits known for their velvety skin and sweet, slightly tart flavor. Originating from China, where they have been cultivated for over 4,000 years, apricots are enjoyed worldwide both fresh and dried. They are particularly prized in health circles for their nutrient density and low-calorie profile, making them a favored snack among those looking to maintain a healthy lifestyle.

Apricots offer a treasure trove of antioxidants, notably beta-carotene and vitamins A and C, which are crucial for immune function and skin health. Their high fiber content supports digestive health and helps manage blood sugar levels, making apricots a great choice for those with diabetes. The presence of potassium aids in maintaining cardiovascular health by regulating blood pressure levels.

NUTRITIONAL INFORMATION PER 100 GRAMS OF APRICOTS	
Total Calories: 48 kcal	
Protein: 1.4 g	
Total Fat: 0.39 g	
Saturated Fat: 0.027 g	
Unsaturated Fat: 0.17 g	
Total Carbohydrates: 11.12 g	
Dietary Fiber: 2 g	
Sugars: 9.24 g	
Sodium: 1 mg	
Vitamins and Minerals: Rich in Vitamin A, Vitamin C, potassium, and contains significant amounts of Vitamin E, iron, and calcium.	
Glycemic Index (GI): Low (34)	

COOKING IDEAS WITH APRICOTS

Start your day with apricot-infused oatmeal. Cook steel-cut oats and stir in chopped apricots during the last few minutes for a naturally sweet flavor that doesn't require added sugars. Top with a sprinkle of cinnamon and a handful of almonds for extra crunch and protein.

Prepare a wholesome apricot and chicken salad. Toss grilled chicken breast, fresh apricot slices, mixed greens, and a sprinkle of goat cheese with a light olive oil and lemon dressing. This meal is refreshing, nutritious, and balanced, providing lean protein, healthy fats, and a variety of vitamins.

Make your own apricot salsa by combining diced apricots with tomato, red onion, cilantro, and a splash of lime juice. This salsa is perfect as a topping for grilled fish or whole grain tortilla chips, offering a burst of sweetness and tanginess that enhances the flavors of your dishes.

Bake apricot halves with a touch of honey and a sprinkle of nutmeg for a delicious, health-friendly dessert. Serve warm with a scoop of low-fat Greek yogurt for a creamy texture that complements the soft and sweet apricots.

Simmer apricots in a small pot with a bit of fresh ginger and water until they form a thick sauce. Use this as a topping for whole grain pancakes or waffles, providing a sweet and slightly spicy flavor that makes a weekend breakfast feel special without the guilt.

Grapes

Grapes, a popular fruit found in many varieties including red, green, and black, originate from the Mediterranean and Central Asia. Throughout history, they have been cherished not only for their direct consumption but also for making wine. Grapes are known for their juicy texture and sweet-tart flavor, making them a favorite among fruit lovers around the world.

NUTRITIONAL INFORMATION PER 100 GRAMS OF GRAPES	
Total Calories: 69 kcal	
Protein: 0.72 g	
Total Fat: 0.16 g	
Saturated Fat: 0.054 g	
Unsaturated Fat: 0.071 g	
Total Carbohydrates: 18.1 g	
Dietary Fiber: 0.9 g	
Sugars: 15.48 g	
Sodium: 2 mg	
Vitamins and Minerals: High in Vitamin C, Vitamin K, and contains potassium and small amounts of various B vitamins.	
Glycemic Index (GI): 56	

Grapes are densely packed with nutrients and antioxidants, including resveratrol, which is found in the skins of red grapes. This compound is noted for its cardiovascular benefits and its ability to reduce inflammation. Although grapes are relatively high in sugar, their high water content help to moderate blood sugar absorption, making them a relatively safe choice in moderation for people with diabetes.

COOKING IDEAS WITH GRAPES

Create a refreshing grape salad by combining halved seedless grapes with slices of cucumber and feta cheese. Dress lightly with olive oil and balsamic vinegar for a crisp, hydrating side dish that pairs beautifully with grilled chicken or fish.

Incorporate grapes into a morning smoothie for a touch of natural sweetness. Blend green grapes with spinach, a small banana for creaminess, and unsweetened almond milk for a nutrient-packed drink that starts the day right.

Roast grapes to intensify their flavor and pair with savory dishes. Toss whole grapes with a little olive oil and roast at a high temperature until they burst. Serve alongside roasted or grilled meats for a delightful contrast in flavors.

Prepare a diabetic-friendly dessert by freezing whole grapes overnight. Enjoy these as a frosty treat that's both sweet and satisfying, perfect for cooling down on hot days without any added sugar.

Simmer grapes down into a sauce with a splash of lemon juice and a sprinkle of cinnamon. Use this as a topping for low-fat cottage cheese or Greek yogurt, providing a healthy snack or dessert option that satisfies sweet cravings without spiking blood sugar levels.

Apples

Apples, celebrated for their crisp texture and a range of sweet to tart flavors, are one of the most beloved fruits worldwide. Originating from Central Asia, these fruits have become a staple in diets across the globe, revered not only for their taste but also for their extensive health benefits. Apples are available in numerous varieties, each offering unique flavors and culinary possibilities, making them incredibly versatile in both raw and cooked forms.

Apples are a low-calorie fruit with a low glycemic index, making them a suitable choice for maintaining stable blood sugar levels. The fiber content, particularly from the skin, helps in digestive health and aids in satiety, which can assist in weight management. Vitamin C boosts immunity and acts as an antioxidant, while potassium contributes to heart health by regulating blood pressure.

NUTRITIONAL INFORMATION PER 100 GRAMS OF APPLES	
Total Calories: 52 kcal	
Protein: 0.3 g	
Total Fat: 0.2 g	
Saturated Fat: 0.03 g	
Unsaturated Fat: 0.17 g	
Total Carbohydrates: 13.81 g	
Dietary Fiber: 2.4 g	
Sugars: 10.39 g	
Sodium: 1 mg	
Vitamins and Minerals: Good source of Vitamin C, potassium, and several B vitamins. Contains small amounts of iron, calcium, and Vitamin A.	
Glycemic Index (GI): 36	

COOKING IDEAS WITH APPLES

Apples can be enjoyed in a variety of ways that complement a diabetes-friendly diet by emphasizing their natural sweetness without adding excess sugars:

Bake apples to concentrate their sweetness and enhance their natural flavors. Core the apples and stuff them with a mixture of nuts, cinnamon, and a small amount of a sweetener like monk fruit or stevia. Bake until tender for a comforting, diabetic-friendly dessert.

Incorporate raw apples into salads for a crunchy texture and a burst of freshness. Combine sliced apples with leafy greens, walnuts, and a vinaigrette made with apple cider vinegar and olive oil for a salad that balances sweetness with acidity and rich flavors.

Create a homemade apple sauce by cooking apples until they are soft and then mashing them. Add cinnamon and a touch of vanilla extract for flavor. Use this applesauce as a natural sweetener in oatmeal or yogurt instead of using added sugars.

Use apples to add flavor and moisture to baked goods. Grate apples and add them to muffin or pancake batter to create moist, flavorful, and healthy breakfast options. Pair with whole-grain flours to keep the recipes diabetes-friendly.

Grill apple slices to serve as a side dish or dessert. Lightly brush the slices with olive oil and grill until caramelized. The grilling process enhances their natural sugars, making them a delicious topping for salads or a sweet treat paired with a sprinkle of cinnamon.

Berries

Berries, the small but mighty fruits of various perennial plants, are celebrated for their delightful blend of sweetness and tang. Popular varieties include strawberries, blueberries, raspberries, and blackberries, each bursting with intense flavor and color. These fruits are not just delicious; they are also incredibly nutritious, offering an array of health benefits. Historically, berries have been a part of the human diet for thousands of years, with their use in traditional medicine being just as valued as their culinary applications.

NUTRITIONAL INFORMATION PER 100 GRAMS OF BERRIES (AVERAGE)	
Total Calories: 57 kcal	
Protein: 0.74 g	
Total Fat: 0.33 g	
Saturated Fat: 0.02 g	
Unsaturated Fat: 0.15 g	
Total Carbohydrates: 13.8 g	
Dietary Fiber: 4.9 g	
Sugars: 8.9 g	
Sodium: 1 mg	
Vitamins and Minerals: Rich in Vitamin C, Vitamin K, manganese, and antioxidants	
Glycemic Index (GI): Low (ranging from 25 to 40, depending on the berry)	

Berries are renowned for their high nutritional value and minimal impact on blood sugar levels, thanks to their low glycemic index. The rich fiber content in berries helps to regulate blood sugar levels by slowing the absorption of sugar into the bloodstream. Additionally, they are a powerhouse of antioxidants, including anthocyanins, which not only give berries their vibrant color but also contribute to reducing inflammation and preventing several chronic diseases. Their high vitamin C content supports the immune system, while manganese plays a crucial role in bone development and metabolism.

COOKING IDEAS WITH BERRIES

Incorporating berries into a diabetes-friendly diet can be both creative and delicious. Prepare a refreshing berry salad by tossing mixed berries with a sprinkle of lemon zest and a drizzle of balsamic reduction to enhance their natural sweetness without added sugars. Another option is to blend berries into a smoothie with spinach and Greek yogurt, creating a nutrient-rich drink that balances proteins, fats, and carbohydrates for a healthy start to the day.

For a dessert that doesn't compromise health, make a berry compote by simmering mixed berries with a touch of cinnamon and vanilla extract; serve it over whole grain pancakes or unsweetened Greek yogurt for a touch of indulgence. Berries can also be added to whole grain muffins or breads, providing moisture and flavor while increasing the fiber content of baked goods. Lastly, freeze whole berries and blend them into a homemade sorbet that can serve as a cool treat during warm weather, perfect for satisfying sweet cravings without spiking blood sugar levels.

LEAN PROTEINS

Lean animal proteins are essential in a diabetes management diet, offering substantial nutritional benefits without the added fats that can negatively impact cardiovascular health. Sources like chicken, turkey, fish, and lean cuts of beef and pork provide high-quality protein that helps stabilize blood sugar levels by minimizing rapid glucose fluctuations often induced by high-carbohydrate foods.

Protein is critical not only for muscle repair and growth but also for maintaining hormonal balance and enzymatic functions within the body. Importantly, animal proteins do not contribute directly to blood glucose levels, which is key for managing diabetes effectively. They also play a vital role in satiety, helping to manage appetite and reduce the likelihood of overeating, which is crucial for maintaining an optimal body weight in diabetes care.

Incorporating these proteins into a diabetic diet can be done in a way that keeps meals interesting and nutritionally balanced. For example, starting the day with a piece of grilled fish or a few slices of turkey in an omelet can provide a morning boost without the risk of sugar spikes. For lunch and dinner, options like grilled chicken breasts, baked fish, or lean pork loin serve as excellent main dishes that can be paired with fiber-rich vegetables and whole grains to create a fulfilling and healthful meal.

The adaptability of lean animal proteins allows for culinary creativity, enabling the preparation of varied dishes that can help sustain long-term dietary satisfaction and adherence.

Chicken

Chicken is a widely consumed meat around the world, known for its versatility, high protein content, and relatively low fat, making it a staple in various cuisines. From grilled and roasted forms to being used in soups and salads, chicken can be prepared in numerous ways to suit any taste. It serves as a crucial source of lean protein in many diets, supporting muscle growth and overall health.

NUTRITIONAL INFORMATION PER 100 GRAMS OF COOKED CHICKEN BREAST
Total Calories: 165 kcal
Protein: 31 g
Total Fat: 3.6 g
Saturated Fat: 1 g
Unsaturated Fat: 1.5 g
Carbohydrates: 0 g
Dietary Fiber: 0 g
Sugars: 0 g
Sodium: 74 mg
Vitamins and Minerals: Rich in niacin, vitamin B6, phosphorus, selenium, and contains traces of iron, zinc, and vitamin B12.

Chicken breast is highly regarded for its high protein and low fat ratio, making it an excellent choice for people looking to maintain or lose weight, as well as for those managing chronic conditions such as diabetes. Its impressive profile of vitamins and minerals supports muscle function, bone health, and the immune system.

COOKING IDEAS WITH CHICKEN

Create a nutritious chicken salad by combining grilled chicken breast strips with mixed greens, cherry tomatoes, avocado, and a sprinkle of walnuts. Dress this salad with a vinaigrette made from olive oil and lemon juice to keep it light and diabetes-friendly.

Simmer chicken in a hearty vegetable soup. Use a base of low-sodium chicken broth and add plenty of vegetables like carrots, celery, and spinach. Season with herbs like thyme and rosemary to enhance the flavors without adding extra salt or sugar.

For a filling main dish, stuff a chicken breast with a mixture of spinach, mushrooms, and a small amount of parmesan cheese. Bake until the chicken is thoroughly cooked and serve with a side of steamed broccoli or asparagus.

Marinate chicken pieces in a blend of Greek yogurt, garlic, and spices, then grill them until cooked through. Serve these flavorful skewers with a side of cucumber yogurt sauce and a small portion of whole-grain rice or a quinoa salad.

Braise chicken thighs in a tomato-based sauce with bell peppers, onions, and a touch of balsamic vinegar for a deliciously tangy and savory dish that pairs well with whole wheat pasta or a bed of leafy greens.

Turkey

Turkey is a popular poultry choice, especially noted for its role in traditional holiday feasts like Thanksgiving and Christmas. However, beyond its festive appeal, turkey is prized for its lean protein, making it a year-round staple in healthy eating diets. It offers a slightly richer flavor than chicken, providing a versatile base for a range of culinary creations from around the world.

NUTRITIONAL INFORMATION PER 100 GRAMS OF COOKED TURKEY BREAST
Total Calories: 135 kcal
Protein: 29 g
Total Fat: 2 g
Saturated Fat: 0.7 g
Unsaturated Fat: 0.5 g
Carbohydrates: 0 g
Dietary Fiber: 0 g
Sugars: 0 g
Sodium: 104 mg
Vitamins and Minerals: Rich in niacin, vitamin B6, selenium, and phosphorus, with traces of zinc and iron.

Turkey's high protein content and low-fat profile make it excellent for weight management and muscle building. Its rich array of B vitamins supports energy metabolism and brain function, while selenium acts as a powerful antioxidant to combat cellular damage.

COOKING IDEAS WITH TURKEY

Sauté ground turkey with garlic, onions, and a mix of bell peppers for a colorful and tasty turkey chili. Spice it up with cumin and chili powder, and simmer with diced tomatoes for a robust flavor without added sugars.

Roast a turkey breast with a rub of olive oil, lemon zest, and fresh herbs such as rosemary and sage. Serve slices over a bed of roasted vegetables like Brussels sprouts and sweet potatoes for a balanced meal rich in nutrients.

Prepare turkey meatballs seasoned with herbs and spices, baked in the oven. Serve them over a bed of spaghetti squash or zucchini noodles, topped with a homemade tomato sauce that's low in sugar.

Grill turkey burgers using finely chopped turkey breast mixed with a small amount of whole-grain breadcrumbs and egg to bind them. Add finely diced onions, parsley, and a touch of Dijon mustard for

flavor. Serve on a whole-grain bun or wrapped in lettuce for a lower carb option.

Create a refreshing turkey salad by mixing shredded cooked turkey with sliced almonds, diced celery, and grapes. Use a dressing made from plain Greek yogurt and fresh dill. Serve this salad chilled, perfect for a light lunch or as a filling for a whole-grain wrap.

Salmon

Salmon is renowned for its incredible health benefits and is a staple in diets that focus on heart health and cognitive function. This oily fish is native to the North Atlantic and Pacific Ocean and is consumed worldwide. It is particularly celebrated in culinary traditions ranging from Scandinavian to Japanese cuisine.

NUTRITIONAL INFORMATION PER 100 GRAMS OF RAW SALMON
Total Calories: 208 kcal
Protein: 20 g
Total Fat: 13 g
Saturated Fat: 3 g
Unsaturated Fat: 10 g
Carbohydrates: 0 g
Dietary Fiber: 0 g
Sugars: 0 g
Sodium: 59 mg
Vitamins and Minerals: High in Vitamin D, B12, selenium, and significant amounts of phosphorus.

Salmon is especially valued for its high content of omega-3 fatty acids, which are essential for cardiovascular health, reducing inflammation, and supporting brain function. The presence of vitamin D and selenium further enhances its status as a superfood, promoting bone health and immune function.

COOKING IDEAS WITH SALMON

Poach salmon fillets gently in a broth made with white wine, garlic, and fresh herbs such as dill and parsley. This method enhances the fish's natural flavors without adding unnecessary fats or sugars.

Grill salmon steaks and serve them with a side of grilled asparagus and a sprinkle of lemon zest. This simple preparation allows the rich flavor of the salmon to shine through while keeping the meal light, healthy, and diabetic-friendly.

Bake salmon topped with a crust of crushed almonds and a sprinkle of Parmesan cheese, adding a delightful crunch and additional protein. Serve with a side salad dressed with olive oil and vinegar to balance the meal.

Create a salmon salad by flaking cooked salmon and mixing it with diced celery, red onion, capers, and a dressing made from Greek yogurt and mustard. Serve this chilled on whole-grain toast or stuffed in a ripe avocado for a dose of healthy fats.

Wrap salmon fillets in parchment paper with slices of lemon, dill, and a drizzle of olive oil, then bake. This en papillote method locks in moisture and flavors without extra oils or fats, making it ideal for a healthy, diabetes-friendly meal.

Tuna

Tuna is a widely popular seafood choice known for its robust flavor and versatility in dishes ranging from salads to grilled entrees. It thrives in warmer waters and comes in several varieties, including bluefin, yellowfin, and albacore, each offering unique flavors and textures. Tuna is not only a staple in many world cuisines but also a significant component of a healthy diet due to its high protein content and beneficial fats.

NUTRITIONAL INFORMATION PER 100 GRAMS OF RAW TUNA
Total Calories: 109 kcal
Protein: 24 g
Total Fat: 0.5 g
Saturated Fat: 0.2 g
Unsaturated Fat: 0.2 g
Carbohydrates: 0 g
Dietary Fiber: 0 g
Sugars: 0 g
Sodium: 39 mg
Vitamins and Minerals: Rich in niacin, Vitamin B6, Vitamin B12, phosphorus, and selenium.

Tuna is exceptionally high in protein while being low in both fat and calories, making it an ideal choice for anyone looking to maintain or improve overall physical health. It is loaded with omega-3 fatty acids which are crucial for cardiovascular health, reducing inflammation, and supporting cognitive function. The vitamins B6 and B12 in tuna help with energy production and the formation of red blood cells, while selenium acts as a powerful antioxidant.

COOKING IDEAS WITH TUNA

Grill tuna steaks with a light brushing of olive oil and a seasoning of black pepper and fresh herbs such as thyme and basil. This method brings out the natural flavors of the fish without adding excessive calories or carbohydrates, adhering to diabetic dietary needs.

Create a Mediterranean tuna salad by mixing flaked grilled tuna with chopped cucumbers, tomatoes, olives, and feta cheese, dressed with olive oil and lemon juice. This salad is rich in nutrients and healthy fats, suitable for a diabetes-friendly diet.

Sear tuna fillets over high heat for a brief period, keeping the center pink. Serve with a side of mixed greens and drizzle with a balsamic reduction to enhance the flavor without adding sugar.

Simmer tuna chunks in a tomato and herb sauce and serve over a bed of zucchini noodles for a low-carbohydrate alternative to pasta dishes. This preparation maintains low sugar levels while being satisfying and flavorful.

Prepare a tuna poke bowl using fresh raw tuna cubes marinated in soy sauce, sesame oil, and a touch of ginger, served over a small portion of brown rice and topped with sliced avocado, scallions, and sesame seeds. This dish balances lean protein, healthy fats, and whole grains to create a fulfilling meal that fits well within a diabetes-friendly diet plan.

Cod

Cod is a widely appreciated white fish known for its mild flavor and flaky texture, making it a staple in many traditional dishes from fish and chips to classic New England chowder. Its subtle taste and versatility make it a favorite among chefs and home cooks alike. Cod is also celebrated for its health benefits, particularly for those seeking a low-calorie, high-protein dietary option.

NUTRITIONAL INFORMATION PER 100 GRAMS OF RAW COD
Total Calories: 82 kcal
Protein: 18 g
Total Fat: 0.7 g
Saturated Fat: 0.1 g
Unsaturated Fat: 0.2 g
Carbohydrates: 0 g
Dietary Fiber: 0 g
Sugars: 0 g
Sodium: 54 mg
Vitamins and Minerals: High in Vitamin B12, niacin, and phosphorus. Good source of iodine, selenium, and other essential minerals.

Cod is an excellent source of high-quality protein and low in fat, making it ideal for those managing their weight or blood sugar levels, such as diabetics. The fish is also rich in vitamins B12 and niacin, which are essential for energy metabolism and maintaining good cardiovascular health. Furthermore, the trace minerals found in cod, like selenium and iodine, are crucial for thyroid function and have antioxidant properties.

COOKING IDEAS WITH COD

Prepare poached cod by gently simmering fillets in a broth of white wine, garlic, and herbs. This method enhances the fish's delicate texture and flavor without adding unnecessary fats or sugars.

Bake cod in parchment with slices of lemon, dill, and a sprinkle of olive oil. This cooking technique seals in moisture and flavor, resulting in a tender and heart-healthy dish suitable for a diabetes management plan.

Create a cod stew by stewing pieces of the fish in a tomato-based sauce with Mediterranean herbs and spices. Serve this over a bed of steamed greens or cauliflower rice for a nutritious, balanced meal.

Make grilled cod tacos using lightly marinated fillets grilled to perfection. Serve on corn tortillas with a slaw of cabbage, cilantro, and lime juice, offering a high-protein meal with minimal impact on blood sugar.

Cook cod curry by simmering the fish in a sauce of coconut milk and curry spices until tender. This flavorful dish pairs well with a small portion of basmati rice or whole grain naan, providing a satisfying meal without the high glycemic load.

Egg Whites

Egg whites are a highly valued food component, especially among health enthusiasts and individuals managing dietary restrictions, such as those with diabetes. Extracted from the whole eggs and devoid of the yolk, egg whites are renowned for their pure protein content and versatility in culinary applications. They offer a low-calorie option for increasing protein intake without the cholesterol and fat associated with egg yolks.

NUTRITIONAL INFORMATION PER 100 GRAMS OF RAW EGG WHITES
Total Calories: 52 kcal
Protein: 11 g
Total Fat: 0.2 g
Saturated Fat: 0 g
Unsaturated Fat: 0 g
Carbohydrates: 0.7 g
Dietary Fiber: 0 g
Sugars: 0.7 g
Sodium: 166 mg
Vitamins and Minerals: Rich in selenium, and contains amounts of potassium, riboflavin, and niacin.

Egg whites stand out due to their high protein content, which is essential for muscle repair and maintenance. They are also low in calories and virtually free of fat, making them an ideal choice for those looking to manage their weight or blood sugar levels. Additionally, the presence of potassium and selenium supports cardiovascular health and antioxidant defenses.

COOKING IDEAS WITH EGG WHITES

Whip up an omelet using egg whites combined with a medley of fresh vegetables such as spinach, mushrooms, and bell peppers. Cook in a non-stick skillet to minimize the need for added fats, creating a nutritious and satisfying meal that is low in carbohydrates and calories.

Create fluffy meringues by whisking egg whites with a pinch of cream of tartar until stiff peaks form, then gently folding in a sugar substitute before baking. This dessert allows for a sweet treat without the high sugar content.

Prepare a protein smoothie by blending egg whites with Greek yogurt, a handful of berries, and a small banana for sweetness. This high-protein shake is perfect for post-workout recovery or a quick breakfast option that stabilizes blood sugar levels.

Make egg white pancakes by mixing egg whites with low-carb flour, a touch of baking powder, and vanilla extract for flavor. Serve with fresh berries and a drizzle of sugar-free syrup for a diabetes-friendly breakfast that feels indulgent yet is health-conscious.

Cook steamed egg white custards, a popular dish in Asian cuisine, by whisking egg whites with a small amount of milk, seasoning with a pinch of salt, and steaming until set. This light, savory custard can serve as an elegant side dish or a main course.

Lean Beef

Lean beef is a staple in many diets around the world, known for its rich flavor and high content of essential nutrients. It is particularly valued in health-conscious circles and among those managing chronic conditions like diabetes for its high-quality protein and relatively low fat content. Choosing cuts like sirloin, tenderloin, or extra lean ground beef ensures that the benefits are maximized without excessive saturated fat intake.

NUTRITIONAL INFORMATION PER 100 GRAMS OF UNCOOKED LEAN BEEF	
Total Calories: 150 kcal	
Protein: 26 g	
Total Fat: 6 g	
Saturated Fat: 2.5 g	
Unsaturated Fat: 2.7 g	
Carbohydrates: 0 g	
Dietary Fiber: 0 g	
Sugars: 0 g	
Sodium: 55 mg	
Vitamins and Minerals: Rich in Vitamin B12, Zinc, Selenium, Iron, and Niacin	

Lean beef is a powerhouse of protein, essential for muscle growth and repair, which is crucial for everyone, including those with diabetes. It's low in carbohydrates, which means it has minimal impact on blood sugar levels. The presence of iron and vitamin B12 makes it especially beneficial in preventing anemia and supporting energy levels. Zinc and selenium are important for a healthy immune system, while the low sodium content makes it a suitable option for heart health.

COOKING IDEAS WITH LEAN BEEF

Create a hearty beef stew by slow-cooking chunks of lean beef with a bounty of vegetables like carrots, celery, and onions in a low-sodium broth. Herbs and spices can be added for flavor without adding sugar or excessive salt.

Grill marinated slices of sirloin or tenderloin, using a blend of olive oil, garlic, and fresh herbs for the marinade. Serve these grilled steaks with a side of grilled vegetables or a fresh salad for a balanced meal that includes fiber to help manage blood sugar levels.

Prepare a lean beef stir-fry with a variety of colorful vegetables such as bell peppers, broccoli, and snap peas. Use a small amount of sesame oil for cooking and flavor with ginger and a splash of low-sodium soy sauce for an Asian-inspired dish that is both nutritious and satisfying.

Make meatballs using extra lean ground beef, mixing in chopped onions, herbs, and a binding agent like beaten eggs or a sprinkle of almond flour. Bake these meatballs and serve them with a homemade tomato sauce over zucchini noodles for a comforting, low-carb meal.

Cook a lean beef burger using ground sirloin, season with salt, pepper, and Worcestershire sauce, and serve on a whole-grain or lettuce bun with plenty of fresh vegetables like lettuce, tomato, and avocado. Opt for mustard or a yogurt-based sauce instead of high-sugar ketchup to keep it diabetes-friendly.

Pork Loin

Pork loin, a popular cut from the area between the shoulder and the beginning of the leg, is prized for its tenderness and lean quality compared to other cuts of pork. It is an excellent choice for a balanced diet due to its favorable nutritional profile, offering a wealth of proteins and essential nutrients with relatively low fat content.

NUTRITIONAL INFORMATION PER 100 GRAMS OF UNCOOKED PORK LOIN	
Total Calories: 143 kcal	
Protein: 26.1 g	
Total Fat: 3.6 g	
Saturated Fat: 1.2 g	
Unsaturated Fat: 1.9 g	
Carbohydrates: 0 g	
Dietary Fiber: 0 g	
Sugars: 0 g	
Sodium: 62 mg	
Vitamins and Minerals: High in Thiamine, Niacin, Vitamin B6, Phosphorus, Zinc, and Selenium	

The lean cut of pork loin is not only low in fat but also rich in high-quality protein, which is vital for muscle repair and maintenance. The vitamin B6 found in pork loin aids in normal nerve function and the production of glucose during times your body needs it, making it particularly beneficial for people managing diabetes. Zinc and selenium contribute to immune health, while thiamine is crucial for converting food into energy, which is essential for maintaining energy levels and overall metabolism.

COOKING IDEAS WITH PORK LOIN

Prepare a savory roast pork loin by seasoning it with a mixture of garlic, rosemary, and thyme, then roasting in the oven until it reaches a perfect tender and juicy state. Serve with a side of roasted Brussels sprouts or a salad of mixed greens for a full meal that is low in carbohydrates and rich in nutrients.

Pork loin can be sliced into medallions and pan-seared with minimal oil. Add a splash of white wine and a squeeze of fresh lemon juice for a flavorful sauce that does not elevate blood sugar levels. Accompany with steamed asparagus or a cauliflower mash to keep the meal balanced and diabetes-friendly.

Try a pork stir-fry by cutting the loin into thin strips and cooking quickly with a variety of vegetables such as bell peppers, broccoli, and snap peas. Flavor the dish with ginger, garlic, and a touch of low-sodium soy sauce for an Asian flair that is both nutritious and delicious.

Another idea is to create a pork loin stew in a slow cooker, combining the pork with low-glycemic vegetables like mushrooms, zucchini, and tomatoes. Let it cook slowly until the pork is exceptionally tender. This method allows flavors to meld together wonderfully, creating a dish that is comforting and suitable for blood sugar management.

Greek Yogurt

Greek yogurt is a thicker, creamier version of regular yogurt, achieved through an extensive straining process that removes much of the liquid whey, lactose, and sugar, giving it a richer texture and a more concentrated nutrient profile. It has become a popular choice among health enthusiasts, particularly for those managing their weight or blood sugar levels due to its high protein and low sugar content.

NUTRITIONAL INFORMATION PER 100 GRAMS OF GREEK YOGURT	
Total Calories: 59 kcal	
Protein: 10 g	
Total Fat: 0.4 g	
Saturated Fat: 0.1 g	
Unsaturated Fat: 0.3 g	
Carbohydrates: 3.6 g	
Dietary Fiber: 0 g	
Sugars: 3.6 g	
Sodium: 36 mg	
Vitamins and Minerals: Rich in Calcium, Phosphorus, Vitamin B12, and Riboflavin	
Glycemic Index (GI): 12	

Greek yogurt's high protein content is excellent for satiety and muscle maintenance, making it a beneficial addition to a diabetic diet. The probiotics found in Greek yogurt help in maintaining a healthy gut flora, which is crucial for overall health and metabolic processes. It's also an excellent source of calcium, which is vital for bone health, and B vitamins, particularly vitamin B12 and riboflavin, which are essential for energy metabolism and red blood cell production.

COOKING IDEAS WITH GREEK YOGURT

Create a refreshing breakfast or snack by layering Greek yogurt with low-glycemic fruits like berries and nuts. This not only adds a variety of textures and flavors but also incorporates healthy fats and antioxidants without a significant spike in blood sugar.

Utilize Greek yogurt as a base for smoothies; blend it with spinach, a small green apple, and flaxseeds for a nutrient-rich drink that balances carbs with high fiber and proteins, maintaining stable blood sugar levels.

Greek yogurt can serve as a healthier alternative to sour cream in dips or toppings. Mix it with herbs and spices to accompany baked sweet potato fries or as a dressing for vegetable salads, enhancing your meals with protein without additional fat or sugar.

Incorporate Greek yogurt into baking by using it as a substitute for butter or oil in recipes for muffins and pancakes. This substitution not only reduces fat content but also adds moisture and protein, making your baked goods more suitable for a health-conscious diet.

PLANT-BASED PROTEINS

Plant-based proteins are an invaluable component of a diabetes-friendly diet, offering diverse health benefits while supporting blood sugar management. Foods like beans, lentils, chickpeas, tofu, and tempeh provide high-quality protein without the saturated fats found in some animal sources, making them ideal for those looking to maintain or improve their cardiovascular health.

Rich in fiber and essential nutrients, plant-based proteins help stabilize blood sugar levels by slowing the digestion process, thereby preventing rapid glucose spikes. This fiber content also enhances satiety, reducing the urge to snack excessively and aiding in weight management—a key factor in controlling Type 2 diabetes.

Incorporating plant-based proteins into meals not only diversifies the diet but also contributes to a lower environmental footprint, aligning with sustainable eating practices. They can be used in a variety of culinary applications, from hearty stews and salads to innovative dishes like veggie burgers and plant-based pastas, ensuring meals are both nutritious and enjoyable.

Moreover, plant proteins can often serve as a direct substitute for animal proteins, making them a versatile choice for any meal. For instance, tofu can be scrambled as an alternative to eggs, lentils can replace ground beef in recipes, and chickpeas can be transformed into a flavorful hummus as a snack or side dish.

Lentils

Lentils, small but mighty legumes, have been a cornerstone of diets around the world for thousands of years. Originating in Central Asia, these pulses have spread globally due to their adaptability to a wide range of climates and soils. They come in a variety of colors, including green, brown, red, and black, each offering a slightly different flavor profile but all equally nutritious. Lentils are highly prized not only for their rich nutrient content but also for their ease of cooking and versatility, making them a popular choice in vegetarian, vegan, and health-conscious diets.

NUTRITIONAL INFORMATION PER 100 GRAMS OF UNCOOKED LENTILS
Total Calories: 352 kcal
Protein: 24.63 g
Total Fat: 1.06 g
Saturated Fat: 0.149 g
Unsaturated Fat: 0.911 g
Total Carbohydrates: 63.35 g
Dietary Fiber: 10.7 g
Sugars: 2.03 g
Sodium: 6 mg
Vitamins and Minerals: Excellent source of folate, good source of iron, magnesium, phosphorus, and zinc. Contains B-vitamins including thiamin and niacin.
Glycemic Index (GI): Approximately 30

Lentils are a powerhouse of nutrition. They offer a high protein content, making them an excellent alternative to meat. Their low glycemic index is ideal for maintaining stable blood sugar levels, beneficial for people with diabetes. The significant fiber content improves digestive health and helps in controlling appetite by promoting feelings of fullness. Rich in iron and folate, lentils support energy production and overall cellular health.

COOKING IDEAS WITH LENTILS

Lentils can be incorporated into a variety of dishes that cater to a diabetes-friendly diet, emphasizing their adaptability and flavor-absorbing properties.

Prepare a hearty lentil soup by simmering lentils with a mixture of diced vegetables like carrots, celery, and onions, along with low-sodium broth and herbs for seasoning. This soup can be a nutritious and filling meal that's low in calories but high in fiber and protein.

Use lentils to make a robust salad. Cook and cool the lentils, then mix with chopped vegetables, such as peppers, cucumber, and tomatoes. Dress with olive oil and lemon juice for a refreshing meal or side dish that's rich in nutrients and fiber.

Create a lentil-based stew with a tomato or coconut milk base. Add spices such as cumin, coriander, and turmeric to enhance the flavors and offer additional anti-inflammatory benefits. Serve this stew over a small portion of whole-grain rice or enjoy it on its own.

Make lentil patties by blending cooked lentils with onions, garlic, and spices, then forming them into patties and baking or lightly frying. These can be served in place of meat burgers, offering a low-fat, high-protein alternative that's also rich in fiber.

Incorporate lentils into breakfast by making a savory lentil porridge. Cook lentils until soft, then mix with sautéed vegetables and season with herbs for a warm, nutritious start to the day.

Chickpeas

Chickpeas, also known as garbanzo beans, are a type of legume that forms an essential part of various cuisines worldwide, particularly in the Mediterranean and the Middle East. These round, beige-colored beans are known for their nutty taste and grainy texture, making them a popular ingredient in many dishes, including hummus, salads, and stews.

NUTRITIONAL INFORMATION PER 100 GRAMS OF UNCOOKED CHICKPEAS
Total Calories: 364 kcal
Protein: 19 g
Total Fat: 6 g
Saturated Fat: 0.6 g
Unsaturated Fat: 2.7 g
Carbohydrates: 61 g
Dietary Fiber: 17 g
Sugars: 11 g
Sodium: 24 mg
Vitamins and Minerals: High in Folate, Iron, Phosphorus, Magnesium, and Manganese
Glycemic Index (GI): 28

Chickpeas are a powerhouse of nutrition, offering substantial plant-based protein and dietary fiber, which are vital for blood sugar control, making them an excellent choice for individuals with diabetes. The low glycemic index of chickpeas helps in maintaining steady blood sugar levels, while their high fiber content aids in digestion and prolongs satiety. Rich in vitamins and minerals, chickpeas support overall health, including enhanced iron absorption, boosted energy levels, and improved digestive health.

COOKING IDEAS WITH CHICKPEAS

Transform chickpeas into a creamy hummus by blending them with tahini, lemon juice, and garlic. Serve with a drizzle of olive oil and a sprinkle of paprika, accompanied by fresh vegetable sticks or whole grain pita bread for a balanced, low GI snack.

Incorporate chickpeas into salads by tossing them with chopped vegetables like cucumbers, tomatoes, and onions, dressed with olive oil and vinegar. This salad is not only refreshing but also provides a good mix of proteins, fats, and fibers.

Create a hearty, flavorful stew with chickpeas, tomatoes, spinach, and spices such as cumin and coriander. Simmer until the flavors meld together beautifully. Serve this stew over a small portion of brown rice or enjoy it as a standalone dish for a filling meal.

Roast chickpeas in the oven with a bit of olive oil and your favorite spices until crispy. This makes for a fantastic snack that is both nutritious and satisfying, perfect for on-the-go snacking or as a crunchy topping for soups and salads.

Beans

Beans, including black, pinto, and kidney varieties, are fundamental foods in many traditional diets around the world. Known for their versatility and dense nutrient content, these legumes are staples in a variety of global cuisines, from Mexican to Mediterranean. They are praised for their ability to act as both a protein source and a fiber-rich carbohydrate, making them a balanced food choice for a wide range of dietary needs, including diabetes management.

NUTRITIONAL INFORMATION PER 100 GRAMS OF RAW MIXED BEANS (BLACK, PINTO, AND KIDNEY)
Total Calories: 341 kcal
Protein: 21.4 g
Total Fat: 1.6 g
Saturated Fat: 0.2 g
Unsaturated Fat: 1.4 g
Total Carbohydrates: 62.3 g
Dietary Fiber: 15.5 g
Sugars: 2.1 g
Sodium: 12 mg
Vitamins and Minerals: High in folate, iron, magnesium, and potassium. Also contains zinc and B-vitamins.
Glycemic Index (GI): Approximately 20-40 (varies by type)

Beans are incredibly beneficial for overall health, particularly for managing diabetes due to their low glycemic index. The high fiber content aids in blood sugar regulation by slowing glucose absorption and promoting satiety, which can prevent overeating. Rich in protein, beans can help maintain muscle mass, which is crucial for metabolic health. Their wealth of vitamins and minerals supports various bodily functions from energy production to immune defense.

COOKING IDEAS WITH BEANS

Beans can be incorporated into a myriad of diabetes-friendly recipes, enhancing dishes with their texture, flavor, and nutritional benefits.

Simmer beans in a tomato-based chili, spiced with cumin, chili powder, and garlic. This hearty dish can be made in large batches and provides a filling meal that pairs well with whole-grain bread or a green salad.

Create a cold bean salad by mixing cooked black, pinto, and kidney beans with chopped bell peppers, onions, and a cilantro-lime dressing. This salad is perfect for meal prep and can serve as a nutritious side dish or a main course.

Use mashed pinto beans as a base for a healthy bean dip, seasoned with paprika, garlic powder, and lime juice. Serve with raw vegetables or whole-grain crackers for a snack that's rich in fiber and protein.

Incorporate kidney beans into a vegetable soup, adding tomatoes, celery, carrots, and spinach for a nutrient-packed meal. Season with herbs like thyme and rosemary to enhance the flavors without adding extra sodium.

Prepare a bean-based burger by blending cooked beans with oats, chopped onions, and spices, then form into patties and grill or bake. These burgers are a fantastic alternative to meat and can be enjoyed with whole-grain buns and fresh vegetable toppings.

Tofu

Tofu, also known as bean curd, is a versatile, plant-based food made by coagulating soy milk and then pressing the resulting curds into solid white blocks. Originating in China, tofu is a staple in many Asian cuisines and has gained popularity worldwide due to its nutritional benefits and adaptability in various dishes.

NUTRITIONAL INFORMATION PER 100 GRAMS OF UNCOOKED TOFU
Total Calories: 76 kcal
Protein: 8 g
Total Fat: 4.8 g
Saturated Fat: 0.7 g
Unsaturated Fat: 3.3 g
Carbohydrates: 1.9 g
Dietary Fiber: 0.3 g
Sugars: 0.3 g
Sodium: 7 mg
Vitamins and Minerals: Rich in Calcium, Iron, and Magnesium
Glycemic Index (GI): 15

Tofu is celebrated for its high protein content and low-calorie count, making it an ideal food for managing diabetes and maintaining a healthy weight. The low amount of saturated fat and the presence of heart-healthy unsaturated fats contribute to cardiovascular health. Being low in carbohydrates, it has little to no impact on blood glucose levels, and the minerals found in tofu, such as calcium and iron, support bone health and energy production.

COOKING IDEAS WITH TOFU

For a satisfying, nutrient-rich breakfast, scramble tofu with turmeric, onions, and spinach. Serve this scramble with a slice of whole-grain toast for a balanced meal that starts the day off right.

Prepare a nutritious stir-fry with tofu cubes, a variety of colorful vegetables, and a sauce made from low-sodium soy sauce, garlic, and ginger. Serve this over a bed of steamed brown rice or quinoa to create a filling meal that's rich in proteins and fibers.

Create a creamy soup by blending silken tofu with cooked pumpkin, onions, and a touch of nutmeg for flavor. This soup is comforting and creamy without the need for heavy cream, making it a healthier option for those managing their blood sugar levels.

Make a tofu kabob by marinating tofu blocks in a mixture of olive oil, lemon juice, and herbs, then threading them onto skewers with bell peppers, onions, and tomatoes. Grill or bake until the vegetables are tender and the tofu is slightly crispy.

Incorporate tofu into a salad by adding baked tofu cubes to mixed greens, cherry tomatoes, and avocado. Dress with a vinaigrette made from balsamic vinegar and extra virgin olive oil for a hearty salad that's both delicious and diabetes-friendly.

Edamame

Edamame, young soybeans harvested before they harden, are a popular snack in East Asia, particularly Japan. These beans are usually steamed or boiled and can be eaten right out of the pod. Known for their bright green color and sweet, slightly nutty flavor, edamame is not only a delicious snack but also a nutrient-rich addition to any diet.

NUTRITIONAL INFORMATION PER 100 GRAMS OF UNCOOKED EDAMAME	
Total Calories: 121 kcal	
Protein: 11.9 g	
Total Fat: 5.2 g	
Saturated Fat: 0.6 g	
Unsaturated Fat: 3.0 g	
Carbohydrates: 9.9 g	
Dietary Fiber: 5.2 g	
Sugars: 2.2 g	
Sodium: 6 mg	
Vitamins and Minerals: High in Vitamin K, Folate, and Iron	
Glycemic Index (GI): 15	

Edamame is an excellent source of high-quality protein, making it particularly valuable in vegetarian and vegan diets. Its high fiber content aids in digestion and helps regulate blood sugar levels, which is crucial for individuals managing diabetes. The presence of essential vitamins and minerals like iron and Vitamin K supports overall health and wellness. Its low glycemic index means it won't cause rapid spikes in blood glucose, making it a safe choice for a diabetes-friendly diet.

COOKING IDEAS WITH EDAMAME

Blend boiled edamame into a smooth paste along with tahini, garlic, lemon juice, and olive oil to create a unique, healthy version of hummus. Serve with fresh vegetable sticks or whole-grain pita bread for a fiber-rich snack.

Toss steamed edamame in a salad with mixed greens, cherry tomatoes, cucumbers, and a light vinaigrette. This salad is refreshing and provides a balanced combination of proteins, fats, and carbohydrates.

Add shelled edamame to whole grain or soba noodle soups. The beans add texture and boost the protein content of your meal, enhancing satiety and nutritional value.

For a simple yet satisfying side, sauté shelled edamame with garlic, a splash of soy sauce, and a hint of chili flakes. This dish pairs well with grilled fish or chicken, offering a flavorful and nutritious complement to your meal.

Incorporate edamame into rice dishes, such as a vegetable fried rice or a pilaf. Cook the rice with onions, carrots, and peas, then stir in steamed edamame towards the end of cooking for an extra protein punch.

Tempeh

Tempeh, originating from Indonesia, is a traditional soy product made by fermenting cooked soybeans with a mold. Unlike tofu, tempeh has a firm texture and a nutty flavor, often enhanced by the fermentation process, which also makes its nutrients more digestible and absorbable. This plant-based protein is highly regarded not only for its taste but also for its substantial nutritional benefits, making it a favorite among vegetarians and health enthusiasts alike.

NUTRITIONAL INFORMATION PER 100 GRAMS OF UNCOOKED TEMPEH	
Total Calories: 193 kcal	
Protein: 18.5 g	
Total Fat: 10.8 g	
Saturated Fat: 2.2 g	
Unsaturated Fat: 5.3 g	
Carbohydrates: 7.6 g	
Dietary Fiber: 3.5 g	
Sugars: 0.0 g	
Sodium: 9 mg	
Vitamins and Minerals: Rich in Iron, Calcium, and Magnesium	
Glycemic Index (GI): 15	

Tempeh stands out in a diet as a rich source of complete protein, containing all essential amino acids necessary for muscle growth and repair. The fermentation process not only enhances its flavor but also increases the bioavailability of its nutrients, making it easier for the body to absorb minerals like iron and calcium. It's low in carbohydrates and has a low glycemic index, ideal for maintaining stable blood sugar levels. The fiber content in tempeh helps promote digestive health and can aid in cholesterol management.

COOKING IDEAS WITH TEMPEH

Marinate slices of tempeh in a blend of soy sauce, garlic, ginger, and a touch of sesame oil then grill or pan-fry them until crispy. These can be served with a side of steamed vegetables and brown rice for a balanced meal.

Incorporate crumbled tempeh into chili or stews instead of meat. Simmer with tomatoes, onions, bell peppers, and kidney beans for a hearty dish that is both satisfying and healthy.

Make a tempeh stir-fry with a variety of colorful vegetables such as bell peppers, snow peas, and carrots. Use a low-sodium soy sauce and serve it over a small portion of quinoa for a fiber-rich dinner.

Use thinly sliced tempeh as a filling for tacos or wraps. Complement with avocado, lettuce, and salsa for a delicious and nutritious meal that is easy to prepare and enjoyable to eat.

Create a tempeh salad by mixing baked tempeh cubes with leafy greens, cherry tomatoes, and a light balsamic vinaigrette. Add nuts or seeds for an extra crunch.

HEALTHY FATS

Healthy fats play an integral role in a diabetes-friendly diet, balancing meals and supporting overall health. Sources such as avocados, nuts, seeds, and olive oil provide monounsaturated and polyunsaturated fats, which are essential for heart health and can help improve insulin sensitivity—a crucial factor for those managing diabetes.

Unlike saturated fats, which can exacerbate cardiovascular risks, these healthy fats help to moderate blood sugar by slowing the absorption of carbohydrates. This process assists in stabilizing blood glucose levels throughout the day, preventing spikes that are common in diets high in unhealthy fats and simple sugars. Additionally, fats are vital for the absorption of fat-soluble vitamins like A, D, E, and K, ensuring that your body receives the full nutritional benefits from your meals.

Incorporating healthy fats into a diabetic diet does not just aid in metabolic health; it also enhances the flavor and texture of foods, making meals more satisfying and enjoyable. For example, dressing salads with olive oil, adding avocado slices to sandwiches, or sprinkling nuts and seeds on breakfast cereals can significantly boost the taste and nutritional profile of these dishes.

Moreover, healthy fats are essential in managing hunger. They provide a sense of fullness and satisfaction after meals, which can help curb overeating—a common challenge in diabetes management. This makes them a crucial component of any meal, supporting dietary adherence and metabolic balance.

Avocado

Avocado, often referred to as a superfruit, is unique among fruits for its high healthy fat content and creamy texture. Originating in the region now known as Mexico, avocados are valued for their rich, buttery flavor and their versatility in various dishes. They are a staple in healthy diets, particularly in vegetarian and ketogenic eating plans, thanks to their beneficial fats and dense nutritional profile.

NUTRITIONAL INFORMATION PER 100 GRAMS OF AVOCADO	
Total Calories: 160 kcal	
Protein: 2 g	
Total Fat: 15 g	
Saturated Fat: 2.1 g	
Unsaturated Fat: 10 g	
Carbohydrates: 9 g	
Dietary Fiber: 7 g	
Sugars: 0.7 g	
Sodium: 7 mg	
Vitamins and Minerals: High in Vitamin K, Folate, Vitamin C, Potassium, and Vitamin E	
Glycemic Index (GI): 40	

Avocados are celebrated for their heart-healthy mono-unsaturated fats, which can help reduce bad cholesterol levels while raising the good cholesterol. This can be particularly beneficial for individuals managing diabetes as it supports cardiovascular health. The high fiber content not only aids in digestion but also helps maintain steady blood glucose levels, which is crucial for diabetes management. The richness in potassium helps balance blood pressure levels, while vitamins and antioxidants support overall health and reduce inflammation.

COOKING IDEAS WITH AVOCADO

Start your day with avocado toast on whole grain bread topped with slices of tomato and a sprinkle of sea salt and pepper for a fiber-rich breakfast.

Blend avocado into smoothies to add creaminess and nutrients without impacting blood sugar levels significantly; try combining with spinach, green apple, and unsweetened almond milk for a refreshing drink.

Make a guacamole by mashing ripe avocados with lime juice, diced onions, tomatoes, and cilantro. Serve with raw vegetables like bell pepper strips and cucumber slices for a healthful snack.

Incorporate diced avocado into salads with mixed greens, grilled chicken, and vinaigrette dressing to create a satisfying meal that is full of texture and nutrition.

Use avocado as a replacement for mayonnaise in chicken or egg salad to enhance the dish with healthy fats and a creamy texture, perfect for a filling lunch that keeps blood sugar steady.

Olive Oil

Olive oil, a central component of Mediterranean cuisine, is renowned for its health benefits and its role in cooking. Extracted from the fruit of the olive tree, this oil is favored not only for its flavorful contribution to dishes but also for its dietary importance. It's primarily used as a cooking oil, in salad dressings, and for sautéing, making it a versatile addition to any kitchen.

NUTRITIONAL INFORMATION PER 100 GRAMS OF OLIVE OIL	
Total Calories: 884 kcal	
Protein: 0 g	
Total Fat: 100 g	
Saturated Fat: 14 g	
Unsaturated Fat: 73 g (Monounsaturated), 11 g (Polyunsaturated)	
Carbohydrates: 0 g	
Dietary Fiber: 0 g	
Sugars: 0 g	
Sodium: 2 mg	
Vitamins and Minerals: Contains Vitamin E and K	

Olive oil is celebrated for its high content of monounsaturated fats, particularly oleic acid, which is known to reduce inflammation and potentially lower the risk of heart disease. Its antioxidative properties, primarily due to Vitamin E, also play a crucial role in preventing cell damage. Regular consumption of olive oil has been linked to improved cardiovascular health and is beneficial in managing type 2 diabetes by enhancing insulin sensitivity and stabilizing blood sugar levels.

COOKING IDEAS WITH OLIVE OIL

Drizzle olive oil over a fresh salad mixed with spinach, walnuts, and sliced strawberries for a heart-healthy meal packed with flavor and nutrients.

Use olive oil as the base for marinades or dressings by blending it with balsamic vinegar, garlic, and herbs, perfect for marinating chicken or dressing a bean salad.

For a simple yet delicious side dish, toss assorted vegetables like zucchini, bell peppers, and onions in olive oil and roast in the oven until tender.

Sauté spinach or kale in a bit of olive oil and garlic for a quick, nutrient-dense side that pairs well with any protein source, enhancing both the taste and the nutritional content of your meals.

Prepare a diabetes-friendly pesto by pulsing together fresh basil, garlic, parmesan cheese, pine nuts, and olive oil, ideal for spreading on whole grain bread or mixing into whole wheat pasta.

Walnuts

Walnuts are a highly nutritious type of tree nut known for their wrinkled, brain-like appearance and a slightly bitter, earthy taste. They are a staple in various cuisines worldwide and are often praised for their high content of healthy fats and antioxidants. Walnuts are typically eaten on their own, added to savory dishes, or used in baking.

NUTRITIONAL INFORMATION PER 100 GRAMS OF WALNUTS	
Total Calories: 654 kcal	
Protein: 15 g	
Total Fat: 65 g	
Saturated Fat: 6 g	
Unsaturated Fat: 51 g (Monounsaturated), 47 g (Polyunsaturated)	
Carbohydrates: 14 g	
Dietary Fiber: 7 g	
Sugars: 3 g	
Sodium: 2 mg	
Vitamins and Minerals: Rich in magnesium, phosphorus, copper, manganese, and B vitamins	
Glycemic Index (GI): 15	

Walnuts are revered for their high levels of polyunsaturated fats, including a significant amount of alpha-linolenic acid (ALA), an essential omega-3 fatty acid. These fats are instrumental in reducing inflammation, supporting brain health, and potentially lowering the risk of heart disease. Their impressive antioxidant content contributes to combating oxidative stress and inflammation, making walnuts particularly beneficial for maintaining heart health and managing metabolic conditions like diabetes.

COOKING IDEAS WALNUTS

Create a nutritious breakfast by adding chopped walnuts to oatmeal or yogurt, providing a satisfying crunch and a boost of omega-3 fatty acids.

Incorporate ground walnuts into whole wheat pancake batter for a heartier, nutrient-rich version of this classic breakfast.

Toss walnuts with mixed greens, sliced pears, and blue cheese for a salad that balances sweet, savory, and crunchy textures while offering a good mix of proteins and healthy fats.

Blend walnuts into smoothies to add thickness and increase the nutritional content, pairing well with bananas and cocoa powder for a delicious treat.

Use walnuts as a topping for grilled fish or chicken, adding texture and flavor, as well as enhancing the meal's satiety and nutritional value.

Flaxseeds

Flaxseeds, also known as linseeds, are small, brown or golden-colored seeds that are known for their health benefits. They have been cultivated for thousands of years and are celebrated for their rich contents of omega-3 fatty acids, lignans, and fiber. These seeds can be ground or used whole and are commonly added to a variety of dishes to boost nutritional content.

NUTRITIONAL INFORMATION PER 100 GRAMS OF FLAXSEEDS	
Total Calories: 534 kcal	
Protein: 18.3 g	
Total Fat: 42.2 g	
Saturated Fat: 3.7 g	
Unsaturated Fat: 36.3 g (Monounsaturated), 28.7 g (Polyunsaturated)	
Carbohydrates: 28.9 g	
Dietary Fiber: 27.3 g	
Sugars: 1.6 g	
Sodium: 30 mg	
Vitamins and Minerals: Rich in thiamine, magnesium, phosphorus, and copper	
Glycemic Index (GI): 35	

Flaxseeds are a powerhouse of nutrition. They offer a substantial amount of alpha-linolenic acid (ALA), a type of plant-based omega-3 fatty acid, which is crucial for heart health and reducing inflammation. The high fiber content promotes digestive health and helps in the management of blood sugar levels, making flaxseeds particularly beneficial for individuals with diabetes. Their rich lignan content, a type of antioxidant, also contributes to their anti-inflammatory and cancer-preventive properties.

COOKING IDEAS WITH FLAXSEEDS

Enhance breakfast cereals or smoothies by sprinkling ground flaxseeds on top, which adds fiber and omega-3s to the meal.

Incorporate ground flaxseeds into bread, muffins, or cookie recipes to increase the fiber content, which can help in managing blood glucose levels more effectively.

Create a flaxseed meal by grinding the seeds and use it as an egg substitute in baking, which adds healthful fats and proteins to vegan recipes.

Stir ground flaxseeds into yogurt or a smoothie bowl for a nutty flavor and extra nutrients, making a simple snack much more beneficial for blood sugar control.

Mix whole or ground flaxseeds into homemade granola bars along with oats, nuts, and seeds for a crunchy texture and a boost of essential fatty acids.

Chia Seeds

Chia seeds are tiny, black seeds from the plant Salvia hispanica, originally grown in Mexico and known for their extensive nutritional benefits. They have gained immense popularity as a modern-day superfood due to their remarkable ability to absorb water and form a gel-like consistency, along with their versatile use in numerous recipes.

NUTRITIONAL INFORMATION PER 100 GRAMS OF CHIA SEEDS	
Total Calories: 486 kcal	
Protein: 16.5 g	
Total Fat: 30.7 g	
Saturated Fat: 3.3 g	
Unsaturated Fat: 23.7 g (Monounsaturated), 24 g (Polyunsaturated)	
Carbohydrates: 42.1 g	
Dietary Fiber: 34.4 g	
Sugars: 0 g	
Sodium: 16 mg	
Vitamins and Minerals: High in calcium, magnesium, phosphorus, and manganese	
Glycemic Index (GI): 30	

Chia seeds are a nutritional powerhouse, rich in fiber and omega-3 fatty acids, which are beneficial for heart health and reducing inflammation. Their high fiber content contributes significantly to weight management by promoting satiety and reducing food intake. The presence of antioxidants, minerals, and vitamins enhances their profile as a food that supports metabolic health, bone health, and overall wellness.

COOKING IDEAS WITH CHIA SEEDS

Prepare chia pudding by soaking chia seeds in almond milk or coconut milk overnight, then top with berries, nuts, and a touch of cinnamon for a hearty breakfast or dessert that helps manage blood sugar levels.

Add chia seeds to smoothies to thicken them naturally while boosting the fiber content, which can help maintain blood sugar stability throughout the day.

Use chia seeds as a vegan thickener in soups and gravies, where they absorb excess liquid and enhance the dish's nutritional value without altering the flavor significantly.

Incorporate chia seeds into homemade breads, muffins, and pancakes to add texture and nutrients, making these staples more diabetes-friendly by enhancing their fiber content.

Sprinkle dry chia seeds over salads or stir into yogurt to add a crunchy texture and a boost of omega-3s, fiber, and protein, all of which are essential for balanced blood sugar management in diabetes.

Almonds

Almonds are the seeds of the fruit of the almond tree. They are native to the Middle East, but the United States is now the largest producer. Known for their versatility and health benefits, almonds can be consumed raw, toasted, or used as a base in various culinary preparations.

NUTRITIONAL INFORMATION PER 100 GRAMS OF ALMONDS	
Total Calories: 575 kcal	
Protein: 21.15 g	
Total Fat: 49.42 g	
Saturated Fat: 3.73 g	
Unsaturated Fat: 39.89 g (Monounsaturated), 12.07 g (Polyunsaturated)	
Carbohydrates: 21.55 g	
Dietary Fiber: 12.5 g	
Sugars: 3.89 g	
Sodium: 1 mg	
Vitamins and Minerals: High in vitamin E, magnesium, and potassium	
Glycemic Index (GI): 15	

Almonds are a heart-healthy snack that is rich in monounsaturated fats, which help to lower cholesterol levels and reduce the risk of heart disease. The high fiber content aids in digestion and helps maintain blood sugar levels, making almonds a great choice for people with diabetes. They are also a good source of protein and essential nutrients like vitamin E, which provides potent antioxidant properties.

COOKING IDEAS WITH ALMONDS

Create a crunchy topping for salads or yogurt by lightly toasting sliced almonds and sprinkling them over your dish for added texture and nutrients.

Grind almonds to use as a gluten-free flour substitute in baking recipes such as breads, muffins, and pancakes, enhancing their nutritional profile and making them suitable for a diabetic diet.

Add chopped almonds to vegetable stir-fries to incorporate a nutty flavor and a satisfying crunch, which also boosts the protein and fiber content of your meals.

Use almond butter as a healthy spread on whole-grain toast or blend it into smoothies for a creamy texture and a protein boost without a significant impact on blood sugar levels.

Prepare a homemade trail mix with raw almonds, seeds, and a small amount of dried fruit for a portable snack that balances healthy fats, proteins, and carbohydrates.

Coconut Oil

Coconut oil is extracted from the meat of mature coconuts harvested from the coconut palm. It has gained popularity in recent years due to its versatile uses in cooking, baking, and even skin and hair care. Known for its unique composition of fatty acids, coconut oil is a staple in tropical regions and is celebrated for its culinary and health benefits.

NUTRITIONAL INFORMATION PER 100 GRAMS OF COCONUT OIL
Total Calories: 892 kcal
Protein: 0 g
Total Fat: 99 g
Saturated Fat: 82.5 g
Unsaturated Fat: 6.5 g (Monounsaturated), 1.7 g (Polyunsaturated)
Carbohydrates: 0 g
Dietary Fiber: 0 g
Sugars: 0 g
Sodium: 0 mg
Vitamins and Minerals: Trace amounts of vitamin E and vitamin K

The unique aspect of coconut oil lies in its high content of saturated fat, predominantly medium-chain triglycerides (MCTs). These fats are metabolized differently from other fats, as they are absorbed directly by the liver and converted into energy or ketone bodies. This process can provide quick energy, which may help stabilize blood sugar levels, making it particularly interesting for those managing diabetes. Additionally, MCTs may have therapeutic effects on brain disorders, including epilepsy and Alzheimer's.

However, due to its high saturated fat content, coconut oil should be used with caution, especially by those with diabetes, as it can also increase LDL (bad) cholesterol levels. Despite its potential to raise HDL (good) cholesterol, the overall impact on cardiovascular health remains a subject of debate, and moderation is advised.

COOKING IDEAS WITH COCONUT OIL

Use coconut oil for sautéing or roasting vegetables to add a hint of tropical flavor while benefiting from its high smoke point, which makes it suitable for high-heat cooking.

Incorporate coconut oil into smoothies or coffee to add richness and a boost of healthy fats, which can help with satiety and energy levels without impacting blood sugar.

Utilize coconut oil in baking to provide moisture and flavor to goods like keto-friendly cookies and cakes that require low carbohydrate content.

Make homemade granola with coconut oil, nuts, seeds, and a touch of sweetener for a crunchy, low-carb snack that's perfect for a diabetes-friendly diet.

Prepare curry dishes using coconut oil to enhance the flavors and pair with vegetables and proteins for a balanced, nutritious meal.

Pumpkin Seeds

Pumpkin seeds, also known as pepitas, are the edible seeds of a pumpkin. These small, flat seeds are encased in a white husk, although they are often shelled when sold commercially. Widely recognized for their nutritional benefits, pumpkin seeds are a common ingredient in many healthy diets, offering a rich source of essential nutrients and a crunchy texture that enhances a variety of dishes.

NUTRITIONAL INFORMATION PER 100 GRAMS OF PUMPKIN SEEDS
Total Calories: 446 kcal
Protein: 19 g
Total Fat: 19 g
Saturated Fat: 3.7 g
Unsaturated Fat: 12 g (Monounsaturated), 9 g (Polyunsaturated)
Carbohydrates: 54 g
Dietary Fiber: 18 g
Sugars: 1 g
Sodium: 18 mg
Vitamins and Minerals: Rich in Magnesium, Iron, Zinc, and Phosphorus; contains Vitamin K, and B-vitamins
Glycemic Index (GI): 25

Pumpkin seeds are a powerhouse of nutrients, offering a substantial amount of fiber, protein, and healthy fats, particularly omega-6 fatty acids. Their high magnesium content supports hundreds of chemical reactions in the body, including glucose control, which is crucial for diabetes management. The zinc found in pumpkin seeds is vital for immune function and skin health, while their iron content helps prevent anemia. The combination of nutrients in pumpkin seeds can aid in heart health, bone health, and diabetes control.

COOKING IDEAS WITH PUMPKIN SEEDS

Roast pumpkin seeds with a sprinkle of salt and a dash of olive oil for a crunchy, nutritious snack that can curb hunger without spiking blood sugar levels.

Add toasted pumpkin seeds to salads or homemade trail mixes for a boost of texture and nutrients, providing a satisfying crunch alongside leafy greens or mixed nuts.

Blend pumpkin seeds into smoothie bowls for added protein and healthy fats, enhancing the nutritional profile of your morning or post-workout meal.

Incorporate ground pumpkin seeds into bread, muffins, or pancake batter to add a nutty flavor and extra nutrients, making your baked goods more filling and healthier.

Stir pumpkin seeds into yogurt or oatmeal to improve the texture and increase the satiety factor of your snacks or breakfast, helping to manage blood sugar levels throughout the day.

Dark Chocolate

Dark chocolate is celebrated not just for its rich flavor and velvety texture, but also for its impressive health benefits when consumed in moderation. Typically containing between 70% to 99% cocoa, dark chocolate is less sweet than milk chocolate and richer in pure cocoa content. This makes it a popular choice among connoisseurs and health-conscious individuals alike.

Dark chocolate is highly nutritious, offering a robust profile of minerals such as iron and magnesium, which are essential for overall health. The high content of antioxidants found in cocoa, including flavonoids, contribute to its health benefits, such as enhancing heart health by improving blood flow and lowering blood pressure. Its low glycemic index makes it a preferable choice for moderating blood sugar levels, particularly beneficial for those managing diabetes.

NUTRITIONAL INFORMATION PER 100 GRAMS OF DARK CHOCOLATE (70-85%)
Total Calories: 598 kcal
Protein: 7.79 g
Total Fat: 42.63 g
Saturated Fat: 24.49 g
Unsaturated Fat: 18.14 g (Monounsaturated), very little Polyunsaturated
Carbohydrates: 45.90 g
Dietary Fiber: 10.9 g
Sugars: 23.99 g
Sodium: 20 mg
Vitamins and Minerals: Rich in Iron, Magnesium, Copper, Manganese, Potassium, Phosphorus, Zinc; contains B-vitamins
Glycemic Index (GI): 23

COOKING IDEAS

Melt dark chocolate to drizzle over fresh berries for a decadent yet healthy dessert, marrying the antioxidant benefits of both chocolate and berries.

Grate or shave dark chocolate over a bowl of oatmeal or Greek yogurt to enrich these staples with a touch of indulgence without overwhelming sweetness.

Prepare homemade dark chocolate bark by melting dark chocolate and mixing it with nuts and seeds, then cooling it in the fridge until set. Break into pieces for a satisfying snack that combines healthy fats and the antioxidant power of dark chocolate.

Use dark chocolate in small amounts to bake diabetes-friendly treats like muffins or cookies, utilizing its rich flavor to add depth without needing excessive sugar.

Create a dark chocolate and nut spread by blending melted dark chocolate with almond butter or cashew butter for a tasty and nutritious topping for whole-grain toast or pancakes.

NON-STARCHY VEGETABLES

Non-starchy vegetables are a cornerstone of a balanced diabetic diet due to their low carbohydrate content, high fiber, and rich nutrient profile. Vegetables such as leafy greens, broccoli, cauliflower, and peppers provide essential vitamins and minerals while having minimal impact on blood glucose levels. These characteristics make them ideal for maintaining stable blood sugar and supporting overall health.

The fiber in non-starchy vegetables aids in digestion and helps regulate blood sugar levels by slowing the absorption of glucose. This is particularly beneficial for individuals managing diabetes, as it helps prevent the rapid blood sugar spikes that can occur after eating high-carbohydrate or sugary foods. Moreover, the high fiber content contributes to a feeling of fullness, aiding in weight management by reducing the urge to snack frequently.

Incorporating a variety of non-starchy vegetables can also significantly enhance the flavor and visual appeal of meals without adding excessive calories or carbohydrates. These vegetables can be steamed, roasted, grilled, or eaten raw, offering versatility in preparation and use in a multitude of recipes from salads and soups to stir-fries and casseroles.

Furthermore, the antioxidants and anti-inflammatory compounds found in these vegetables play a critical role in reducing the risk of chronic diseases and improving overall health. They support immune function, reduce inflammation, and provide protective benefits against cardiovascular diseases, which are of particular concern to those with diabetes.

Spinach

Spinach is a versatile and nutrient-packed leafy green vegetable that has been recognized for its health benefits and culinary flexibility. Rich in color and dense with nutrients, spinach can be enjoyed raw or cooked and is a staple in a variety of cuisines around the world.

Spinach is a low-calorie food that is exceptionally rich in vitamins and minerals, especially Vitamin A, Vitamin C, and Vitamin K, as well as iron and calcium. It is also a great source of dietary fiber, which helps in controlling blood sugar levels and maintaining a healthy digestive system. The antioxidants present, such as lutein and zeaxanthin, are known for their roles in promoting eye health and preventing age-related macular degeneration. Its low glycemic index makes it an excellent choice for individuals with diabetes, contributing to a balanced diet without spiking blood sugar levels.

NUTRITIONAL INFORMATION PER 100 GRAMS OF RAW SPINACH	
Total Calories: 23 kcal	
Protein: 2.9 g	
Total Fat: 0.39 g	
Saturated Fat: 0.063 g	
Unsaturated Fat: 0.165 g	
Carbohydrates: 3.6 g	
Dietary Fiber: 2.2 g	
Sugars: 0.4 g	
Sodium: 79 mg	
Vitamins and Minerals: High in Vitamin A, Vitamin C, Vitamin K, Iron, Calcium, Folate, Magnesium, Manganese	
Glycemic Index (GI): Very Low	

COOKING IDEAS WITH SPINACH

Create a nutritious spinach salad by tossing fresh spinach leaves with sliced strawberries, a sprinkle of walnuts, and a light vinaigrette. The sweetness of the strawberries complements the earthy flavor of the spinach, while walnuts add a crunchy texture and healthy fats.

Sauté spinach with minced garlic and a dash of olive oil for a simple, flavorful side dish. Add a squeeze of lemon juice just before serving to enhance the flavors and add a bit of zesty freshness.

Incorporate spinach into smoothies for a nutrient boost. Blend fresh spinach with Greek yogurt, a small banana, and a handful of blueberries for a delicious, fiber-rich drink.

Use spinach as a base for a hearty, diabetic-friendly soup. Simmer spinach with low-sodium vegetable broth, diced carrots, and onions, then puree the mixture until smooth for a warm, comforting meal.

Prepare a spinach and feta cheese stuffed chicken breast for a satisfying main dish. Simply stuff the chicken with a mixture of chopped spinach, feta, and herbs, then bake until the chicken is thoroughly cooked.

Broccoli

Broccoli is a cruciferous vegetable known for its distinctive green color and tree-like shape. It is a staple on many dinner tables around the world, celebrated not only for its robust flavor but also for its array of health benefits. This vegetable originates from the Mediterranean and was cultivated in Italy centuries ago before spreading to other parts of the world. Rich in vitamins, minerals, and bioactive compounds, broccoli offers a host of health benefits, making it a favorite among those looking to maintain a healthy diet.

Broccoli is a nutritional powerhouse that provides numerous health benefits. Its high fiber content aids in digestion and helps maintain stable blood sugar levels, making it ideal for diabetes management. The vegetable is also loaded with vitamin C, which boosts the immune system, and vitamin K, essential for bone health and wound healing. The compounds found in broccoli, such as sulforaphane, are known to have anti-inflammatory, anti-cancer, and heart-protective properties. These benefits make broccoli an excellent addition to a healthy diet, particularly for those managing chronic conditions like diabetes.

NUTRITIONAL INFORMATION PER 100 GRAMS OF UNCOOKED BROCCOLI	
Total Calories: 34 kcal	
Protein: 2.82 g	
Total Fat: 0.37 g	
Saturated Fat: 0.039 g	
Unsaturated Fat: 0.031 g	
Total Carbohydrates: 6.64 g	
Dietary Fiber: 2.6 g	
Sugars: 1.7 g	
Sodium: 33 mg	
Vitamins and Minerals: Excellent source of Vitamin C and K, provides folate, potassium, and manganese.	
Glycemic Index (GI): Low (approximately 15)	

COOKING IDEAS WITH BROCCOLI

Broccoli can be incorporated into a variety of dishes suitable for a diabetes-friendly diet, offering both nutritious and tasty options. One way to enjoy this vegetable is by steaming broccoli florets until just tender and then tossing them with olive oil, fresh lemon juice, and minced garlic to create a flavorful side dish that pairs well with any main course. Alternatively, you can prepare a hearty broccoli and chickpea salad by mixing raw or lightly steamed broccoli with cooked chickpeas and red onion, dressed with yogurt and dill, making it substantial enough to serve as a main dish while being rich in fiber and protein. Another simple yet delicious method is to roast broccoli with cauliflower florets coated lightly in olive oil until they are crisp and browned, seasoned with just a pinch of salt and pepper. For a quick meal, sauté broccoli florets with slices of bell pepper, onions, and either tofu or chicken for an easy stir-fry, seasoned with a splash of low-sodium soy sauce and served over a modest portion of brown rice or whole grain noodles. Lastly, for a comforting dish, blend steamed broccoli with low-sodium vegetable stock and sautéed onions until smooth, seasoned with your choice of herbs and spices to create a warm and inviting broccoli soup suitable for any season.

Cauliflower

Cauliflower is a cruciferous vegetable that has gained immense popularity for its versatility and health benefits. With its mild, slightly nutty flavor and its impressive adaptability in recipes, cauliflower can serve as a lower-carbohydrate substitute for starches like potatoes and grains, making it a favorite in many dietary regimens, including those for diabetes management.

NUTRITIONAL INFORMATION PER 100 GRAMS OF RAW CAULIFLOWER	
Total Calories: 25 kcal	
Protein: 1.9 g	
Total Fat: 0.3 g	
Saturated Fat: 0.1 g	
Unsaturated Fat: 0.1 g	
Carbohydrates: 5 g	
Dietary Fiber: 2 g	
Sugars: 1.9 g	
Sodium: 30 mg	
Vitamins and Minerals: High in Vitamin C, Vitamin K, Folate, Pantothenic Acid	
Glycemic Index (GI): 15	

Cauliflower stands out as a nutrient-dense vegetable that is low in calories but high in vitamins C and K, and folate, essential for overall health and wellness. Its high fiber content aids in digestion and helps maintain steady blood sugar levels, which is crucial for managing diabetes. The low calorie and carbohydrate content make cauliflower an excellent choice for those looking to manage their weight without sacrificing flavor or satisfaction.

COOKING IDEAS WITH CAULIFLOWER

Transform cauliflower into a rice alternative by pulsing raw florets in a food processor until they resemble grains of rice. Sauté in a pan with a bit of olive oil and a selection of herbs for a flavorful side dish that pairs well with a variety of proteins.

Create a creamy cauliflower mash as a low-carb substitute for mashed potatoes. Steam the cauliflower until very tender, then blend with garlic, a touch of cream cheese, and a sprinkle of chives for a comforting side that's low in carbohydrates and high in taste.

Roast cauliflower steaks by slicing the head into thick slabs, brushing with olive oil, and seasoning with salt, pepper, and your favorite spices. Roast in a hot oven until the edges are caramelized and crispy, offering a hearty, satisfying dish that's perfect alongside a main protein.

Make a nutritious cauliflower and turmeric soup to take advantage of its anti-inflammatory properties. Simmer cauliflower with onions, garlic, turmeric, and low-sodium vegetable stock until soft. Puree until smooth and serve warm, garnished with a swirl of yogurt and a sprinkle of fresh herbs.

Incorporate cauliflower into a diabetes-friendly stir-fry by using it as a base. Add colorful vegetables like bell peppers, snap peas, and scallions, along with lean protein such as chicken or shrimp, and stir-fry with a splash of low-sodium soy sauce for a complete meal that's both filling and nutritious.

Asparagus

Asparagus is a perennial vegetable that heralds the arrival of spring. Its spear-like stalks are tender and packed with flavor, ranging from slightly bitter to sweet. Known for its distinct, vibrant green color, asparagus is a staple in healthy kitchens due to its robust nutritional profile and versatility in cooking.

NUTRITIONAL INFORMATION PER 100 GRAMS OF RAW ASPARAGUS	
Total Calories: 20 kcal	
Protein: 2.2 g	
Total Fat: 0.1 g	
Saturated Fat: 0.04 g	
Unsaturated Fat: 0.06 g	
Carbohydrates: 3.9 g	
Dietary Fiber: 2.1 g	
Sugars: 1.9 g	
Sodium: 2 mg	
Vitamins and Minerals: High in Vitamin K, Folate, Vitamins A, C, E, and Iron	
Glycemic Index (GI): 15	

Asparagus offers a wealth of nutrients with few calories, making it an excellent choice for weight management and diabetes control. It's rich in fiber, which promotes digestive health and helps to maintain blood sugar levels. The high levels of antioxidants and anti-inflammatory compounds in asparagus can help reduce oxidative stress and may support heart health. Its low glycemic index makes it an ideal vegetable for maintaining stable blood glucose levels.

COOKING IDEAS WITH ASPARAGUS

Grill whole asparagus spears brushed lightly with olive oil and sprinkled with sea salt and pepper. This method enhances their natural sweetness and adds a smoky flavor, making them a great side dish or a feature in warm salads.

Wrap asparagus in thinly sliced prosciutto and roast until the prosciutto is crispy for a delightful contrast in textures and flavors, suitable as an appetizer or a side.

Simmer asparagus in a light broth with a touch of lemon and herbs for a simple yet elegant soup. Blend until smooth for a creamy texture without heavy cream, serving as a healthy first course.

Stir-fry chopped asparagus with other colorful vegetables like bell peppers and carrots in a touch of sesame oil. Add ginger, garlic, and a splash of tamari for an Asian-inspired dish that pairs well with grilled chicken or tofu.

Blanch asparagus briefly then chop and add to a spring vegetable frittata with eggs and a sprinkle of feta cheese. Serve for brunch or a light dinner; the combination of protein and fiber will help manage blood sugar levels throughout the meal.

Bell Peppers

Bell peppers, known for their vibrant colors and sweet, mild flavor, are a popular vegetable in many cuisines around the world. Available in a spectrum of colors including red, yellow, orange, and green, each hue of bell pepper has its own unique set of nutrients and antioxidants, making them a delightful and attractive addition to dishes.

NUTRITIONAL INFORMATION PER 100 GRAMS OF RAW BELL PEPPERS	
Total Calories: 31 kcal	
Protein: 1 g	
Total Fat: 0.3 g	
Saturated Fat: 0.03 g	
Unsaturated Fat: 0.17 g	
Carbohydrates: 6 g	
Dietary Fiber: 2.1 g	
Sugars: 4.2 g	
Sodium: 4 mg	
Vitamins and Minerals: Exceptionally high in Vitamin C, good amounts of Vitamin B6, Vitamin A, and Folate	
Glycemic Index (GI): 15	

Bell peppers are not only low in calories but are also a powerhouse of nutrients, particularly Vitamin C, which is crucial for immune function and skin health. The high fiber content aids in digestion and helps control blood sugar levels, making bell peppers an excellent food for managing diabetes. Their low glycemic index ensures that they have a minimal impact on blood glucose levels.

COOKING IDEAS WITH BELL PEPPERS

Create a colorful stir-fry using thinly sliced bell peppers, onions, and chicken breast or tofu. Season with garlic, a hint of soy sauce, and fresh ginger for a quick and nutritious meal that balances protein and vegetables.

Stuff bell peppers with a mixture of ground turkey, quinoa, tomatoes, and spices, then bake until the peppers are tender and the filling is cooked through. This meal is high in protein and fiber, ideal for a satisfying diabetes-friendly lunch or dinner.

Slice bell peppers and use them raw in salads or as part of a veggie platter. Combine with a yogurt-based dip or hummus to add protein and healthy fats, which can help slow carbohydrate absorption and stabilize blood sugar levels.

Roast a mix of red, yellow, and orange bell peppers with a drizzle of olive oil until they are soft and slightly charred. Blend them into a smooth, flavorful soup or sauce that can be served with grilled chicken or mixed into whole wheat pasta dishes.

Add chopped bell peppers to omelets or frittatas along with spinach and mushrooms for a fiber-rich, low-carb breakfast that starts the day with plenty of nutrients.

Green Beans

Green beans, also known as string beans, are a staple vegetable that can be found in many kitchens worldwide. They are valued for their crisp texture and versatile nature, making them a favorite ingredient in both cold and hot dishes. Green beans are an excellent addition to a healthy diet due to their rich content of vitamins and low-calorie profile.

Green beans are an exceptional source of fiber and several essential nutrients including Vitamin K and Vitamin C, which are vital for health maintenance and disease prevention. The dietary fiber in green beans helps with digestion and provides a feeling of fullness, aiding in weight management and glycemic control, which is particularly beneficial for individuals with diabetes.

NUTRITIONAL INFORMATION PER 100 GRAMS OF RAW GREEN BEANS	
Total Calories: 31 kcal	
Protein: 1.83 g	
Total Fat: 0.22 g	
Saturated Fat: 0.05 g	
Unsaturated Fat: 0.17	
Carbohydrates: 7 g	
Dietary Fiber: 3.4 g	
Sugars: 3.26 g	
Sodium: 6 mg	
Vitamins and Minerals: Rich in Vitamin C, Vitamin K, Vitamin A, and Folate	
Glycemic Index (GI): 30	

COOKING IDEAS WITH GREEN BEANS

Sauté green beans in a minimal amount of olive oil and garlic for a simple yet flavorful side dish that pairs well with lean meats or tofu for a balanced meal.

Blanch green beans quickly in boiling water and then chill them in ice water to preserve their color and crunch. Toss them in a salad with cherry tomatoes, feta cheese, and a light vinaigrette for a refreshing and nutritious addition to any meal.

Include green beans in a vegetable stir-fry with bell peppers, broccoli, and carrots. Serve over a small portion of brown rice or whole grain noodles, using a low-sodium soy sauce and plenty of spices like turmeric and ginger to enhance the flavor without adding sugar.

For a hearty, one-pot meal, simmer green beans with chunks of potato and lean cuts of beef or chicken in a tomato-based stew. Season with herbs like rosemary and thyme to add depth to the dish while keeping it diabetes-friendly.

Roast green beans with a sprinkle of almond slivers for an added crunch. Drizzle with a bit of balsamic vinegar before serving to bring out their natural sweetness and add a gourmet touch to this simple preparation.

Zucchini

Zucchini, also known as courgette, is a summer squash that ranges in color from deep green to a pale yellow. It has a delicate flavor that makes it a popular addition to many dishes, and its high water content makes it low in calories but rich in essential nutrients. Zucchini can be eaten raw, cooked, or shredded and added to a variety of recipes, from baked goods to savory meals.

NUTRITIONAL INFORMATION PER 100 GRAMS OF RAW ZUCCHINI	
Total Calories: 17 kcal	
Protein: 1.21 g	
Total Fat: 0.32 g	
Saturated Fat: 0.07 g	
Unsaturated Fat: 0.25 g	
Carbohydrates: 3.11 g	
Dietary Fiber: 1 g	
Sugars: 2.5 g	
Sodium: 8 mg	
Vitamins and Minerals: High in Vitamin C, Vitamin B6, Riboflavin, and Manganese	
Glycemic Index (GI): 15	

Zucchini is particularly beneficial for individuals with diabetes as it is low in carbohydrates and sugars, which helps maintain blood glucose levels. The presence of dietary fiber in zucchini aids in digestion, slows down sugar absorption, and can help in managing blood sugar levels. Additionally, its rich vitamin and mineral content supports overall health, enhancing immune function and reducing inflammation.

COOKING IDEAS WITH ZUCCHINI

Grate zucchini into spaghetti-like strands to use as a low-carb pasta substitute, top with a homemade tomato sauce and grilled chicken for a nutritious and satisfying meal.

Incorporate sliced zucchini into frittatas or omelets, combined with other low-carb vegetables like spinach and mushrooms for a fiber-rich breakfast or brunch option.

Grill zucchini slices brushed lightly with olive oil and seasoned with herbs such as thyme and basil. Serve alongside grilled fish or tofu steaks as part of a balanced meal.

Create a refreshing cold salad by slicing zucchini thinly and marinating it in lemon juice, olive oil, and herbs. Add chopped nuts for a crunchy texture and a boost of healthy fats.

Stuff hollowed-out zucchini boats with a mixture of lean ground turkey, diced vegetables, and a sprinkle of low-fat cheese, then bake until tender for a delightful dish that's both low in calories and high in flavor.

Kale

Kale is a leafy green vegetable that has risen in popularity due to its exceptional nutrient profile and health benefits. This hardy cabbage relative is available in various forms, including curly, ornamental, and dinosaur varieties, each with a slightly different texture and taste. Kale can be consumed raw, cooked, or as part of juices and smoothies, making it a versatile ingredient in a health-conscious kitchen.

NUTRITIONAL INFORMATION PER 100 GRAMS OF RAW KALE	
Total Calories: 49 kcal	
Protein: 4.3 g	
Total Fat: 0.9 g	
Saturated Fat: 0.1 g	
Unsaturated Fat: 0.8 g	
Carbohydrates: 8.8 g	
Dietary Fiber: 3.6 g	
Sugars: 2.3 g	
Sodium: 38 mg	
Vitamins and Minerals: High in Vitamin A, Vitamin C, Vitamin K, Calcium, and Iron	
Glycemic Index (GI): Very Low	

Kale's rich content of vitamins A, C, and K, along with iron and calcium, supports immune function, bone health, and vision. Its high dietary fiber content aids in digestion and helps stabilize blood sugar levels, making it an excellent choice for diabetes management. The antioxidant properties of kale also play a role in reducing inflammation and protecting against chronic diseases.

COOKING IDEAS WITH KALE

Simmer kale in soups and stews where it adds texture and absorbs flavors from spices and herbs, enhancing the dish's nutritional profile without overwhelming it with calories.

Sauté kale with garlic and a splash of olive oil for a simple yet tasty side dish that pairs well with proteins like grilled chicken or baked fish, providing a hearty dose of fiber and essential nutrients.

Blend kale into green smoothies with low GI fruits like green apples and kiwi to kickstart your morning with a burst of energy and vital nutrients without spiking your blood sugar.

Create a warm kale salad by wilting the leaves slightly and then tossing with roasted butternut squash, pomegranate seeds, and a light balsamic dressing for a dish rich in flavors and textures.

Bake kale chips by tearing the leaves into bite-size pieces, massaging them with a touch of olive oil and your choice of seasoning, and baking at a low temperature until crisp for a healthy, crunchy snack.

Mushroom

Mushrooms, with their earthy flavors and meaty texture, serve as a staple in many culinary traditions worldwide. Available in various types, such as button, portobello, shiitake, and more, mushrooms are renowned not only for their taste but also for their minimal calorie content and impressive nutritional benefits. They are a non-starchy vegetable that can be incorporated into numerous dishes, ranging from soups to stir-fries, making them a favored choice for health-conscious eaters and those managing diabetes.

NUTRITIONAL INFORMATION PER 100 GRAMS OF RAW MUSHROOMS	
Total Calories: 22 kcal	
Protein: 3.1 g	
Total Fat: 0.3 g	
Saturated Fat: 0.05 g	
Unsaturated Fat: 0.25 g	
Carbohydrates: 3.3 g	
Dietary Fiber: 1.0 g	
Sugars: 2.0 g	
Sodium: 5 mg	
Vitamins and Minerals: Rich in B vitamins, Selenium, Potassium, Copper	
Glycemic Index (GI): Very Low	

Mushrooms are a low-calorie food that packs a nutritional punch. Rich in B vitamins and essential minerals like selenium and potassium, they help in energy production and regulate antioxidant functions in the body. The fiber in mushrooms aids in digestion and helps manage blood sugar levels, which is crucial for those with diabetes. Their low GI makes them an excellent addition to any meal, supporting overall health without spiking glucose levels.

COOKING IDEAS WITH MUSHROOMS

Incorporate mushrooms into omelets or frittatas, adding herbs and a sprinkle of cheese for a protein-rich breakfast or brunch that keeps blood sugar levels steady.

Simmer mushrooms in broth with herbs like thyme and a splash of white wine to create a flavorful soup that's both nourishing and comforting, perfect for any meal.

Sauté mushrooms with garlic and onions until they're golden and tender, then toss them into a salad with mixed greens and a vinaigrette for a delicious side or main dish.

Stuff large portobello mushrooms with a mixture of spinach, feta, and pine nuts, then bake them until

everything is deliciously melded together for a satisfying main course that's low in carbs but high in flavor.

Add sliced mushrooms to stir-fries with lean protein sources like chicken or tofu and a variety of vegetables for a quick, healthy meal packed with nutrients suitable for a diabetic diet.

Tomatoes

Tomatoes are a cornerstone in kitchens around the world, known for their vibrant color and versatile use in dishes from salads to sauces. Botanically a fruit but commonly treated as a vegetable in culinary contexts, tomatoes are celebrated not just for their flavor but also for their impressive health benefits, especially their high vitamin C and lycopene content.

NUTRITIONAL INFORMATION PER 100 GRAMS OF RAW TOMATOES	
Total Calories: 18 kcal	
Protein: 0.9 g	
Total Fat: 0.2 g	
Saturated Fat: 0.03 g	
Unsaturated Fat: 0.17 g	
Carbohydrates: 3.9 g	
Dietary Fiber: 1.2 g	
Sugars: 2.6 g	
Sodium: 5 mg	
Vitamins and Minerals: High in Vitamin C, Vitamin K, Potassium, Folate	
Glycemic Index (GI): Low (approx. 15)	

Tomatoes offer a rich source of antioxidants, notably lycopene, which has been linked to many health benefits, including reduced risk of heart disease and cancer. They are also a good source of vitamin C, potassium, folate, and vitamin K. The low calorie and carbohydrate content coupled with a low glycemic index make tomatoes an excellent food choice for managing diabetes, promoting heart health, and supporting overall well-being.

COOKING IDEAS WITH TOMATOES

Prepare a fresh tomato salsa with chopped onions, cilantro, lime juice, and a pinch of salt, which can be used as a flavorful topping for grilled chicken or fish, providing a burst of flavor and nutrients without significantly impacting blood sugar levels.

Create a hearty tomato soup by simmering chopped tomatoes with garlic, onions, and a touch of olive oil, blending into a smooth consistency and finishing with fresh basil. Serve hot for a comforting meal that pairs well with a whole-grain roll.

Use sliced tomatoes as a vibrant base for a breakfast dish by topping them with avocado and poached eggs, offering a balanced meal with healthy fats, protein, and minimal impact on blood sugar.

Roast cherry tomatoes with a drizzle of olive oil and herbs until they burst open and caramelize, then toss with whole wheat pasta and a sprinkle of Parmesan cheese for a simple yet delicious diabetic-friendly dinner.

Layer slices of tomatoes in a baking dish with zucchini and eggplant, sprinkle with low-fat cheese and bake as a gratin for a low-carb side dish that complements any protein source.

STARCHY VEGETABLES

Starchy vegetables, such as potatoes, corn, peas, and winter squash, are packed with essential nutrients including vitamins, minerals, and fiber. They are an important part of a balanced diet, even for individuals managing diabetes. However, due to their higher carbohydrate content, it's crucial to integrate these vegetables carefully into meals to avoid spikes in blood sugar levels.

One effective strategy for including starchy vegetables in a diabetes-friendly diet is to adhere to the rule of the 1/4 plate. This means filling no more than one-quarter of your plate with starchy vegetables in any given meal. This portion control technique helps manage carbohydrate intake while allowing you to enjoy the variety and nutritional benefits of these foods.

Additionally, the way starchy vegetables are cooked can significantly affect their impact on blood sugar. To help lower their glycemic index—a measure of how quickly foods raise blood sugar levels—opt for cooking methods that preserve the integrity of the vegetable's fiber. For instance, steaming or boiling can be more beneficial than baking or frying. Incorporating acidic ingredients such as vinegar or lemon juice can also reduce the glycemic index. Furthermore, cooling starchy vegetables after cooking, such as letting boiled potatoes cool down before making a potato salad, can alter the structure of the carbohydrates and reduce their impact on blood sugar.

Potatoes

Potatoes are one of the most commonly consumed vegetables worldwide, cherished for their versatility and ability to complement a wide range of dishes. Originating in the Andes mountains of South America, potatoes have become a staple in many cultures due to their adaptability in various climates and recipes.

NUTRITIONAL INFORMATION PER 100 GRAMS OF RAW POTATOES
Total Calories: 77 kcal
Protein: 2.0 g
Total Fat: 0.1 g
Saturated Fat: 0.03 g
Unsaturated Fat: 0.07 g
Carbohydrates: 17 g
Dietary Fiber: 2.2 g
Sugars: 0.8 g
Sodium: 6 mg
Vitamins and Minerals: High in Vitamin C, Vitamin B6, Potassium
Glycemic Index (GI): High (varies from 78 for boiled potatoes to lower for cooled and reheated potatoes)

Potatoes are often viewed with caution by those managing diabetes due to their high glycemic index, which can lead to spikes in blood sugar levels if not managed properly. However, when incorporated carefully, potatoes can be a nutritious part of your diet. They are an excellent source of vitamin C, essential not only for immune function but also for skin health and enhancing iron absorption. Additionally, potatoes provide significant amounts of potassium, which can help lower blood pressure, and vitamin B6, which is crucial for energy metabolism.

The fiber content in potatoes also plays an important role in digestive health and helps to regulate blood sugar levels. To make the most of these benefits while mitigating the risk of blood sugar spikes, it's important to practice portion control and be mindful of how they are prepared. For instance, eating a small serving of potatoes with the skin on can increase the fiber content, and pairing them with a source of healthy fats or proteins can help slow the absorption of carbohydrates.

COOKING IDEAS WITH POTATOES

Opt for boiling potatoes and letting them cool to create a resistant starch, which is less impactful on blood glucose levels, serving them in a salad with fresh greens and a vinegar-based dressing.

Prepare a diabetic-friendly potato hash by sautéing pre-boiled, diced potatoes with onions, peppers, and spices in a minimal amount of olive oil, serving with a side of scrambled eggs for a balanced breakfast.

Make a comforting soup by combining diced potatoes with low-sodium vegetable broth, carrots, celery, and herbs, simmering until the vegetables are tender. Puree the mixture for a creamy texture without cream.

Roast slices of potatoes with a light coating of olive oil and a sprinkle of rosemary and garlic, making sure to include a protein source like chicken or fish to balance the meal.

Incorporate potatoes in small quantities into stews with lots of non-starchy vegetables and lean meats, ensuring the dish provides fiber and protein to help mitigate the potatoes' high glycemic impact.

Sweet Potatoes

Sweet potatoes are a vibrant and nutritious root vegetable known for their sweet flavor and bright orange color, though they can also be found in white, purple, and yellow varieties. Native to the Americas, sweet potatoes are not only delicious but also highly versatile in the kitchen. They offer a wealth of health benefits and are especially popular in both savory and sweet culinary applications.

Sweet potatoes are renowned for their high beta-carotene content, which the body converts into vitamin A, essential for vision, immune function, and skin health. They also provide ample dietary fiber, which can help manage blood sugar levels by slowing the absorption of sugar into the bloodstream. Additionally, their content of vitamins C and B6 supports general health and energy production. While their glycemic index is moderate, pairing them with a source of healthy fats or proteins can help minimize their impact on blood sugar levels.

NUTRITIONAL INFORMATION PER 100 GRAMS OF RAW SWEET POTATOES
Total Calories: 86 kcal
Protein: 1.6 g
Total Fat: 0.1 g
Saturated Fat: 0.02 g
Unsaturated Fat: 0.03 g
Carbohydrates: 20.1 g
Dietary Fiber: 3.0 g
Sugars: 4.2 g
Sodium: 55 mg
Vitamins and Minerals: High in Vitamin A (beta-carotene), Vitamin C, Manganese, and several B vitamins
Glycemic Index (GI): Medium (approx. 70 when boiled)

COOKING IDEAS WITH SWEET POTATOES

Bake whole sweet potatoes until tender and stuff with a mixture of sautéed greens, beans, and a sprinkle of feta cheese for a filling meal that balances carbohydrates with fiber and protein.

Slice sweet potatoes into wedges, toss with olive oil and your choice of spices, and roast until crispy for a healthier alternative to traditional French fries.

Grate sweet potatoes and mix with egg and almond flour for a high-fiber, low-GI pancake, perfect for a nutritious breakfast or brunch option.

Simmer chunks of sweet potato in a hearty stew with lean meats and plenty of aromatic vegetables like garlic, onions, and celery to enrich the flavor without adding sugar.

Create a colorful salad by combining roasted sweet potato cubes with quinoa, black beans, red onion, cilantro, and a lime dressing for a dish rich in vitamins and minerals.

Corn

Corn, also known as maize, is a cereal grain first domesticated by indigenous peoples in southern Mexico about 10,000 years ago. Today, it is a staple food in many parts of the world, enjoyed for its sweet flavor when fresh and its versatility in processed forms. Corn can be found in everything from popcorn and cornmeal to sweet corn on the cob.

Corn is highly valued for its high fiber content, which can aid in digestion and help regulate blood sugar levels, making it a favorable option for those managing diabetes when consumed in moderation. Its rich vitamin B content supports energy metabolism and brain function. The phytochemicals found in corn, particularly lutein and zeaxanthin, contribute to eye health.

NUTRITIONAL INFORMATION PER 100 GRAMS OF RAW CORN
Total Calories: 86 kcal
Protein: 3.2 g
Total Fat: 1.2 g
Saturated Fat: 0.2 g
Unsaturated Fat: 0.6 g
Carbohydrates: 19 g
Dietary Fiber: 2.7 g
Sugars: 3.2 g
Sodium: 15 mg
Vitamins and Minerals: Rich in Vitamin C, B vitamins (especially Thiamine and Folate), Magnesium, and Phosphorus
Glycemic Index (GI): 52

COOKING IDEAS WITH CORN

Grill whole cobs of corn until slightly charred, then brush lightly with olive oil and sprinkle with a mix of herbs and spices for a flavorful side dish that adds excitement to any barbecue.

Add corn kernels to a vibrant vegetable soup featuring low-GI vegetables like zucchini and tomatoes, seasoned with garlic and herbs for a nourishing meal that's both satisfying and good for blood sugar management.

Combine cooked corn kernels with chopped bell peppers, cucumber, and red onion, dress with a light vinaigrette, and garnish with fresh cilantro for a refreshing salad that pairs well with grilled chicken or fish.

Create a wholesome salsa by mixing corn with diced tomatoes, avocado, jalapeño, and lime juice; serve with whole-grain tortilla chips or over grilled fish tacos for a meal rich in nutrients and flavors but low in unhealthy fats.

Incorporate corn into a whole-grain salad with barley or quinoa, black beans, diced peppers, and a tangy lime dressing for a fiber-rich dish that helps keep blood sugar levels stable.

Peas

Peas, belonging to the legume family, have been cultivated for thousands of years and are valued not only for their versatility in the culinary world but also for their nutritional benefits. Fresh, frozen, or dried, peas are commonly used in a variety of cuisines around the world, ranging from hearty soups to vibrant salads.

NUTRITIONAL INFORMATION PER 100 GRAMS OF RAW PEAS
Total Calories: 81 kcal
Protein: 5.4 g
Total Fat: 0.4 g
Saturated Fat: 0.1 g
Unsaturated Fat: 0.2 g
Carbohydrates: 14.5 g
Dietary Fiber: 5.1 g
Sugars: 5.7 g
Sodium: 5 mg
Vitamins and Minerals: Rich in Vitamin C, Vitamin K, several B vitamins (Thiamine, Folate), Manganese, Iron, and Magnesium
Glycemic Index (GI): 35

Peas are an excellent source of protein and fiber, which aid in digestion and help maintain stable blood sugar levels, making them ideal for diabetes management. The high content of vitamins and antioxidants supports overall health, boosting the immune system and reducing inflammation.

COOKING IDEAS WITH PEAS

Simmer peas with mint and onions until tender, then blend into a smooth, creamy soup that balances their natural sweetness with the freshness of mint—ideal for a light lunch or starter.

Stir-fry peas with chicken and mixed vegetables like carrots and bell peppers in a ginger-soy sauce for a quick and nutritious dinner that incorporates lean protein and fiber.

Toss peas into a salad with chunks of feta cheese, cherry tomatoes, and a sprinkle of dill, dressed with olive oil and lemon juice for a Mediterranean-flavored side dish that pairs well with grilled meats.

Mix peas with whole grains such as barley or quinoa, along with chopped red onions and herbs, for a filling and healthful salad that can serve as a meal on its own or as a side dish.

Incorporate peas into a hearty risotto, using brown rice and low-sodium chicken broth, and finish with a handful of grated Parmesan for a comforting meal that is both satisfying and diabetic-friendly.

Butternut Squash

Butternut squash, a type of winter squash, boasts a sweet, nutty taste akin to that of a pumpkin. This versatile vegetable is not only a fall favorite but also a nutritional powerhouse, popular for both its flavor and health benefits.

NUTRITIONAL INFORMATION PER 100 GRAMS OF RAW BUTTERNUT SQUASH
Total Calories: 45 kcal
Protein: 1 g
Total Fat: 0.1 g
Saturated Fat: 0.02 g
Unsaturated Fat: 0.08 g
Carbohydrates: 11.7 g
Dietary Fiber: 2 g
Sugars: 2.2 g
Sodium: 4 mg
Vitamins and Minerals: High in Vitamin A, Vitamin C, Vitamin E, B vitamins (especially folate), magnesium, and potassium
Glycemic Index (GI): 51

Butternut squash is especially noted for its high vitamin A content, which supports eye health and immune function. Its low calorie and high fiber content make it ideal for weight management and improving digestive health. The antioxidants present in butternut squash help reduce inflammation and protect against chronic diseases.

COOKING IDEAS BUTTERNUT SQUASH

Roast cubes of butternut squash with a light drizzle of olive oil and a sprinkle of cinnamon and nutmeg for a sweet and savory side dish that enhances any main meal.

Create a heartwarming soup by blending cooked butternut squash with low-sodium vegetable broth, sautéed onions, and a touch of ginger for added warmth and spice.

Incorporate butternut squash into a hearty chili by adding it to ground turkey, tomatoes, and kidney beans, simmering until the squash is tender and the flavors meld beautifully.

Toss roasted butternut squash into a salad with arugula, red onion, pomegranate seeds, and a light balsamic dressing for a refreshing and nutritious lunch option.

Make a healthy alternative to pasta by using spiralized butternut squash noodles sautéed with garlic, spinach, and cherry tomatoes, topped with a sprinkle of Parmesan cheese.

Carrots

Carrots, known for their vibrant orange color and sweet, crunchy texture, are among the most popular and versatile vegetables in the world. Originating from Persia, where they were initially cultivated for their leaves and seeds, today's carrots are bred for their thick, nutrient-rich taproots. Carrots are celebrated not only for their appealing flavor but also for their significant health benefits, including high levels of beta-carotene, which the body converts into vitamin A.

NUTRITIONAL INFORMATION PER 100 GRAMS OF UNCOOKED CARROTS
Total Calories: 41 kcal
Protein: 0.93 g
Total Fat: 0.24 g
Saturated Fat: 0.037 g
Unsaturated Fat: 0.183 g
Total Carbohydrates: 9.58 g
Dietary Fiber: 2.8 g
Sugars: 4.74 g
Sodium: 69 mg
Vitamins and Minerals: Exceptional source of vitamin A (from beta-carotene), good source of biotin, vitamin K1, potassium, and vitamin B6.
Glycemic Index (GI): Low (16 to 49 depending on preparation and variety)

Carrots offer numerous health benefits. The high fiber content helps regulate blood sugar levels and aids in digestion. Rich in beta-carotene, carrots are excellent for improving eyesight and skin health, and their antioxidants may reduce the risk of cancer. The vitamins and minerals in carrots support immune function and bone health, while their low glycemic index makes them an excellent choice for managing diabetes.

COOKING IDEAS WITH CARROTS

Carrots can be prepared in various ways to fit into a diabetes-friendly diet, enhancing meals with their natural sweetness and satisfying crunch. One delicious method is roasting whole or sliced carrots with a touch of olive oil until tender, seasoned with herbs like rosemary or thyme to enhance their natural sweetness, making them a delicious side dish that complements a variety of main courses. Alternatively, for a warming, nutritious soup, simmer sliced carrots with onions, garlic, and low-sodium vegetable broth until soft, then puree the mixture until smooth and season with ginger. This soup pairs beautifully with a protein-rich sandwich or salad. Another option is a refreshing carrot salad made by grating raw carrots and mixing them with apple cider vinegar, a sprinkle of olive oil, and fresh herbs like parsley or cilantro, adding raisins or diced apples for a hint of sweetness. This salad is fiber-rich and makes a great addition to any meal. For a simpler preparation, steam carrot slices or baby carrots until just tender to preserve their texture and nutrients, season with a dash of salt, pepper, and a drizzle of lemon juice, and serve alongside grilled or baked lean proteins such as chicken or fish. Lastly, for a balanced, fiber-rich meal, add thinly sliced carrots to a stir-fry with other non-starchy vegetables like bell peppers and snow peas, use a low-sodium soy sauce and serve over a small portion of brown rice or quinoa.

Parsnips

Parsnips, a root vegetable closely related to the carrot and parsley root, offer a distinctly sweet flavor, especially after the first frost. Often overlooked, this creamy white vegetable is a staple in many winter dishes and is valued for its versatility and rich nutritional profile.

NUTRITIONAL INFORMATION PER 100 GRAMS OF RAW PARSNIPS
Total Calories: 75 kcal
Protein: 1.2 g
Total Fat: 0.3 g
Saturated Fat: 0.05 g
Unsaturated Fat: 0.25 g
Carbohydrates: 18 g
Dietary Fiber: 4.9 g
Sugars: 4.8 g
Sodium: 10 mg
Vitamins and Minerals: Rich in Vitamin C, folate, and manganese; contains significant amounts of potassium and magnesium
Glycemic Index (GI): 85

Parsnips are high in fiber, which helps to regulate blood sugar and cholesterol levels, making them beneficial for heart health and diabetes management. They are also a good source of antioxidants and essential minerals that support immune function and overall health.

COOKING IDEAS WITH PARSNIPS

Cooking parsnips in ways that highlight their natural flavors while managing their glycemic impact is essential for incorporating them into a diabetes-friendly diet. Roasting parsnips can enhance their innate sweetness—try slicing them and tossing with a little olive oil and herbs, then baking until golden and tender. This method brings out a rich flavor without the need for added sugars or excessive fats.

For a comforting side dish, mashed parsnips are a fantastic alternative to mashed potatoes. Cook them until soft, then mash with a touch of olive oil and garlic for a creamy texture. Pairing this dish with a lean protein can make for a satisfying meal that doesn't significantly spike blood sugar levels.

Parsnip puree offers another versatile option; blend steamed parsnips with unsweetened almond milk and season with just a touch of salt and pepper. This puree works well as a creamy base for other dishes or as a light side that complements a variety of main courses without adding a heavy carbohydrate load.

Adding parsnips to a vegetable soup can also be a great way to enjoy their flavor while keeping the overall glycemic index low. Use a low-sodium broth and include plenty of non-starchy vegetables like spinach and mushrooms to create a filling, nutrient-rich meal that's gentle on blood sugar.

Incorporating sliced parsnips into a stir-fry with chicken or tofu, bell peppers, and snap peas can round out a meal nicely. Opt for low-sodium soy sauce or tamari and serve over a modest portion of brown rice to ensure a balanced meal that includes fiber and other nutrients to help manage the absorption of sugars and maintain overall dietary balance.

When introducing parsnips into your diet, it's advisable to watch the portion sizes and observe how your blood sugar responds. This can help you determine the appropriate amounts and combinations that best support your health goals.

Beets

Beets, known for their vibrant color and earthy flavor, are a nutritious root vegetable that can be a valuable addition to a healthy diet. They are not only rich in vitamins and minerals but also contain unique bioactive compounds that provide various health benefits.

NUTRITIONAL INFORMATION PER 100 GRAMS OF RAW BEETS
Total Calories: 43 kcal
Protein: 1.6 g
Total Fat: 0.2 g
Saturated Fat: 0.03 g
Unsaturated Fat: 0.17 g
Carbohydrates: 10 g
Dietary Fiber: 2.8 g
Sugars: 7 g
Sodium: 78 mg
Vitamins and Minerals: High in folate and manganese, contains good amounts of potassium and vitamin C
Glycemic Index (GI): 64

Beets are particularly notable for their high levels of nitrates, which are converted into nitric oxide in the body. This process aids in blood flow and blood pressure regulation, which is beneficial for heart health. The fiber in beets helps to regulate blood sugar levels and supports digestive health, making them a great choice for managing diabetes.

COOKING IDEAS WITH BEETS

Roast whole beets with a drizzle of olive oil to concentrate their sweetness and create a tender, flavorful dish that pairs well with greens and grains for a balanced meal.

Prepare a beetroot salad by mixing thinly sliced raw beets with arugula, goat cheese, and a sprinkle of walnuts. Dress with a simple vinaigrette made from olive oil and lemon juice for a refreshing side dish that is low in calories yet high in nutrients.

Blend cooked beets into a smooth soup with a base of vegetable broth and season with thyme and black pepper. Serve this vibrant soup with a dollop of Greek yogurt for added protein and a creamy texture.

Incorporate grated beets into whole wheat pancake batter to add sweetness and moisture without the need for excess sugar, creating a colorful and nutritious breakfast option.

Use pickled beets as a flavorful addition to sandwiches and wraps, combining them with lean proteins such as turkey or chicken breast and plenty of leafy greens for a tasty and healthful meal.

Plantains

Plantains, often mistaken for bananas, are a staple food in tropical regions around the world. Unlike bananas, plantains are typically cooked before eating and are highly versatile in both savory and sweet dishes due to their high starch content.

NUTRITIONAL INFORMATION PER 100 GRAMS OF RAW PLANTAINS
Total Calories: 122 kcal
Protein: 1.3 g
Total Fat: 0.3 g
Saturated Fat: 0.1 g
Unsaturated Fat: 0.2 g
Carbohydrates: 31.9 g
Dietary Fiber: 2.3 g
Sugars: 14.8 g
Sodium: 4 mg
Vitamins and Minerals: Rich in vitamin A, vitamin C, and potassium
Glycemic Index (GI): Approximately 40

Plantains are a good source of complex carbohydrates, dietary fiber, and essential vitamins like A and C, which support immune function and eye health. The resistant starch in green plantains acts as a prebiotic, feeding beneficial gut bacteria, which is crucial for overall health and particularly beneficial for managing blood sugar levels.

COOKING IDEAS WITH PLANTAINS

Grill slices of green plantains until they are caramelized and tender, then serve with a sprinkle of cinnamon and a side of low-fat cottage cheese for a balance of flavors and a boost of protein.

Make a plantain mash by boiling green plantains until soft, then mashing them with a touch of olive oil and seasoning with garlic and herbs. This can be a diabetic-friendly substitute for mashed potatoes.

Create a plantain stir-fry by slicing them thinly and sautéing with onions, bell peppers, and lean pieces of chicken or shrimp. Add a splash of low-sodium soy sauce and a bit of ginger for an Asian-inspired dish that's rich in nutrients and flavor.

Prepare baked plantain chips by slicing green plantains thinly, tossing them with a small amount of olive oil and paprika, and baking until crispy. This makes a great snack that's much healthier than traditional fried chips.

Use ripe plantains to sweeten dishes naturally without the need for added sugars. Cook them in a minimal amount of oil until they develop a rich, sweet flavor and serve alongside savory dishes like roast chicken or fish.

Yams

Yams are a type of tuber vegetable that are highly valued in many parts of the world for their earthy taste and substantial nutritional benefits. They are distinctly different from sweet potatoes, though the two are often confused in some countries. Yams are starchier and drier, making them a versatile component of both sweet and savory dishes.

Yams are a good source of complex carbohydrates and fiber, which can help manage blood sugar levels by slowing the rate of glucose absorption. Their high potassium content supports heart health by maintaining proper blood pressure and fluid balance. The presence of vitamin C not only boosts immunity but also acts as an antioxidant, protecting the body against free radicals and supporting skin health.

NUTRITIONAL INFORMATION PER 100 GRAMS OF RAW YAMS
Total Calories: 118 kcal
Protein: 1.5 g
Total Fat: 0.1 g
Saturated Fat: 0.02 g
Unsaturated Fat: 0.08 g
Carbohydrates: 27.9 g
Dietary Fiber: 4.1 g
Sugars: 0.5 g
Sodium: 9 mg
Vitamins and Minerals: Rich in vitamin C, potassium, and manganese
Glycemic Index (GI): 65

COOKING IDEAS WITH YAMS

Create a hearty yam stew by simmering chunks of yam in a tomato-based sauce with onions, garlic, lean meats like turkey or chicken, and a generous helping of spices like cumin and chili powder. This rich dish can be served as a fulfilling main course that delivers nutrition and flavor without spiking blood sugar.

Bake yams whole in the oven until they are soft and their natural sweetness is enhanced. Split them open and top with a dollop of Greek yogurt and a sprinkle of chives for a satisfying dish that pairs well with a protein-rich main.

Incorporate yams into breakfast by grating them and forming them into patties to be lightly fried in a non-stick pan. Serve these yam hash browns with a side of scrambled egg whites for a balanced breakfast.

Make a yam puree by boiling them until tender, then blending with a touch of olive oil and seasonings such as garlic and rosemary. This puree can be a delightful substitute for mashed potatoes and can be paired with any main dish.

Prepare a cold yam salad by boiling them until just tender, then dicing and mixing with a vinaigrette made from olive oil, vinegar, mustard, and fresh herbs. Add some chopped red onions and celery for crunch, and chill before serving. This salad is refreshing and makes a great side dish for picnics and lunches.

DAIRY AND DAIRY ALTERNATIVES

Navigating the dairy aisle as a diabetic involves carefully weighing the options between low-fat, full-fat, and plant-based products to align with dietary needs that support both blood sugar management and overall health. This decision-making process extends beyond simple calorie counting, focusing more critically on how these dairy choices influence blood sugar control and insulin sensitivity.

Traditionally, low-fat dairy products have been recommended to those aiming to reduce calorie intake and improve heart health. Options like 1% milk or low-fat yogurt offer fewer calories and less saturated fat than their full-fat counterparts, and they are often fortified with vitamins A and D, which are lost when fat is removed. For diabetics, particularly those managing their weight, low-fat dairy can be a wise choice. These products provide essential nutrients and high-quality protein without the added fats that can exacerbate insulin resistance. However, it's crucial for diabetics to remain vigilant about added sugars, commonly used to enhance the flavor of reduced-fat dairy products.

Conversely, recent research suggests that full-fat dairy products may also have a beneficial role in a diabetic's diet. Full-fat options like whole milk and regular cheese contain more fat-soluble vitamins and contribute to a feeling of satiety, which can aid in weight management—a critical aspect of Type 2 diabetes management. Some studies indicate that the fats found in full-fat dairy might even improve insulin sensitivity, challenging the previous notion that these fats heighten the risk of heart disease. The inclusion of full-fat dairy should be practiced with moderation, allowing diabetics to gain the nutritional benefits without excessive calorie intake.

Low-Fat Yogurt

Low-fat yogurt is a dairy product made by fermenting milk with live bacteria cultures, which results in a creamy, tangy food that's both nutritious and versatile. It is particularly popular among those managing their weight and blood sugar levels, as it offers the nutritional benefits of dairy without the high fat content of full-fat versions.

Low-fat yogurt is a great source of high-quality protein and essential nutrients, including calcium and vitamin B-12, which are crucial for bone health and energy metabolism, respectively. The presence of probiotics in yogurt helps enhance digestive health and may improve gut flora, which is important for overall wellness. Its low glycemic index makes it an excellent choice for those managing diabetes, as it has minimal impact on blood sugar levels.

NUTRITIONAL INFORMATION PER 100 GRAMS OF LOW-FAT YOGURT
Total Calories: 63 kcal
Protein: 5.25 g
Total Fat: 1.55 g
Saturated Fat: 1.0 g
Unsaturated Fat: 0.55 g
Carbohydrates: 7.04 g
Dietary Fiber: 0 g
Sugars: 7.04 g
Sodium: 70 mg
Vitamins and Minerals: Rich in calcium, vitamin B-12, phosphorus, and riboflavin
Glycemic Index (GI): 33

COOKING IDEAS WITH LOW-FAT YOGURT

Incorporate low-fat yogurt into a morning smoothie by blending it with a handful of berries, a scoop of protein powder, and a touch of cinnamon for a nutritious breakfast that starts the day right.

Use low-fat yogurt as a base for a tangy dressing or dip by mixing it with herbs like dill or parsley, garlic powder, and a squeeze of lemon. This can be used to dress salads or as a dip for veggies and whole-grain crackers.

Create a creamy soup by using low-fat yogurt as a thickener. After cooking your choice of vegetables, such as pumpkin or carrot, blend them with low-fat yogurt and season with nutmeg and black pepper for a comforting bowl that is rich in flavor and low in calories.

Prepare a marinade for chicken or fish using low-fat yogurt, mixed with spices like turmeric, coriander, and a bit of chili powder. The yogurt not only infuses the meat with flavor but also tenderizes it, making for a juicy and delicious meal.

Make a dessert parfait by layering low-fat yogurt with chopped nuts, diced fruits, and a sprinkle of oats. This delightful treat can be enjoyed as a snack or a light dessert, offering sweetness without a significant sugar rush.

Skim Milk

Skim milk, also known as nonfat milk, is cow's milk from which the fat has been removed. It serves as a lower-calorie alternative to whole milk, retaining all the nutrients except for the fat-soluble vitamins, which are reduced due to the removal of fat. It's particularly favored by those looking to reduce fat intake or manage calorie consumption effectively.

NUTRITIONAL INFORMATION PER 100 GRAMS OF SKIM MILK
Total Calories: 34 kcal
Protein: 3.4 g
Total Fat: 0.1 g
Saturated Fat: 0.1 g
Unsaturated Fat: 0 g
Carbohydrates: 5 g
Dietary Fiber: 0 g
Sugars: 5 g
Sodium: 42 mg
Vitamins and Minerals: Rich in calcium, vitamin D (fortified), phosphorus, and vitamin B-12
Glycemic Index (GI): 27

Skim milk offers a good source of high-quality protein and essential nutrients like calcium and vitamin B-12, which are crucial for bone health and energy metabolism. The low fat content helps those managing their cholesterol levels or cardiovascular health. It's also beneficial for weight management due to its lower

calorie content compared to whole milk. Being low in fat and high in protein makes it a valuable addition to a diabetic diet as it does not significantly impact blood glucose levels.

COOKING IDEAS WITH SKIM MILK

Prepare a morning oatmeal using skim milk instead of water for a creamier texture without the added fat. Enhance the flavor with cinnamon and top with fresh berries for a filling breakfast that helps maintain steady blood sugar levels.

Use skim milk in smoothies by blending it with a combination of fruits such as peaches and bananas for natural sweetness, and add a handful of spinach for extra nutrition without altering the taste significantly.

Create lighter versions of soups and sauces by substituting cream with skim milk. For instance, in a mushroom stroganoff, use skim milk thickened with a little flour instead of cream for a healthy yet satisfying dish.

Make a low-fat custard with skim milk, a little sugar substitute, and egg yolks. Flavor it with vanilla and serve with a fruit salad for a dessert that is both indulgent and friendly to blood sugar management.

Prepare a skim milk latte by frothing hot skim milk and adding it to a strong shot of espresso for a café-style beverage that's low in calories and fat but high in calcium and protein.

Low-Fat Cottage Cheese

Low-fat cottage cheese is a fresh cheese curd product with a mild flavor that is a staple in many health-conscious diets. Its lower fat content compared to traditional cottage cheese makes it an appealing choice for those looking to reduce their dietary fat intake while still enjoying a rich source of protein.

NUTRITIONAL INFORMATION PER 100 GRAMS OF LOW-FAT COTTAGE CHEESE
Total Calories: 72 kcal
Protein: 10.5 g
Total Fat: 1.0 g
Saturated Fat: 0.7 g
Unsaturated Fat: 0.3 g
Carbohydrates: 4.3 g
Dietary Fiber: 0 g
Sugars: 4.3 g
Sodium: 406 mg
Vitamins and Minerals: Rich in calcium, phosphorus, and contains some B vitamins like B-12
Glycemic Index (GI): 30

Low-fat cottage cheese is especially valued for its high protein content, which helps in muscle repair and satiety. It is low in carbohydrates, making it an excellent choice for individuals managing their blood sugar levels. The calcium found in cottage cheese is vital for bone health, and its overall nutrient profile supports healthy metabolism and weight management.

COOKING IDEAS

Create a nutritious breakfast by layering low-fat cottage cheese with nuts and berries. The combination of protein from the cheese and fiber from the berries helps to stabilize blood sugar levels and start the day off right.

Incorporate low-fat cottage cheese into smoothies for added creaminess and protein without significantly impacting the carbohydrate content. Blend with spinach, a small banana, and unsweetened almond milk for a refreshing and nutritious drink.

Use low-fat cottage cheese as a filling for omelets, adding herbs and diced vegetables for a protein-rich breakfast or lunch that is low in carbs but high in flavor and nutritional value.

Mix low-fat cottage cheese with chopped herbs, garlic, and a bit of lemon zest for a savory spread on whole-grain crackers or slices of cucumber. This snack is low in carbohydrates and fats but high in taste and satisfaction.

Prepare a diabetic-friendly dessert by blending low-fat cottage cheese until smooth, then mix with a touch of vanilla extract and stevia. Top with cinnamon and diced apples for a sweet treat that mimics the flavors of apple pie without the high sugar content.

Low-Fat Kefir

Low-fat kefir is a cultured, fermented milk drink similar to a thin yogurt, known for its tangy flavor and probiotic benefits. Originating from parts of Eastern Europe and Southwest Asia, kefir is made by adding kefir grains to milk, which initiates the fermentation process. This beverage is celebrated for its contributions to gut health and its versatility in various dietary plans, particularly for those seeking low-fat options.

Low-fat kefir is esteemed for its probiotic content, which supports a healthy digestive system and can improve gut flora. The protein in kefir aids in satiety and muscle maintenance, making it an excellent choice for weight management. Its low glycemic index makes it particularly suitable for those managing diabetes, as it does not cause significant spikes in blood sugar.

NUTRITIONAL INFORMATION PER 100 GRAMS OF LOW-FAT KEFIR	
Total Calories: 41 kcal	
Protein: 3.3 g	
Total Fat: 1.0 g	
Saturated Fat: 0.6 g	
Unsaturated Fat: 0.4 g	
Carbohydrates: 4.0 g	
Dietary Fiber: 0 g	
Sugars: 4.0 g	
Sodium: 50 mg	
Vitamins and Minerals: Rich in calcium, phosphorus, and vitamins B12 and D	
Glycemic Index (GI): 25	

COOKING IDEAS WITH LOW-FAT KEFIR

Enhance your morning smoothie by adding low-fat kefir for a probiotic boost and a creamy texture without significantly increasing the fat content. Blend with low-GI fruits like berries and a handful of spinach for a nutritious, balanced meal.

Create a light, flavorful dressing for salads by mixing low-fat kefir with lemon juice, fresh herbs, and a touch of garlic. This dressing adds a probiotic punch to your greens without the added sugars and fats found in commercial dressings.

Use low-fat kefir in place of buttermilk or yogurt in baking to add moisture and a slight tanginess to baked goods like muffins and pancakes. This substitution can help reduce fat content while still creating fluffy and delicious treats.

Prepare a chilled soup, such as cucumber or gazpacho, using low-fat kefir as the soup base. This adds a creamy texture and a boost of probiotics, making for a refreshing and stomach-friendly meal.

Marinate chicken or fish in low-fat kefir with spices and herbs before cooking. The kefir acts as a tenderizer, and its mild acidity adds flavor while keeping the meat moist and tender.

Low-Fat Cheese

Low-fat cheese is a staple in many healthy diets, offering the beloved flavors and textures of traditional cheeses with fewer calories and saturated fats. It comes in many varieties, including cheddar, mozzarella, and Swiss, allowing it to easily substitute for full-fat cheeses in most recipes. This makes it a popular choice for those managing weight, cholesterol levels, or diabetes.

NUTRITIONAL INFORMATION PER 100 GRAMS OF LOW-FAT CHEESE	
Total Calories: 174 kcal	
Protein: 28 g	
Total Fat: 4.5 g	
Saturated Fat: 2.9 g	
Unsaturated Fat: 1.6 g	
Carbohydrates: 3.4 g	
Dietary Fiber: 0 g	
Sugars: 0.5 g	
Sodium: 621 mg	
Vitamins and Minerals: High in calcium and phosphorus, contains vitamins A and B12	
Glycemic Index (GI): Low	

Low-fat cheese is an excellent source of high-quality protein and calcium, crucial for bone health and muscle function. Its low carbohydrate content makes it ideal for diabetes management, helping to prevent spikes in blood sugar while still allowing the enjoyment of cheese in meals.

COOKING IDEAS WITH LOW-FAT CHEESE

Incorporate low-fat cheese into a vegetable omelet for breakfast. This addition provides a good source of protein and makes the meal more filling without adding excessive fat.

Create a flavorful grilled cheese sandwich using whole-grain bread and low-fat cheese. Add slices of tomato or a spread of pesto for extra flavor without compromising blood sugar levels.

Sprinkle shredded low-fat cheese over a homemade pizza topped with lots of vegetables and a thin whole-grain crust. This approach maintains the cheesy delight of pizza while keeping the meal balanced and health-friendly.

Use low-fat cheese as a topping for salads or steamed vegetables to enhance flavor and add calcium, transforming plain dishes into more appealing and nutritious meals.

Prepare a light macaroni and cheese using whole-grain pasta, low-fat cheese, and skim milk. Add a pinch of mustard powder and black pepper to boost the flavor. This version of the classic comfort food is lower in fat and suitable for a diabetes-friendly diet.

Whole Milk

Whole milk is a traditional dairy product known for its rich taste and creamy texture. It is the least processed form of milk, retaining all of its natural fats, which are crucial for the absorption of fat-soluble vitamins.

Whole milk is often a key dietary source of calcium, protein, and vitamin D.

NUTRITIONAL INFORMATION PER 100 GRAMS OF WHOLE MILK	
Total Calories: 61 kcal	
Protein: 3.15 g	
Total Fat: 3.25 g	
Saturated Fat: 1.865 g	
Unsaturated Fat: 1.385 g	
Carbohydrates: 4.8 g	
Dietary Fiber: 0 g	
Sugars: 5.1 g	
Sodium: 41 mg	
Vitamins and Minerals: High in calcium, vitamin D, and B vitamins	
Glycemic Index (GI): 31	

Whole milk provides a balanced mix of nutrients. It is an excellent source of calcium, essential for bone health, and vitamin D, which facilitates the absorption of calcium and boosts immune function. The presence of whole fats in milk has been studied for potential benefits in reducing the risk of diabetes and aiding in weight management by promoting satiety.

COOKING IDEAS WITH WHOLE MILK

Prepare a morning smoothie using whole milk, a handful of berries, and a scoop of protein powder for a nutritious start to the day that doesn't spike blood sugar levels.

Create a creamy soup base with whole milk instead of cream. Use it in soups such as mushroom or pumpkin for a rich texture without excessive fat.

Make a homemade custard with whole milk, flavored with vanilla and sweetened with a diabetic-friendly sweetener. Serve this as a dessert or a sweet snack.

Use whole milk to make oatmeal or porridge, adding a rich flavor and creamy texture. Enhance it with cinnamon and nuts for a filling breakfast.

Whip up a béchamel sauce using whole milk as a base. This can be used in casseroles or lasagna, adding creamy texture and flavor without the need for heavy cream.

Regular Yogurt

Regular yogurt is a fermented dairy product known for its creamy texture and slightly tangy flavor. It is made by bacterial fermentation of milk, where beneficial bacteria ferment lactose, the natural sugar found in milk, producing lactic acid which acts on milk protein. Regular yogurt contains live probiotics, which are beneficial for digestive health.

NUTRITIONAL INFORMATION PER 100 GRAMS OF REGULAR YOGURT	
Total Calories: 61 kcal	
Protein: 3.5 g	
Total Fat: 3.3 g	
Saturated Fat: 2.1 g	
Unsaturated Fat: 1.2 g	
Carbohydrates: 4.7 g	
Dietary Fiber: 0 g	
Sugars: 4.7 g	
Sodium: 46 mg	
Vitamins and Minerals: Rich in calcium, phosphorus, and B vitamins	
Glycemic Index (GI): 35	

Regular yogurt is an excellent source of calcium, essential for bone health, and also provides significant amounts of protein and B vitamins, particularly B12, which is vital for brain health and maintaining red blood cells. The presence of live probiotics supports gut health, which can positively influence everything from immunity to mental well-being.

COOKING IDEAS WITH REGULAR YOGURT

Mix regular yogurt with fresh or frozen berries and a sprinkle of flaxseed for a nutrient-dense breakfast or snack that supports blood sugar control.

Use yogurt as a base for smoothies; combine it with a high-fiber fruit like pears or apples and a handful of spinach for a refreshing and nutritious drink.

Create a marinade for chicken or turkey by mixing yogurt with spices like turmeric, garlic, and cilantro, which not only adds flavor but also helps in tenderizing the meat.

Make a healthier version of tzatziki, a Greek yogurt-based dip, by combining it with grated cucumber, garlic, and herbs, perfect as a dip for vegetables or a topping for grilled meats.

Prepare a creamy dressing for salads by blending yogurt with herbs, lemon juice, and a touch of olive oil, providing a delicious way to enhance the taste of raw vegetables without adding excess calories.

Cheddar Cheese

Cheddar cheese, originating from the village of Cheddar in England, is among the most popular cheeses worldwide, known for its rich, sharp flavor and firm texture. This cheese varies in taste depending on the length of aging and can range from mild to extra sharp. Cheddar is not only a staple in culinary traditions around the world but also offers several nutritional benefits.

NUTRITIONAL INFORMATION PER 100 GRAMS OF CHEDDAR CHEESE	
Total Calories: 402 kcal	
Protein: 25 g	
Total Fat: 33 g	
Saturated Fat: 21 g	
Unsaturated Fat: 10 g	
Carbohydrates: 1.3 g	
Dietary Fiber: 0 g	
Sugars: 0.5 g	
Sodium: 621 mg	
Vitamins and Minerals: Rich in calcium, phosphorus, and vitamin A	
Glycemic Index (GI): Low	

Cheddar cheese is a significant source of high-quality protein and essential fats, with a richness in calcium and phosphorus, which are crucial for maintaining bone health. Its high content of saturated fat calls for moderation in consumption, particularly for individuals managing cholesterol levels. The low carbohydrate content makes it a favorable choice for those on a low-carb or ketogenic diet.

COOKING IDEAS WITH CHEDDAR CHEESE

Grate cheddar cheese over a vegetable gratin comprising cauliflower, broccoli, and spinach, then bake until the cheese is bubbly and golden for a comforting, low-carb meal.

Incorporate small cubes of cheddar into salads with leafy greens, nuts, and a vinaigrette dressing to add flavor and protein without significantly increasing the dish's carbohydrate content.

Prepare a diabetes-friendly snack by slicing cheddar cheese and pairing it with apple slices or whole-grain crackers, balancing the fat and protein with a modest amount of healthy carbohydrates.

Use cheddar in a stuffed chicken breast recipe, filling the chicken with cheese and herbs, then baking it. This provides a protein-rich meal that is low in carbs but high in satisfaction.

Create a low-carb version of "mac" and cheese using chopped cauliflower as a substitute for pasta, mixed with a creamy cheddar sauce, which delivers all the comfort-food feel without the high carbs of traditional versions.

Cream Cheese

Cream cheese is a soft, mild-tasting cheese known for its smooth texture and versatility in both sweet and savory dishes. Originating from the United States in the 19th century, it has become a staple ingredient in various recipes, including frostings, dips, and spreads. Its creamy texture makes it a favorite for enhancing the richness of dishes.

NUTRITIONAL INFORMATION PER 100 GRAMS OF CREAM CHEESE
Total Calories: 342 kcal
Protein: 6 g
Total Fat: 34 g
Saturated Fat: 19 g
Unsaturated Fat: 10 g
Carbohydrates: 4.1 g
Dietary Fiber: 0 g
Sugars: 3.2 g
Sodium: 321 mg
Vitamins and Minerals: Contains Vitamin A, small amounts of calcium
Glycemic Index (GI): Low

Cream cheese offers moderate protein levels and a high fat content, making it a good choice for low-carbohydrate diets. It's particularly rich in Vitamin A, which is essential for good vision, skin health, and immune function. The presence of saturated fat means that it should be consumed in moderation, especially by those monitoring their heart health.

COOKING IDEAS WITH CREAM CHEESE

Meld cream cheese into a smooth sauce with herbs and spices to drizzle over steamed vegetables or grilled meats, adding a rich flavor without adding excessive carbohydrates.

Whip cream cheese with a bit of vanilla extract and a sugar substitute to make a keto-friendly frosting for cakes or muffins made from almond or coconut flour, catering to those managing their sugar intake.

Incorporate cream cheese into scrambled eggs or omelets, giving them a creamy texture and rich taste while keeping the dish low in carbs, perfect for a diabetic-friendly breakfast.

Blend cream cheese with avocado and lime juice to create a creamy dip for raw vegetables, which can be a satisfying snack or appetizer that is both nutritious and low in sugar.

Use cream cheese as a base for a savory cheesecake, incorporating ingredients like chopped spinach, artichokes, and garlic, baked in a nut-based crust for a delightful, low-carb main course or side dish.

PLANT-BASED ALTERNATIVES

For individuals managing dietary restrictions such as lactose intolerance or veganism, or for those simply seeking to broaden their dietary horizons, plant-based dairy alternatives offer an array of nutritious and versatile choices. These alternatives include options like almond milk, soy milk, oat milk, and coconut milk, each offering unique flavors and health benefits that make them popular not just among those with dietary restrictions, but also with health-conscious consumers.

As the popularity of plant-based diets continues to rise, these dairy alternatives have become integral for providing essential nutrients typically found in traditional dairy, such as calcium and vitamin D. However, when incorporating these options into a diabetes-friendly diet, selecting unsweetened varieties is crucial. Many commercial plant-based milks are often laden with added sugars that can lead to unnecessary spikes in blood sugar levels, undermining the management of diabetes.

By choosing unsweetened versions of these products, individuals can enjoy the creamy texture and various health benefits of plant-based dairy while keeping their carbohydrate intake in check. This careful selection helps ensure that the integration of plant-based dairy alternatives into one's diet not only diversifies their food choices but also contributes positively to their overall health management, especially for those monitoring blood sugar levels.

Soy Milk

Soy milk, derived from soybeans, is a popular dairy-free alternative to cow's milk. It has been a staple in Asian cuisine for centuries and has gained widespread popularity worldwide for its nutritional benefits and versatility. This plant-based milk is produced by soaking and grinding soybeans, boiling the mixture, and then filtering out the particulates.

Soy milk is an excellent source of protein and essential fatty acids. It's naturally low in saturated fat and free from cholesterol, making it a heart-healthy choice. Fortified versions provide additional nutrients such as calcium and vitamins D and B12, which are important for bone health. The low glycemic index makes it suitable for those managing diabetes, as it does not cause a significant spike in blood sugar levels.

NUTRITIONAL INFORMATION PER 100 GRAMS OF SOY MILK	
Total Calories: 54 kcal	
Protein: 3.3 g	
Total Fat: 1.8 g	
Saturated Fat: 0.2 g	
Unsaturated Fat: 1.4 g	
Carbohydrates: 6.3 g	
Dietary Fiber: 0.6 g	
Sugars: 4 g	
Sodium: 51 mg	
Vitamins and Minerals: Rich in Vitamin D, Vitamin B12, and calcium (when fortified)	
Glycemic Index (GI): 30	

NUTRITIONAL INFORMATION PER 100 GRAMS OF ALMOND MILK	
Total Calories: 17 kcal	
Protein: 0.42 g	
Total Fat: 1.49 g	
Saturated Fat: 0.11 g	
Unsaturated Fat: 1.38 g	
Carbohydrates: 0.59 g	
Dietary Fiber: 0.2 g	
Sugars: 0.15 g	
Sodium: 64 mg	
Vitamins and Minerals: Contains Vitamin E; often fortified with calcium and Vitamin D	
Glycemic Index (GI): 30	

COOKING IDEAS WITH SOY MILK

Create a smoothie by blending unsweetened soy milk with low-GI fruits like berries and a scoop of protein powder, offering a nutrient-rich start to the day or a refreshing post-workout snack.

Use soy milk as a base in creamy soup recipes, such as mushroom or broccoli soup, to add richness without the added sugars found in some cream-based soups.

Prepare a dairy-free béchamel sauce using soy milk, flour, and olive oil, perfect for making healthier versions of classic dishes like lasagna or a creamy casserole.

Make a chai latte with soy milk, steeping black tea with spices like cinnamon, cardamom, and ginger, then sweetening with a diabetes-friendly sweetener for a warming, aromatic beverage.

Incorporate soy milk into oatmeal or breakfast cereals instead of water or cow's milk, enriching your first meal with additional protein without raising blood sugar levels excessively.

Almond Milk

Almond milk, a creamy and nutty beverage, is made from ground almonds and water. It has become a popular plant-based alternative to traditional dairy milk, favored not only by vegans and those with lactose intolerance but also by individuals looking to reduce their intake of animal products. This milk alternative is low in calories and carbohydrates, making it a suitable choice for a variety of dietary needs, including diabetes management.

Almond milk is naturally rich in Vitamin E, an antioxidant known for its skin health benefits and its ability to protect cells from oxidative damage. Its low calorie and carbohydrate content make it an excellent option for those monitoring their blood sugar levels. Fortified versions of almond milk can also provide a significant amount of calcium and Vitamin D, comparable to that of cow's milk, which is essential for bone health.

COOKING IDEAS WITH ALMOND MILK

Whip up a smoothie using unsweetened almond milk, a handful of spinach, a small portion of avocado, and a serving of protein powder for a nourishing and filling meal that won't spike your blood sugar.

Create a morning porridge by cooking steel-cut oats or whole grain cereal in almond milk, topping it with nuts and seeds for added texture and a boost of healthy fats.

Use almond milk in baking recipes like muffins or pancakes to add moisture without the extra sugars, ensuring treats that are lower in calories and carbohydrates.

Prepare a creamy almond milk-based curry using turmeric, ginger, and cinnamon to infuse flavor into dishes such as chicken or vegetable curry, which can be served over cauliflower rice for a full meal.

Make a dairy-free hot chocolate by heating almond milk with cocoa powder and a sweetener like stevia, perfect for a cozy evening drink that keeps blood sugar in check.

Coconut Milk

Coconut milk, derived from the meat of mature coconuts, is a creamy, rich liquid that's a staple in many tropical cuisines, particularly in Southeast Asia, the Caribbean, and parts of South America. Its luxurious texture and sweet, nutty flavor make it a popular choice in both savory dishes and desserts. Coconut milk is also a favored ingredient in various dietary regimens, including vegan and paleo diets, due to its high content of medium-chain triglycerides (MCTs).

Coconut milk is renowned for its content of MCTs, which are believed to aid in weight management, energy production, and glucose regulation, making it suitable for diabetics when used in moderation. The saturated fat in coconut milk is primarily lauric acid, which has been linked to improved cholesterol levels and heart health. It also provides vital minerals and electrolytes that support muscle and nerve function.

NUTRITIONAL INFORMATION PER 100 GRAMS OF COCONUT MILK
Total Calories: 230 kcal
Protein: 2.3 g
Total Fat: 23.8 g
Saturated Fat: 21.1 g
Unsaturated Fat: 1.7 g
Carbohydrates: 5.5 g
Dietary Fiber: 2.2 g
Sugars: 3.3 g
Sodium: 15 mg
Vitamins and Minerals: Contains manganese, copper, phosphorus, magnesium, iron, and potassium
Glycemic Index (GI): 40

COOKING IDEAS WITH COCONUT MILK

Simmer a flavorful Thai green curry using coconut milk, fresh herbs, spices, and lean meats or tofu to create a balanced dish that infuses subtle sweetness and rich flavors.

Prepare a coconut chia pudding by mixing unsweetened coconut milk with chia seeds and letting it sit overnight. Top with nuts and a few slices of kiwi or berries for a refreshing and filling breakfast or snack.

Use coconut milk to make a creamy soup base for pumpkin or butternut squash soup, enhancing the natural sweetness of the vegetables while keeping the dish hearty and satisfying.

Incorporate coconut milk into smoothies for added creaminess and flavor; blend with low GI fruits like berries and a scoop of protein powder for a well-rounded snack.

Create a dairy-free rice pudding using coconut milk, a cinnamon stick, and arborio rice, slow-cooked until tender. Sweeten with a minimal amount of maple syrup and serve with a sprinkle of cinnamon to enhance flavor without a significant sugar addition.

Oat Milk

Oat milk is a plant-based milk alternative made by blending water and oats, then straining the mixture to produce a smooth, creamy liquid. It has gained popularity as a vegan-friendly option that mimics the mouthfeel and flavor of traditional cow's milk, making it a favorite among those who prefer non-dairy products. Oat milk is not only appealing for its taste and texture but also for its nutritional benefits, especially for individuals with dietary restrictions or lactose intolerance.

NUTRITIONAL INFORMATION PER 100 GRAMS OF OAT MILK
Total Calories: 50 kcal
Protein: 1 g
Total Fat: 1.5 g
Saturated Fat: 0.2 g
Unsaturated Fat: 1.3 g
Carbohydrates: 9 g
Dietary Fiber: 0.8 g
Sugars: 4 g
Sodium: 100 mg
Vitamins and Minerals: Often fortified with vitamins A, D, B2, and B12; contains small amounts of calcium
Glycemic Index (GI): Medium

Oat milk provides a beneficial alternative for those managing diabetes due to its beta-glucan content, a type of soluble fiber that helps to slow digestion and modulate blood sugar spikes. Although it is higher in carbohydrates than other plant milks, the presence of fiber helps to stabilize glucose levels. The fortification of oat milk with vitamins and minerals supports overall health, complementing a balanced diet.

COOKING IDEAS WITH OAT MILK

Create a warming morning porridge by cooking oats in oat milk until thick and creamy. Enhance the dish with a sprinkle of cinnamon, which can help regulate blood sugar levels, and top with a handful of fresh berries for natural sweetness.

Whip up a smoothie using unsweetened oat milk, a spoonful of almond butter, and a blend of spinach and frozen blueberries for a nutritious snack that balances sugars and provides essential fatty acids.

Use oat milk as a base for homemade creamy soups, such as mushroom or broccoli, to enrich the texture without adding excessive calories or sugars, ensuring a hearty meal suitable for those monitoring their carbohydrate intake.

Bake diabetes-friendly treats by substituting oat milk for regular milk in recipes for muffins or pancakes, which allows for a reduction in lactose while still achieving a tender, fluffy texture.

Prepare a dairy-free béchamel sauce with oat milk, using whole grain flour and a touch of olive oil for dishes like lasagna or a cauliflower gratin, offering a lower GI alternative to traditional recipes.

Foods to Avoid or Limit

Managing diabetes requires an attentive approach to diet, particularly when it comes to avoiding foods that can exacerbate the condition by causing rapid spikes in blood sugar levels. While a balanced diet is crucial, certain foods are particularly detrimental for those with diabetes due to their high glycemic index (GI) and glycemic load (GL), which measure how quickly foods release glucose into the bloodstream and the volume of glucose they release, respectively. Below is a detailed discussion on foods that individuals with diabetes should avoid to maintain better health and blood glucose control.

Sugary Beverages: One of the most harmful items in a diabetic diet is sugary drinks, including sodas, fruit punches, and energy drinks. These beverages are loaded with sugar and lack fiber, causing a swift rise in blood sugar and insulin levels. They contribute significantly to weight gain, which can complicate diabetes management and increase the risk of cardiovascular disease.

Refined Grains: White bread, white rice, and pasta made from white flour have high GI scores and offer little nutritional benefit due to the removal of the fiber-rich outer bran and nutrient-rich germ during processing. These foods break down quickly into glucose and can lead to significant spikes in blood sugar levels. Opting for whole grains can help manage the GI impact and provide sustained energy.

Pastries and Sweets: Cakes, cookies, pastries, and other desserts are typically high in sugar and fats, which may increase blood glucose dramatically. These foods are not only bad for blood sugar levels but are also high in calories, potentially leading to weight gain and increased insulin resistance.

Fried Foods and High-Fat Snacks: Fried foods and snacks like potato chips and fries are high in unhealthy fats and calories, leading to weight gain and increased blood sugar levels. The high content of trans and saturated fats in these foods can also contribute to heart disease, a common complication for those with diabetes.

Candy and Chocolate: Except for dark chocolate, which should be consumed in moderation, candy and milk chocolate are concentrated sources of sugar and can have a swift and substantial effect on blood sugar levels. These treats are energy-dense, offer little satiety, and can lead to overeating.

Fruit Juices: While fruit juice might seem like a healthy choice, it often contains as much sugar as sugary soft drinks. Whole fruits are a better option because they contain fiber, which helps slow down sugar absorption and reduces the overall GI load.

Alcohol: Alcohol can interfere with blood sugar control. Some alcoholic beverages, especially sweet wines and cocktails, are high in sugar and can lead to a spike in glucose levels. Moderation is key, and it is advisable to consult with healthcare providers on safe alcohol consumption levels.

Highly Processed Foods: Convenience foods like instant noodles, microwave meals, and canned soups are often high in sugars, unhealthy fats, and salts. They are usually low in nutrients and high in GI, making them unsuitable for a diabetes-friendly diet.

Setting Up Your Diabetic Diet

Managing diabetes effectively goes beyond medication—it involves a holistic approach that includes tailored diet planning. Understanding and personalizing your dietary needs is not just a part of treatment; it's a cornerstone of daily diabetes management that empowers you to control your blood glucose levels actively.

Every individual's metabolic response to different foods and the timing of their intake can vary significantly, influenced by factors such as age, activity level, and existing health conditions. This diversity in physiological responses highlights the critical importance of understanding and adapting to one's unique dietary needs. Personalized diet planning is not a one-size-fits-all approach; it's a meticulous process that involves identifying the optimal mix and balance of nutrients tailored to each individual. This tailored approach not only aids in maintaining stable blood sugar levels but also plays a crucial role in holistic health management.

By optimizing nutrient intake, personalized diets do more than just control glucose levels—they enhance physical energy and can have a profound effect on emotional well-being. Stable blood sugar levels contribute to improved mood and mental clarity, reducing the emotional stress that can often accompany chronic illness management. Additionally, a well-structured diet can help mitigate the risk of serious diabetes-related complications such as cardiovascular disease, nerve damage, and kidney issues. Thus, effective diet planning becomes a fundamental strategy in the long-term management of diabetes, aiming for both immediate benefits in daily glucose control and long-term health outcomes.

Determine Your Daily Caloric Needs

Managing diabetes effectively involves a comprehensive understanding of nutritional needs, particularly how many calories you should consume daily. Calories are essentially the energy you derive from the food and drinks you consume. Balancing your caloric intake is pivotal not only for weight management but also for controlling blood glucose levels, which is crucial for individuals with diabetes.

UNDERSTANDING CALORIC NEEDS

The number of calories each person needs can vary dramatically based on several factors. These include age, gender, activity level, and specific weight goals, such as losing, maintaining, or gaining weight.

- **Age:** Metabolic rate tends to decrease with age. As you grow older, your body requires fewer calories due to a natural decline in muscle mass, unless you offset this with strength training and an active lifestyle.

- **Gender:** Typically, men have a higher caloric requirement than women. This difference is due to men usually having more muscle mass and less body fat, which increases their resting metabolic rate.

- **Activity Level:** The more active you are, the more calories you'll burn. Activity levels can be categorized into sedentary, moderately active, or highly active. Sedentary lifestyles need fewer calories, while active lifestyles require more to maintain energy levels and bodily functions.

- **Weight Goals:** Your caloric needs adjust depending on whether you aim to lose, maintain, or gain weight. To lose weight, you would typically consume fewer calories than your body burns. To gain weight, the opposite is true. For maintaining weight, you aim to match your caloric intake with your energy expenditure.

Understanding your daily caloric needs is also critical for managing your blood glucose levels effectively. Consuming too many calories can lead to weight gain, which may increase insulin resistance and make blood glucose harder to control. Conversely, consuming too few calories can lead to weight loss and potentially destabilize your blood glucose levels, which could be dangerous if not monitored carefully.

CALCULATING YOUR DAILY CALORIC NEEDS

The Basal Metabolic Rate (BMR) is the cornerstone of calculating your total daily caloric requirements. It represents the minimum number of calories your body requires to perform fundamental life-sustaining functions, such as breathing, circulation, cellular production, and nutrient processing. In simpler terms, BMR is the energy expended by your body at rest to maintain normal body functions without any physical activities.

Several methods exist to calculate BMR, with the Mifflin-St Jeor Equation being one of the most widely accepted due to its accuracy. The equation takes into account your weight, height, and age, providing a tailored approach to understanding your basal energy needs. The formula differs slightly between genders to accommodate physiological differences:

- **Men**: BMR = 10 * weight (kg) + 6.25 * height (cm) - 5 * age (y) + 5
- **Women**: BMR = 10 * weight (kg) + 6.25 * height (cm) - 5 * age (y) - 161

ADJUSTING FOR PHYSICAL ACTIVITY LEVEL (PAL)

After determining your BMR, you must adjust this number to reflect your daily activity levels. This adjustment is crucial because it accounts for the additional energy expended through your day-to-day activities beyond resting. The Physical Activity Level (PAL) factor is used to modify the BMR based on how active you are:

- **Sedentary (little or no exercise)**: BMR x 1.2
- **Lightly active (light exercise/sports 1-3 days/week)**: BMR x 1.375
- **Moderately active (moderate exercise/sports 3-5 days/week)**: BMR x 1.55
- **Very active (hard exercise/sports 6-7 days a week)**: BMR x 1.725
- **Super active (very hard exercise/physical job & exercise 2x/day)**: BMR x 1.9

The result of this calculation gives you your Total Daily Energy Expenditure (TDEE), which is the total number of calories you should consume each day to maintain your current weight, given your level of physical activity.

ADJUSTING CALORIC INTAKE FOR WEIGHT MANAGEMENT

Adjusting your caloric intake is vital for weight management, especially for individuals with diabetes, as it directly influences blood glucose control and reduces the risk of complications associated with the condition. Managing weight effectively involves creating a caloric deficit, which is the difference between the calories consumed and the calories expended through daily activities and metabolic processes.

To effectively adjust your calorie intake for weight loss, begin by setting realistic weight loss goals. Aiming to lose 1-2 pounds per week is considered safe and sustainable; achieving this typically involves reducing your daily caloric intake by 500 calories below your Total Daily Energy Expenditure (TDEE). For instance, if your calculated TDEE is 2,500 calories per day, reducing your intake to 2,000 calories can help you reach your weight loss targets.

Regular monitoring of your weight and blood glucose levels is essential in this process. This ongoing assessment helps in determining if further adjustments to your caloric intake are needed. As weight loss progresses, your caloric needs might decrease, which would require recalculating your Basal Metabolic Rate (BMR) and TDEE to reflect your new body weight.

It is also crucial to consult with healthcare providers before making significant changes to your diet or physical activity levels, particularly if you are managing diabetes. They can offer personalized advice and adjustments based on your health status and medical needs, ensuring that your weight management strategy complements your overall diabetes care plan.

Allocating Macronutrients in a Diabetic Diet

After calculating your Total Daily Energy Expenditure (TDEE), the crucial next step in managing diabetes through diet involves the effective allocation of macronutrients. Carbohydrates, proteins, and fats must be balanced to manage blood glucose levels efficiently and meet overall health needs.

Macronutrient distribution should align with an individual's health goals, activity levels, and specific diabetes management plans. Here is a general guideline on how to distribute macronutrients:

- **Carbohydrates:** Typically, 45-60% of total daily calories. However, if you experience high blood glucose spikes during the day, it may be beneficial to lower this percentage and increase your intake of proteins and healthy fats, which have less of an immediate impact on blood glucose levels.

- **Proteins:** 15-20% of total daily calories. Proteins are crucial for repairing tissues and maintaining muscle mass and have minimal impact on blood glucose, making them a stable source of energy.

- **Fats:** 20-35% of total daily calories. Healthy fats are essential for cardiovascular health and help absorb vitamins. They are calorie-dense and should be consumed in controlled amounts.

EXAMPLE OF CALCULATING TDEE AND ALLOCATING MACRONUTRIENTS

Consider a 40-year-old woman with diabetes, weighing 70 kg and 165 cm tall, leading a lightly active lifestyle, and aiming to maintain her weight.

Step 1: Calculate BMR

Using the Mifflin-St Jeor Equation:

- $BMR = 10 * weight (kg) + 6.25 * height (cm) - 5 * age (y) - 161$
- $BMR = 10 * 70 + 6.25 * 165 - 5 * 40 - 161 = 1364$ calories/day

Step 2: Adjust for Activity Level

- $TDEE = BMR * 1.375$
- $TDEE = 1364 * 1.375 = 1876$ calories/day

Step 3: Allocate Macronutrients

- **Carbohydrates (50% of TDEE):** $1876 * 0.50 = 938$ calories from carbohydrates.
  - Since each gram of carbohydrate provides 4 calories, that's $938 / 4 = 234.5$ grams of carbohydrates per day.
- **Proteins (20% of TDEE):** $1876 \times 0.20 = 375$ calories from protein.
  - Since each gram of protein provides 4 calories, that's $375 / 4 = 93.75$ grams of protein per day.
- **Fats (30% of TDEE):** $1876 \times 0.30 = 563$ calories from fats.
  - Since each gram of fat provides 9 calories, that's $563 / 9 = 62.56$ grams of fat per day.

If this individual finds that her blood glucose levels spike too frequently, she might consider reducing her carbohydrate intake to 40% of her daily calories and redistributing these calories to increase her protein and fat intake. This adjustment can help stabilize her blood glucose levels throughout the day.

Planning Meal Timing and Frequency

Effective diabetes management is heavily dependent on not just what you eat, but also when and how often. Structuring your meals and snacks with strategic timing can play a pivotal role in maintaining stable blood sugar levels, enhancing medication efficacy, and preventing both hyperglycemia and hypoglycemia.

Consistency in meal times is crucial for individuals managing diabetes. Eating at regular intervals helps stabilize blood glucose levels throughout the day and can prevent the spikes and drops that are common when meals are skipped or delayed. Regularly scheduled eating times align with the body's circadian rhythm, optimizing metabolic functions such as insulin secretion and cellular energy production.

Moreover, adhering to a fixed meal schedule can enhance the effectiveness of diabetes medications. For those on insulin or oral diabetes medications that increase insulin production, syncing medication timing with meals can maximize the medication's efficacy in controlling blood sugar.

By consuming food at consistent times, the body is better able to regulate glucose levels in the bloodstream. When meals are eaten sporadically, the pancreas is put under stress to manage fluctuating blood sugar levels, which can lead to insulin resistance over time. Regular meal times also mitigate the risk of overeating, which can occur when there is too long a gap between meals, leading to significant blood sugar elevation post-meals.

SCHEDULING MEALS AND SNACKS

When planning your meal and snack times, consider your daily routine, your body's response to different foods, and the timing of your diabetes medications. Here's a structured approach to meal and snack scheduling:

- **Determine the Number of Meals and Snacks:** Most diabetes meal plans consist of three meals and two to three snacks per day. This framework helps in spreading out calorie intake and reduces the burden on the digestive system to metabolize large amounts of food at once, thereby maintaining steady blood sugar levels.

- **Set Fixed Times for Meals:** Aim to eat your meals at the same times each day to help regulate your body's internal clock, which can aid in better blood sugar control. For example, plan to eat breakfast at 7 AM, lunch at noon, and dinner at 6 PM. Adjust the times based on your personal schedule, but once set, try to stick to these times as closely as possible.

- **Incorporate Snacks Wisely:** Snacks are important in a diabetes diet as they can help prevent blood sugar dips, especially for those on insulin or certain diabetes medications. Plan for a mid-morning snack around 9:30 AM, an afternoon snack around 3:00 PM, and a bedtime snack at 9:00 PM if needed. Choose snacks that are rich in fiber and protein to promote satiety and minimize blood sugar spikes.

- **Account for Physical Activity:** If you engage in regular exercise, you may need to adjust your meal and snack times to accommodate your activity levels. Eating a small, carbohydrate-rich snack before exercise can help prevent hypoglycemia, especially if you take insulin or insulin-producing medications. Post-exercise, a combination of protein and carbohydrate can help replenish energy stores and aid in muscle recovery.

- **Adjust Based on Blood Sugar Monitoring:** Use your blood glucose monitoring results to make adjustments to your meal and snack times. If you notice certain trends in your blood sugar levels (e.g., a consistent rise or drop at a certain time of the day), you might need to adjust what and when you eat next.

The Plate Method

The Plate Method is a straightforward and visually intuitive way to plan balanced meals, particularly useful for individuals managing diabetes. This method helps ensure that each meal contains a proper balance of nutrients, without the need for meticulous calorie counting or food weighing. By using the dinner plate itself as a guide for portion sizes and food group distribution, it simplifies dietary planning and can aid in maintaining blood sugar levels within a healthy range.

The Plate Method centers on dividing your plate into sections, each representing a portion of food groups necessary for a well-balanced diet. The beauty of this method lies in its simplicity; it transforms the abstract concept of nutrient ratios into a tangible and easy-to-follow visual guide. It encourages a healthy eating pattern by emphasizing portion control and the inclusion of diverse food groups at each meal.

This method is particularly endorsed by dietitians and diabetes educators because it naturally limits the intake of higher-calorie foods, which can spike blood sugar levels, while promoting sufficient intake of fiber-rich vegetables and lean proteins, which are beneficial for glucose management. The visual nature of the Plate Method also helps in making immediate decisions about food, a key advantage for those needing to make quick meal choices that fit within their dietary guidelines.

When using the Plate Method, envision your plate divided into three sections. The largest section, making up half of the plate, is reserved for non-starchy vegetables. These are low in calories but high in vitamins, minerals, and fiber, which are crucial for overall health and help manage hunger and blood sugar levels. Examples include leafy greens, carrots, broccoli, cauliflower, and bell peppers.

One-quarter of the plate should contain lean protein sources. Protein is essential for body repair and maintenance and has minimal impact on blood glucose levels. Suitable protein choices for this section include grilled or baked fish, skinless poultry, lean beef, tofu, or eggs.

The remaining quarter of the plate is designated for carbohydrates, preferably from whole grains, starchy vegetables, or legumes. These carbohydrates should be high in fiber, which slows digestion and helps prevent spikes in blood sugar following meals. Good options might include brown rice, quinoa, whole wheat pasta, sweet potatoes, or whole grain breads.

Eating Out with Diabetes

Navigating the culinary world outside the familiar comfort of one's kitchen presents a unique set of challenges for individuals managing diabetes. The act of dining out, which many take for granted as a simple pleasure, can become fraught with potential pitfalls for those who must constantly monitor their blood sugar levels. Restaurants, with their tempting arrays of dishes, often do not cater specifically to the needs of those on a strict diabetic diet. This can make sticking to a healthy eating plan more difficult, as diners are confronted with unpredictable menu options and the irresistible aromas of foods that might lead them astray.

Despite these challenges, maintaining a balanced diabetic diet while dining out is not only possible but also essential. The ability to adapt one's dietary management to different settings is crucial. It requires not only a solid foundation in the nutritional needs specific to diabetes but also an understanding of how various foods and their preparation methods can impact glucose levels. More than just knowing what to eat, it's about understanding how to make safe choices in an environment you don't control.

However, this chapter aims to transform dining out from a source of anxiety into an enjoyable experience. Equipped with the right knowledge and strategies, individuals with diabetes can responsibly enjoy meals at restaurants without fear. Preparation is key: by planning ahead, making informed menu choices, and understanding how to adjust meals to fit their dietary needs, diners can navigate most restaurant menus safely.

Moreover, this guide encourages diners to communicate their needs clearly with restaurant staff. Many chefs and servers are willing to accommodate dietary requests if they're made aware of them. This proactive approach not only ensures a safer dining experience but also empowers individuals with diabetes to enjoy a broader range of culinary experiences.

Thus, let this chapter serve as both a practical guide and a source of encouragement. Managing diabetes effectively while eating out is an achievable goal that can lead to enriching experiences. With careful planning and informed choices, dining out can remain one of life's great pleasures, ensuring that individuals with diabetes can both protect their health and enhance their quality of life. This empowerment comes with the knowledge that they can confidently handle any dining situation, turning potential dietary challenges into opportunities for enjoyment and discovery.

Planning Ahead

The ability to enjoy dining out begins well before stepping into a restaurant. Effective planning is crucial to ensure that each meal is enjoyable and consistent with your health needs. This proactive approach involves a couple of key strategies: conducting research before your visit and setting personal dietary guidelines.

Starting your restaurant experience with some preliminary homework can greatly enhance your dining satisfaction. Many restaurants now post their menus online, allowing you to peruse the offerings at your convenience. This is an excellent opportunity to assess the ingredients and nutritional content of various dishes, helping you make informed decisions that align with your meal plan. If nutritional details are not provided online, a quick phone call to the restaurant can clarify how dishes are prepared and whether they can cater to specific dietary requirements.

Timing your visit can also play a significant role in the quality of your experience. Opting to dine during off-peak hours can lead to better service and a more attentive staff. Restaurants tend to be less crowded, and the kitchen less rushed, making it easier for your dietary needs to be meticulously accommodated.

In addition to doing your research, establishing personal guidelines for dining out is crucial. Decide in advance to choose water or sugar-free beverages over sugary drinks or alcohol, which can disrupt your blood sugar control.

It's also beneficial to decide on your meal choices beforehand. Restaurants are designed to entice the senses, often leading diners to make impulsive decisions that may not align with their nutritional goals. By determining what you will order ahead of time, you can steer clear of high-carb or high-fat options that are tempting yet unsuitable.

Understanding Menu Descriptions

Navigating a restaurant menu with an eye toward healthy eating involves more than just avoiding obvious pitfalls like desserts and fried foods. Understanding the subtle cues and keywords that indicate how a dish is prepared can help you make choices that align with a nutritious, balanced diet.

Menus often use enticing language to describe dishes, but these descriptions can also give clues about the nutritional content. Words like "fried", "battered", and "creamy" typically indicate that a dish is high in fats and calories, which can be less ideal for blood sugar management. Similarly, terms like "buttery" or "smothered" suggest that the food will have added fats, while "crispy" usually means the food is fried.

On the flip side, there are plenty of terms that signify a healthier preparation method. Dishes described as "grilled", "baked", "roasted", "steamed", or "broiled" generally involve less oil and are cooked in ways that retain more of the food's natural nutrients without adding unnecessary fats. Similarly, descriptions such as "light", "fresh", or "tossed" often indicate that a dish is not overly heavy or laden with calorie-dense ingredients.

When assessing menu options, it's also helpful to look for specific words that point to healthier ingredients. Dishes featuring "whole grain", "fiber", "lean protein", and "low-fat" signal that the meal might be more in line with dietary guidelines for managing diabetes. Foods labeled as "seasonal" or "market" are often prepared using fresh, minimally processed ingredients, which can be beneficial for nutrient intake and overall health.

Another tip for identifying healthier menu options is to pay attention to the order of ingredients in dish descriptions. Often, ingredients listed first are used in the largest amounts, so dishes that lead with vegetables or lean proteins are typically better choices than those that start with cheese or cream.

Cuisine-Specific Advice

With a myriad of global cuisines available, it's entirely possible to enjoy a rich tapestry of flavors while adhering to a health-conscious diet. This section delves into the subtleties of various popular cuisines—each offering its unique dishes and potential pitfalls for those with dietary considerations.

From the robust, hearty options found in American fare to the delicate and nuanced flavors of Asian cooking, understanding how to navigate these menus is crucial. Each cuisine comes with its own set of guidelines for making the healthiest choices. For instance, while enjoying Italian dishes, you can indulge in vibrant tomato-based sauces instead of heavier cream-based options, or opt for grilled meats and seafood instead of succumbing to the allure of fried appetizers.

In this comprehensive guide, we'll explore specific strategies for making diabetes-friendly choices across a range of cuisines, including Italian, Mexican, Asian, and classic American settings. Learn how to start your meal with healthier appetizers, like fresh salads or broth-based soups, and make informed decisions about main courses, ensuring they align with your dietary needs.

PIZZA

Enjoying pizza in a way that aligns with a diabetic diet might seem challenging, but with a few strategic choices, it can be incorporated into a balanced meal plan. The key is to focus on selecting healthier options that minimize high glycemic index ingredients and saturated fats.

When indulging in pizza, starting with a side dish can make a significant difference. Opting for a garden or house salad is an excellent way to fill up on fiber-rich vegetables, which not only add nutrients but also help to slow the absorption of sugar into the bloodstream. Dress the salad with a light vinaigrette or lemon juice to keep the calorie count in check.

The type of toppings you choose for your pizza can also have a big impact on its nutritional value. Vegetable toppings such as bell peppers, onions, mushrooms, spinach, and artichokes are not only delicious but also add texture and flavor without the excess fat and calories found in traditional meat toppings. Instead of high-fat meats like pepperoni or sausage, consider healthier alternatives like grilled chicken or even a small amount of lean ham. Be cautious with cheeses; opting for less cheese or a lower-fat cheese can significantly reduce the calorie and fat content of your pizza.

Portion control is crucial when enjoying pizza. Limit yourself to one large slice or two smaller slices to keep carb intake under control. Choosing a thin-crust pizza can also help reduce the amount of carbohydrate per slice, making it easier to fit into your meal plan. By being mindful of the crust, toppings, and portion size, you can enjoy pizza while still adhering to a health-conscious eating strategy.

SUBS

Sub sandwiches offer a fantastic canvas for creating a meal that's both satisfying and suitable for a diabetic diet, provided you make mindful choices about the components. The flexibility of subs allows you to control the ingredients and tailor your meal to support your health goals.

When choosing a sub, the bread you select plays a fundamental role in how the sandwich fits into your diabetic meal plan. Opt for whole-grain bread, which is rich in fiber and helps slow the absorption of glucose into your bloodstream, thereby maintaining more stable blood sugar levels. Whole grains also provide a nutritious boost from essential nutrients and minerals, unlike their refined white bread counterparts.

For the fillings, lean proteins are your best choice. Turkey, lean ham, and roast beef are excellent options that offer high-quality protein without the excessive fats found in more traditional sandwich meats like salami or bologna. These leaner meats satisfy your hunger and provide lasting energy without negatively impacting your blood sugar.

Adding plenty of vegetables to your sub not only enhances the flavor and texture but also increases the nutritional value of your meal. Load up on options like lettuce, tomatoes, onions, cucumbers, green peppers, and spinach. These vegetables are low in calories and carbohydrates while being high in fiber and essential vitamins, making them perfect for enriching your sub without adding unnecessary sugars or fats.

When it comes to condiments, making a wise choice can drastically reduce the intake of hidden sugars and fats. Mustard and vinegar are excellent choices for adding flavor without the added calories and fats associated with dressings like mayonnaise or oil-based vinaigrettes. Mustard, in particular, can offer a potent taste with minimal caloric impact, while vinegar provides a tangy freshness to complement the other flavors in your sub.

FAST FOOD

Navigating the fast food menu for healthier options requires careful consideration, especially for those looking to maintain a diabetic-friendly diet. While fast food often conjures images of unhealthy choices, it is entirely possible to enjoy these meals responsibly by focusing on what to choose and what to avoid.

Prioritize grilled items over fried whenever possible. Grilled chicken, for example, is a healthier choice available at many fast food outlets. It provides high-quality protein without the unhealthy fats and extra calories that come with fried foods.

When it comes to sandwiches and burgers, opting for whole-grain buns or wraps can make a significant difference. These options add necessary fiber to your meal, aiding in blood sugar control and providing a slower release of energy, which helps in maintaining satiety for extended periods. Snack wraps, often featuring a combination of lean proteins and vegetables, are excellent for keeping carbohydrate intake in check and avoiding spikes in blood sugar levels.

Salads are a staple for adding a variety of vegetables and sometimes fruits to your meal, boosting intake of essential vitamins and minerals. However, it's crucial to be cautious of high-fat toppings like cheese and bacon, as well as dressings laden with added sugars and fats. Opt for simple dressings like vinaigrettes and always request them on the side to control the amount you consume.

It's also important to be vigilant about hidden sources of added sugars, which are prevalent in fast food. Many sauces and dressings, as well as flavored yogurts and beverages, can contain high levels of added sugars, quickly increasing the carbohydrate content of your meal. Whenever possible, choose plain options or those labeled as low-sugar or sugar-free.

For side dishes, traditional choices like French fries are not ideal due to their high glycemic index and fat content. Healthier substitutions such as apple slices or a side salad are preferable, providing nutrients and fiber without excessive carbohydrates or fats. Some fast food restaurants also offer low-fat yogurt, a better alternative that can help satisfy your sweet tooth without the added sugars found in typical fast food desserts.

SOUP AND SANDWICHES

Soup and sandwich combinations offer a comforting and potentially healthy option for dining out, provided you make informed choices. Whether you're sitting down to a casual lunch or grabbing a quick bite, focusing on the composition and preparation of these dishes can help you enjoy your meal while adhering to a diabetic-friendly diet.

When selecting soups, opt for broth-based or tomato-based varieties rather than cream-based soups. Broth and tomato-based soups tend to be lower in calories and fat and can be rich in nutrients if they include a variety of vegetables. Cream soups, on the other hand, are typically high in saturated fats and calories, which can negatively impact blood sugar levels. Additionally, avoid soups served in bread bowls. While appealing, bread bowls significantly increase the carbohydrate content of the meal, which can lead to higher blood sugar levels.

Sandwiches present a fantastic opportunity to incorporate whole grains and lean proteins into your diet. Choose sandwiches made with whole-grain breads as they provide more fiber, which helps slow the absorption of sugar into the bloodstream. For fillings, select lean proteins like turkey, chicken, or even plant-based options, and stack your sandwich with plenty of fresh vegetables for added nutrition and flavor.

The combo meal of a soup, sandwich, and salad can be an excellent way to enjoy a balanced meal. This combination allows for a variety of nutrients and textures, making the meal satisfying and healthy. When it comes to salads, however, it's crucial to be mindful of the dressing. Salad dressings can be deceptive; they may seem like a minor component but often contain high amounts of fats and sugars. Always ask for the dressing on the side so you can control the amount you consume, ensuring it complements your meal without overpowering it.

AMERICAN FARE

When it comes to enjoying American cuisine, there are several strategies you can adopt to ensure that your meal is not only delicious but also aligns with a diabetic-friendly diet. By choosing the right dishes and requesting specific preparation methods, you can indulge in traditional American fare without compromising your health.

Starting your meal with a healthy appetizer is a great way to set a nutritious tone. Opt for a fresh salad or a hearty vegetable soup. These options are typically lower in calories and carbohydrates and can help fill you up before the main course, reducing the temptation to overindulge in richer foods later. When choosing a salad, focus on a variety of colorful vegetables, and ask for the dressing on the side to control the amount you consume. For soups, select broth-based varieties which are more likely to be lower in fat and calories compared to cream-based soups.

For main dishes, there are plenty of satisfying and healthy options within American cuisine. Grilled chicken, poached fish, and veggie burgers are excellent choices as they are high in protein and low in unhealthy fats. These cooking methods, such as grilling and poaching, do not require much, if any, added fat and help retain the natural flavors and textures of the food. When ordering, be mindful of how these dishes are prepared and request no extra butter or oil to be used.

It's also crucial to steer clear of fried foods, fatty cuts of meat, and high-fat side dishes. Instead of French fries or onion rings, ask for a side of steamed vegetables or a baked sweet potato. These sides are not only nutritious but also beneficial for blood sugar management thanks to their higher fiber content and lower glycemic index.

Adding vegetable side dishes to your meal is another effective way to increase your intake of fiber and essential nutrients while keeping carbohydrate consumption in check. Vegetables like steamed green beans, broccoli, or spinach are flavorful options that complement any main dish without adding excess calories.

ITALIAN FARE

Italian cuisine, celebrated for its rich flavors and diverse dishes, can be enjoyed even within the constraints of a diabetic-friendly diet with some mindful choices and specific requests. When dining at an Italian restaurant, navigating the menu strategically can help you avoid pitfalls and select dishes that align well with your health goals.

One of the first encounters at an Italian restaurant is often the bread basket. Tempting as it may be, it's wise to skip it altogether. Bread, especially when eaten before the main course, can cause a rapid increase in blood sugar levels. Instead, opt for lighter appetizers to start your meal. Salads with a vinaigrette dressing, grilled calamari, or a caprese salad (tomatoes, basil, and mozzarella) offer satisfying flavors without the heavy carbohydrates.

When selecting your main dish, focus on those with broth or tomato-based sauces rather than cream-based ones. Dishes like marinara sauce, minestrone soup, or cioppino (seafood stew) are flavorful and lower in fat and calories, making them better options for managing blood sugar levels. Tomato-based sauces are rich in lycopene, an antioxidant that's beneficial for heart health, a particular concern for those managing diabetes.

Be mindful of the preparation of dishes. Italian cuisine can often include hidden fats like butter and olive oil, which can add up quickly. Requesting less butter or oil and avoiding heavier dishes such as risotto, which is typically rich in butter and cheese, or lasagna packed with cheese and meat, can significantly reduce your intake of saturated fats and refined carbohydrates.

Grilled fish and meat specials are excellent choices. These dishes usually focus on simple, high-quality ingredients cooked in a way that enhances their natural flavors without the need for excess fat. When it comes to side dishes, ask for vegetables instead of pasta. Many Italian restaurants will accommodate this request, offering steamed or grilled vegetables which can make a nutritious and delicious alternative to the traditional pasta accompaniment.

MEXICAN FARE

Mexican cuisine offers a vibrant tapestry of flavors and ingredients, providing ample opportunity for those on a diabetic-friendly diet to enjoy without compromise. With its emphasis on fresh vegetables, beans, and lean proteins, Mexican food can be both nutritious and delicious when selected carefully.

When exploring the appetizer section of a Mexican menu, consider starting with a light salad dressed with lime juice or a tangy vinaigrette, or opt for a bowl of hearty black bean soup. These choices are not only flavorful but also high in fiber, which helps to regulate blood sugar levels and promote satiety. Avoid creamy or cheese-laden starters, which can add excessive amounts of fat and calories early in the meal.

For the main course, grilled fajitas are an excellent choice. This dish typically consists of grilled vegetables and your choice of lean protein such as chicken, beef, or shrimp, served with warm tortillas. When assembling your fajitas, be mindful of high-fat toppings such as extra cheese and sour cream. These add unnecessary fats and calories and can disrupt blood sugar management. Instead, enhance your dish with guacamole and salsa, which provide good fats and a rich flavor without adversely affecting your dietary goals.

It's also wise to steer clear of fried items, which are common in Mexican cuisine. Dishes like tacos dorados (fried tacos), chimichangas, and churros are tempting but can significantly increase your intake of unhealthy fats and simple carbohydrates. When choosing sides, opt for rice and black beans instead of refried beans, which are often prepared with lard. The combination of rice and black beans not only offers a balance of carbohydrates and protein but also adds fiber, which is beneficial for blood sugar control.

ASIAN FARE

Asian cuisine, with its emphasis on fresh ingredients and vibrant flavors, offers many opportunities for healthy eating, especially for those mindful of their dietary intake. By focusing on dishes that incorporate plenty of vegetables, lean proteins, and complex carbohydrates, you can enjoy the rich culinary traditions of Asia without compromising your health.

Starting your meal with a light appetizer is a great way to indulge in the authentic tastes without overloading on calories and carbs. Miso soup, with its soothing broth and beneficial probiotics, makes for a healthy beginning. Edamame, young soybeans served in their pods, are rich in protein and fiber, making them a perfect diabetic-friendly snack. Steamed dumplings filled with vegetables or lean meats can also be a good choice, provided they are not dipped in excessive sauces which may contain hidden sugars.

When selecting entrees, look for dishes like teriyaki chicken, which should be grilled, not fried, and served with a side of steamed vegetables rather than smothered in sauce. Sushi can be a healthy choice, particularly when it includes fresh fish and vegetables. Opt for sushi made with brown rice to increase your intake of fiber, which helps manage blood sugar levels. Stir-fried dishes are also a staple in Asian cuisine and can be a great option if they're loaded with a variety of colorful vegetables and lean proteins like chicken, shrimp, or tofu. Request that these dishes be cooked with less oil to reduce fat content.

It is crucial to be cautious with fried items, which are prevalent in many Asian restaurants. Items like spring rolls, tempura, and fried dumplings are high in unhealthy fats and calories. Whenever possible, choose steamed versions of these dishes to keep your meal lighter and healthier.

Sauces in Asian cuisine can be a hidden source of a lot of sugar and sodium. Always ask for sauces to be served on the side so you can control how much you use. This simple request can significantly cut down on hidden sugars and enhance your ability to manage your meal's impact on your blood sugar.

Finally, whenever there's an option, choose brown rice over white. Brown rice offers more fiber and nutrients compared to white rice, which has a higher glycemic index and can cause a quicker spike in blood sugar levels.

Dealing with Social Pressure

Dining out is often a social affair, bringing with it the potential for pressure to conform to the dietary choices of others. For individuals managing diabetes, this can pose unique challenges, as well-meaning friends and family might encourage choices that don't align with health goals. Successfully navigating these situations requires a blend of assertiveness and tact, ensuring you maintain your dietary regimen without compromising the social enjoyment of dining out.

When engaging in social dining situations, it's important to plan ahead. Anticipating potential pressures or tempting situations can help you prepare responses and decide on your menu choices in advance. This proactive approach lessens the likelihood of being swayed by what others are ordering or by recommendations from well-intentioned companions.

Communicating your dietary needs begins with confidence in your health priorities. It's beneficial to be upfront about your dietary restrictions right from the start. You might say, "I'm managing my carbohydrate intake tonight, so I'm going to skip the bread", or "I need to choose dishes with less sugar for health reasons". This not only sets the stage for your meal choices but also educates those around you about your needs, potentially reducing future pressure.

Assertiveness should be balanced with politeness to keep the social atmosphere light and enjoyable. It's helpful to express gratitude when others show consideration for your dietary needs, such as when a host chooses a restaurant with diabetes-friendly options or when a friend skips dessert with you in solidarity. A simple "Thank you for understanding" goes a long way in acknowledging their efforts and reinforcing your appreciation.

It's also practical to suggest alternatives that meet your dietary needs while still appealing to your dining companions. For example, proposing a restaurant known for its great salads or a place with a renowned selection of grilled dishes can guide the group toward choices that are delicious and suitable for your diet.

In scenarios where your choices are questioned or challenged, maintain a calm and informative demeanor. You might explain, "My body reacts to certain foods differently, so I have to be careful with what I eat". Often, a brief explanation is enough to satisfy curiosity and deter further pressure.

Smart Shopping for Diabetics

Navigating grocery shopping with diabetes involves more than avoiding sugary snacks; it's about making informed choices crucial for managing blood glucose levels effectively. Supermarkets, designed to maximize consumer spending, often promote less healthy options through strategic placement and enticing promotions. For diabetics, this presents a challenge as these strategies do not align with their health needs.

Understanding the impact of each food choice is fundamental. Diabetics need to scrutinize labels for carbohydrate content, added sugars, fats, and overall nutritional values, going beyond front-of-package claims to assess the real impact on their blood sugar levels. Knowledge of the glycemic index (GI) and glycemic load (GL) is also vital, as these indices help identify foods that manage glucose levels more effectively.

Psychologically, grocery shopping can sometimes feel restrictive for diabetics due to necessary dietary limitations. However, with the right knowledge, it can become an empowering activity that promotes health and well-being. Making healthy choices also sets a positive example for family and friends, fostering a supportive environment for maintaining these habits.

How to Read Food Labels Accurately

For individuals managing diabetes, understanding nutritional labels is crucial for grocery shopping. These labels are particularly important because they do not include glycemic index (GI) or glycemic load (GL) data—key metrics that indicate how foods might impact blood sugar levels. Without these values, people with diabetes must rely on other nutritional information provided on packaging to make informed dietary choices, helping them maintain stable blood glucose control.

The cornerstone of diabetes management lies in comprehending the nutritional content of foods. Labels detail the amounts of macronutrients, such as carbohydrates, fats, and proteins, which significantly influence blood glucose levels. Since carbohydrates have the most immediate impact on blood sugar, understanding how to calculate net carbs (total carbs minus dietary fiber) is essential.

Consider a comparison between two breakfast cereals. The first is a high-fiber, whole grain cereal, while the second is a popular sugar-coated cereal. The nutritional labels for each might read as follows:

HIGH-FIBER WHOLE GRAIN CEREAL

- Total carbohydrates: 30 grams

- Dietary fiber: 8 grams

- Sugars: 5 grams (includes 0 grams of added sugars)

- Total fat: 2 grams

- Saturated fat: 0 grams

- Protein: 5 grams

SUGAR-COATED CEREAL

- Total carbohydrates: 30 grams

- Dietary fiber: 1 gram

- Sugars: 12 grams (includes 12 grams of added sugars)
- Total fat: 0.5 grams
- Saturated fat: 0 grams
- Protein: 2 grams

When assessing foods for diabetes management, several nutritional label values are pivotal:

- **Carbohydrates**: Total carbohydrates include all sugars, starches, and dietary fibers in food. Diabetics need to pay close attention to this number because carbs affect blood glucose levels most significantly. However, the type of carbohydrate also matters.

- **Fiber**: Dietary fiber is a part of carbohydrates that the body cannot digest. High-fiber foods can help manage blood sugar levels by slowing the breakdown of other carbohydrates, which reduces blood glucose spikes after eating. Foods high in fiber are generally recommended for diabetics because they promote a slower, more controlled rise in blood sugar.

- **Sugars and Added Sugars**: Sugars contribute directly to the total carbohydrate content that can raise blood glucose levels. Added sugars are particularly important to note as they indicate sugars that are not naturally present in food but rather added during processing. Diabetics are advised to limit added sugars as much as possible to avoid rapid increases in blood glucose.

- **Fats**: While fats have less direct impact on blood sugar than carbohydrates, the type of fat is crucial. Diabetics should look for foods low in saturated fats and trans fats to maintain heart health, as diabetes increases the risk of heart disease.

ANALYSIS OF SUITABLE FOOD

The high-fiber whole grain cereal is an excellent option for diabetics. With 30 grams of total carbohydrates and 8 grams of dietary fiber, the net carbs (total carbs minus fiber) amount to 22 grams. This lower net carb count, combined with high fiber content, helps mitigate blood sugar spikes. Additionally, the low amount of saturated fats and absence of added sugars aligns with the dietary needs of someone managing diabetes.

ANALYSIS OF UNSUITABLE FOOD

Conversely, the sugar-coated cereal, while also containing 30 grams of total carbohydrates, only provides 1 gram of dietary fiber. This results in a much higher net carb load of 29 grams. Moreover, the presence of 12 grams of added sugars is a significant concern, as this can lead to quick rises in blood sugar levels. The low fiber content and high added sugars make this cereal a poor choice for diabetics looking to control their glycemic response.

IDENTIFYING HIDDEN SUGARS

One of the critical challenges in label reading is identifying hidden sugars, which can often go unnoticed due to the variety of terms used to denote them. Sugar can appear under many names on ingredient lists, such as sucrose, high-fructose corn syrup, dextrose, and maltose, among others. Recognizing these terms is vital for people with diabetes to manage their disease effectively. For example, a product like salad dressing might list ingredients like agave nectar or cane juice, which are essentially sugars and can significantly affect blood sugar levels.

Navigating Supermarkets and Health Food Stores

Grocery stores are typically divided into several key areas: fresh produce, meats and proteins, dairy and alternatives, frozen foods, and the middle aisles, which usually contain packaged and processed foods. For someone with diabetes, how you shop in each of these areas can significantly impact your diet and blood sugar levels.

Starting with the produce section, this is generally the safest area for those managing diabetes. It's filled with nutrient-rich vegetables and fruits essential for a balanced diet. However, it's important to differentiate between high-fiber, low-glycemic options and those fruits and vegetables that might spike blood sugar levels. Vegetables like leafy greens, broccoli, and cauliflower are excellent choices due to their low carbohydrate content and high nutritional value. Fruits, while healthy, can be trickier due to their natural sugars; opting for berries or avocados, which are lower in sugar and high in fiber, can be more beneficial.

As you move from the perimeter of the store towards the inner aisles, caution is needed. These aisles typically house processed foods, snacks, and other packaged goods that are often high in added sugars and refined carbohydrates. These are the common pitfalls for anyone, but especially those on a diabetic diet. Products in these aisles might also include 'diet' or 'low-fat' labels but can still be high in carbohydrates and sugars, which are detrimental to blood sugar control.

To efficiently find diabetic-friendly options, it is essential to become proficient at reading labels. Look for foods that have whole food ingredients and minimal added sugars or unhealthy fats. Learning the typical layout of your local grocery store can also help in planning your shopping route, allowing you to spend more time in the fresh produce and meats sections, and less time in the middle aisles where temptations lurk.

For those managing diabetes, it is also wise to avoid shopping on an empty stomach, as this can lead to impulse purchases of sugary or high-carb foods. Instead, go prepared with a list of needed items based on a meal plan that includes lots of vegetables, lean proteins, and whole grains. This preparation helps in resisting the allure of convenience foods that offer little nutritional value and could disrupt glucose levels.

SELECTING FRESH PRODUCE

Among the plethora of options in the produce section, avocados stand out as a superior choice for those on a diabetic diet. Avocados are not only rich in healthy monounsaturated fats, which are beneficial for heart health, but they are also extremely high in fiber. This combination helps to stabilize blood sugar levels and support overall metabolic health. When selecting avocados, look for ones that yield slightly under gentle pressure, indicating they are ripe and ready to eat. Unripe avocados can be ripened at home at room temperature over a few days, making them a practical choice even if planning ahead.

Artichokes are another excellent choice for those managing diabetes. They are one of the most fiber-rich vegetables available in the grocery store, making them an excellent tool for blood sugar management. However, preparing fresh artichokes can be somewhat daunting due to their tough exterior. An effective alternative without sacrificing health benefits is to choose jarred or canned artichoke hearts that have been preserved in water or healthy oils like olive oil. These pre-prepared options retain most of the nutritional benefits of fresh artichokes without the inconvenience of extensive preparation. When shopping for artichoke hearts, always check the label to ensure there are no added sugars or unhealthy oils which could undermine their health benefits.

Leafy greens such as kale, spinach, and lettuce are also staples in a diabetes-friendly diet due to their high fiber content and wealth of nutrients including iron, calcium, and vitamins A, C, and K. For these vegetables, the choice between organic and non-organic can be guided by the Environmental Working Group's (EWG) Dirty Dozen list, which highlights vegetables and fruits that are prone to high pesticide residue levels. Kale and spinach often appear on this list, suggesting that purchasing organic versions is a safer option, whereas vegetables like broccoli and cabbage, which have natural pest-resistant properties, are usually safe to purchase non-organically.

Making cost-effective choices in the produce section doesn't necessarily mean skimping on quality. While organic produce can sometimes be more expensive, the health benefits they offer, especially for individuals with chronic conditions like diabetes, can outweigh the cost. However, when budget constraints are tight, prioritize buying organic for those items known to have higher pesticide residues and choose conventional for those known to be safer. Additionally, shopping for seasonal produce can also reduce costs and increase freshness, adding more variety and flavor to your diet throughout the year.

CHOOSING MEATS AND PROTEINS

Lean proteins, such as chicken breast, turkey, and lean cuts of beef or pork, are excellent choices. These meats are lower in fat, which is beneficial for heart health—a significant concern for those with diabetes, as they are at an increased risk for cardiovascular diseases. When selecting meat, it's advisable to look for labels such as "lean" or "extra lean," indicating lower fat content. Additionally, preparing these meats through baking, grilling, or steaming rather than frying can help maintain their healthfulness.

The benefits of choosing grass-fed and pasture-raised meats extend beyond mere fat content. These meats are typically higher in omega-3 fatty acids and conjugated linoleic acids, both of which are known for their anti-inflammatory properties. Inflammation is a key concern in diabetes, as it can exacerbate insulin resistance and complicate blood sugar control. Grass-fed and pasture-raised options also tend to have a more favorable omega-6 to omega-3 fat ratio, further supporting cardiovascular health.

For those exploring meat alternatives or looking to diversify their protein sources, plant-based proteins offer a wealth of suitable options for a diabetic diet. Foods such as legumes, lentils, chickpeas, and a variety of beans provide high protein content along with fiber, which can help manage blood sugar levels by slowing glucose absorption into the bloodstream. These sources are not only beneficial for blood sugar management but also contribute to a lower overall glycemic load of the diet.

Additionally, incorporating seeds like chia, flax, and hemp into the diet can boost protein intake while also providing omega-3 fatty acids, which are beneficial for reducing inflammation. Nuts, another excellent source of protein and healthy fats, can be a nutritious snack option, though portion control is important due to their high calorie density.

For those on a vegetarian or vegan diet, tofu and tempeh are excellent protein-rich alternatives that also fit well within a diabetic diet. These soy-based products are versatile and can be used in a variety of dishes, mimicking meats in texture and flavor when prepared appropriately. Moreover, they are low in carbs and high in protein, making them ideal for blood sugar management.

DAIRY AND DAIRY ALTERNATIVES

When choosing dairy products, it's essential to consider the sugar content, particularly for those with diabetes. Many flavored yogurts and dairy-based desserts contain high levels of added sugars, which can spike blood glucose levels rapidly. Instead, opting for plain, unsweetened varieties provides the dairy benefits without the unnecessary sugar intake. Greek yogurt is an excellent choice in this category; its production process involves straining excess whey, which not only concentrates the protein content but also reduces the lactose, or natural sugar, found in dairy. This makes Greek yogurt a high-protein, lower-carbohydrate option that is ideal for maintaining stable blood sugar levels.

The benefits of Greek yogurt extend beyond its macronutrient profile. The thicker, creamier texture and increased satiety it offers make it a satisfying choice for meals or snacks. Additionally, it serves as a versatile base in recipes, capable of substituting for higher-fat ingredients like sour cream or mayonnaise, thus enabling a richer diet without compromising diabetic dietary needs.

For those interested in the highest quality dairy, grass-fed products are a superior choice. Dairy from grass-fed cows not only boasts a lower environmental impact but also contains higher levels of omega-3 fatty acids and conjugated linoleic acid, which have been shown to improve heart health and decrease inflammation. These factors are particularly beneficial for individuals with diabetes, as they help manage both the direct and indirect effects of the condition.

However, dairy isn't suitable for everyone. Lactose intolerance, allergies, or personal dietary choices may lead individuals to seek plant-based alternatives. Fortunately, the market for non-dairy substitutes has expanded significantly, offering numerous options that can complement a diabetic diet. Almond, soy, coconut, and oat milks are popular choices, each with its unique nutritional profile. When selecting a plant-based milk, it's crucial to opt for unsweetened versions to avoid the added sugars commonly found in flavored alternatives. Among these, soy milk stands out for its high protein content, closely mirroring the protein levels found in cow's milk, making it a suitable substitute in a protein-conscious diabetic diet.

For those seeking a dairy-free yogurt alternative, products like almond-based Greek yogurt can provide a similar texture and protein content to traditional Greek yogurt. These alternatives often incorporate protein isolates to achieve a higher protein content while maintaining low sugar levels, making them appropriate for blood sugar management.

SMART SELECTIONS IN FATS AND OILS

The use of healthy oils like olive oil and avocado oil is advocated due to their rich content in monounsaturated fats, which support cardiovascular health and reduce inflammatory responses in the body. Olive oil, especially extra virgin olive oil, is beneficial due to its minimal processing and rich antioxidant profile, making it suitable for both cooking and dressings. Avocado oil is noted for its high smoke point, making it ideal for high-temperature cooking without degrading its nutritional value.

Conversely, the negative implications of using certain plant-based oils such as canola, sunflower, soybean, and safflower oils are significant, particularly for those with diabetes. These oils often undergo extensive processing and are typically high in omega-6 fatty acids, which can promote inflammation when consumed in excess relative to omega-3 fatty acids. This inflammatory response can exacerbate insulin resistance, a core issue in diabetes management.

76

Furthermore, many of these oils are extracted using chemicals like hexane, and their high processing levels can include deodorizing and bleaching, which strips away beneficial nutrients and potentially introduces harmful compounds. For example, canola oil, commonly modified genetically and highly processed, can induce inflammation due to its altered omega-6 to omega-3 ratio and the presence of trans fats formed during hydrogenation, making it less desirable for consumption.

Instead of these heavily processed oils, selecting options like grass-fed butter or ghee can offer better health benefits. Grass-fed dairy products are higher in omega-3 fatty acids compared to their grain-fed counterparts, making them a healthier choice for managing blood sugar levels. The presence of conjugated linoleic acid in grass-fed dairy has also been shown to have anti-diabetic properties, making it a favorable option for dietary fats.

Coconut oil deserves a special mention; though it is a saturated fat, it comprises medium-chain triglycerides (MCTs) that are metabolized differently, providing quick energy without a significant impact on blood sugar levels. This makes it a potentially useful oil for diabetic diets, though it should be used judiciously due to its high caloric content.

THE MIDDLE AISLES: SNACKS AND PROCESSED FOODS

When exploring the middle aisles, the key is to focus on low-carb and sugar-free options that minimize blood sugar spikes. For instance, chicharrones (pork rinds) are an excellent choice for a snack as they contain zero carbohydrates and can satisfy the craving for something crispy and salty without impacting glucose levels. Their high protein content also helps in feeling fuller longer, making them a practical snacking option.

Chocolate, a common craving, can also be enjoyed in a diabetes-friendly form. Dark chocolate with high cocoa content is preferable because it contains less sugar and more fiber compared to its milk chocolate counterparts. Opting for dark chocolate that is 85% cocoa or higher ensures lower sugar content and the presence of antioxidants beneficial for overall health. Additionally, some newer options on the market such as chocolates sweetened with stevia or monk fruit offer a sweet treat without added sugars, providing a guilt-free way to satisfy a sweet tooth.

Label reading is critical when selecting snacks from the middle aisles. Many products marketed as "healthy" or "natural" can still contain high amounts of added sugars and unhealthy fats. It's essential to scrutinize the ingredients list for hidden sugars, which can appear under various names like corn syrup, dextrose, fructose, or sucrose. Moreover, understanding the types of fats used in these snacks is crucial; it's advisable to avoid items containing trans fats or highly processed vegetable oils like palm or soybean oil, which are often used in commercial baked goods and snacks.

Additionally, paying attention to the nutritional content beyond just the sugar and fat is important. Looking at the fiber content can be beneficial, as foods high in dietary fiber can help regulate blood sugar levels. Some snacks may also be fortified with vitamins and minerals, enhancing their nutritional profile and adding value to their consumption.

SELECTING WHOLE GRAINS AND ALTERNATIVE PASTAS

For those managing diabetes, the choice of pasta can play a crucial role in dietary planning. Traditional pastas made from white flour are high on the glycemic index and can cause rapid spikes in blood sugar. Fortunately, there are numerous alternatives available that are made from legumes and other low-glycemic materials, providing better options for those looking to maintain a stable blood glucose level.

Pasta alternatives made from legumes such as chickpeas or lentils are excellent choices. These pastas not only mimic the texture and taste of traditional pasta but also bring significant nutritional benefits, including higher protein and fiber content. For example, chickpea pasta boasts a high protein level and an impressive amount of fiber, offering about nine grams of fiber per serving. This high fiber content is instrumental in managing blood sugar spikes, making chickpea pasta a superior choice for a diabetic diet.

Similarly, lentil pasta stands out as another nutritious alternative. It also provides a substantial amount of protein and fiber, which are essential for blood sugar regulation and can help in creating a feeling of fullness, aiding in weight management — an important aspect for many individuals with diabetes. The glycemic index of these pastas is considerably lower than that of traditional wheat pasta, making them a smarter choice for maintaining more consistent blood sugar levels.

Beyond legume-based pastas, exploring other high-fiber, low-carbohydrate alternatives can further diversify dietary choices without compromising blood sugar goals. Shirataki noodles, often made from the konjac plant, are virtually carb-free and rich in glucomannan, a type of fiber that can aid digestive health and improve glycemic control. While they have a unique texture that may require some getting used to, they are an exceptional pasta substitute for those strictly managing carbohydrate intake.

THE BREAKFAST AISLE: CEREALS AND MORE

Choosing the right breakfast foods is crucial for individuals managing diabetes, as the morning meal can significantly impact blood glucose levels throughout the day. The breakfast aisle in most grocery stores is laden with options, but many are high in sugars and refined carbohydrates that can cause undesirable spikes in blood sugar. However, with thoughtful selection and a few strategic choices, those with diabetes can enjoy satisfying and healthy breakfasts that support stable glucose levels.

Steel-cut oats are a particularly good choice for a diabetes-friendly breakfast. Unlike their more processed counterpart, rolled oats, steel-cut oats undergo minimal processing and offer a denser, nuttier texture, which aids in slower digestion and a more gradual release of glucose into the bloodstream. This slower digestion process is key in preventing the rapid spikes in blood sugar associated with more refined grains. Steel-cut oats also have a slightly higher fiber content, which not only helps with blood sugar management but also contributes to a feeling of fullness, aiding in weight control.

While steel-cut oats are a healthy option, they still contain carbohydrates that can impact blood sugar levels. To mitigate this and enhance the nutritional profile of your breakfast, supplementing oats with low-carb options like chia seeds or flaxseeds is advisable. These seeds are not only low in carbohydrates but are also high in fiber and healthy fats, which further stabilize blood sugar levels and improve satiety.

Chia seeds are particularly beneficial because they form a gel-like substance when mixed with liquids, slowing the conversion of carbohydrates into sugar. They are also a good source of omega-3 fatty acids, which are known for their anti-inflammatory properties and cardiovascular health benefits. Adding a tablespoon of chia seeds to your oatmeal can enhance its texture and nutritional value without significantly increasing the carbohydrate content.

Similarly, flaxseeds are a fantastic addition to a diabetic diet. They are rich in lignans and omega-3 fatty acids, providing anti-inflammatory benefits while helping to maintain healthy blood sugar levels. Ground flaxseeds can be sprinkled over hot or cold cereal, providing a nutty flavor and a boost in fiber. This addition not only helps in controlling blood sugar levels but also supports digestive health, which is often a concern for those with diabetes.

When selecting breakfast cereals, it's important to avoid those with added sugars and instead choose whole-grain options that are naturally low in sugar. Always read labels carefully to check for hidden sugars and opt for cereals that list whole grains as the first ingredient. Combining these cereals with low-carb supplements like chia or flaxseeds can further help in creating a breakfast that is both nutritious and conducive to maintaining good blood sugar control.

Breakfast Recipes

Berry Protein Smoothie

PREPARATION TIME: 5 minutes

COOKING TIME: 0 minutes

TOTAL TIME: 5 minutes

SERVING SIZE: 2 servings

INGREDIENTS:

- 1 cup mixed berries (blueberries, strawberries, raspberries), fresh or frozen
- 1 cup unsweetened almond milk
- 1/2 cup Greek yogurt, plain
- 2 tablespoons chia seeds
- 1 scoop protein powder (vanilla or unflavored)
- Optional: Ice cubes (if using fresh berries)

NUTRITIONAL INFORMATION (PER SERVING):

- **Total Calories:** 230 kcal
- **Total Carbohydrates:** 24 g
    - Dietary Fiber: 8 g
    - Sugars: 10 g
- **Protein:** 20 g
- **Total Fat:** 7 g
    - Saturated Fat: 1 g
    - Unsaturated Fat: 5 g
- **Sodium:** 125 mg

INSTRUCTIONS:

1. **Prepare Ingredients:** If using frozen berries, measure out 1 cup into a blender. For fresh berries, wash and prepare them accordingly.
2. **Blend the Smoothie:** Add the mixed berries, unsweetened almond milk, Greek yogurt, chia seeds, and protein powder to a blender. Include a handful of ice cubes if using fresh berries for a chilled effect.
3. **Process Until Smooth:** Blend on high speed until all ingredients are thoroughly combined and the texture is smooth.
4. **Serve Immediately:** Pour the smoothie into two glasses and serve immediately for the best taste and texture.

INGREDIENT SUBSTITUTIONS:

- **Almond Milk:** Substitute with coconut milk or soy milk for a similar low-carbohydrate profile.
- **Greek Yogurt:** Use a dairy-free yogurt like coconut yogurt or soy yogurt to maintain protein content and achieve a similar texture.
- **Chia Seeds:** Flaxseeds can be used as an alternative; both are rich in omega-3 fatty acids and fiber.
- **Mixed Berries:** Feel free to choose any combination of low-glycemic berries such as blackberries or more of any berry you prefer for varied flavor profiles without significantly altering the nutritional content.

Green Goddess Smoothie

PREPARATION TIME: 5 minutes
COOKING TIME: 0 minutes
TOTAL TIME: 5 minutes
SERVING SIZE: 2 servings

INGREDIENTS:

- 1 cup spinach leaves, fresh
- 1/2 ripe avocado, peeled and pitted
- 1/2 cucumber, peeled and sliced
- Juice of 1 lime
- 1 cup unsweetened coconut water

NUTRITION PER SERVING:

- **Total Calories:** 150 kcal
- **Total Carbohydrates:** 19 g
  - Dietary Fiber: 7 g
  - Sugars: 6 g
- **Protein:** 3 g
- **Total Fat:** 8 g
  - Saturated Fat: 1 g
  - Unsaturated Fat: 5 g
- **Sodium:** 60 mg

INSTRUCTIONS:

1. **Prepare Ingredients:** Wash spinach leaves thoroughly. Peel the avocado and remove the pit. Slice the cucumber and prepare the lime for juicing.
2. **Blend the Smoothie:** Place the spinach, avocado, cucumber, lime juice, and unsweetened coconut water into a blender.
3. **Process Until Smooth:** Blend on high until the mixture becomes completely smooth. Add more coconut water if needed to adjust the consistency.
4. **Serve Immediately:** Pour the smoothie into two glasses and serve fresh to retain the nutrients and flavors.

INGREDIENT SUBSTITUTIONS:

- **Spinach:** Kale or Swiss chard can be used as alternatives for varied nutrient profiles but maintaining low calories and carbohydrates.
- **Avocado:** If desired, you can substitute with Greek yogurt to increase protein content while keeping a creamy texture.
- **Cucumber:** Celery can be a crisp substitute, offering a slightly different flavor but similar hydration and nutrient levels.
- **Unsweetened Coconut Water:** You may switch to plain water for lower sugar content or almond milk for a creamier texture without significantly affecting the carbohydrate count.

Chia & Flaxseed Smoothie

PREPARATION TIME: 5 minutes
COOKING TIME: 0 minutes
TOTAL TIME: 5 minutes
SERVING SIZE: 2 servings

INGREDIENTS:

- 1 tablespoon flaxseeds
- 1 tablespoon chia seeds
- 100 grams tofu, silken or soft
- 1 cup strawberries, fresh or frozen
- 2 cups unsweetened soy milk

NUTRITION PER SERVING:

- **Total Calories:** 220 kcal
- **Total Carbohydrates:** 18 g
  - Dietary Fiber: 6 g
  - Sugars: 7 g
- **Protein:** 14 g
- **Total Fat:** 11 g
  - Saturated Fat: 1.5 g
  - Unsaturated Fat: 7.5 g
- **Sodium:** 95 mg

INSTRUCTIONS:

1. **Prepare Ingredients:** If using fresh strawberries, wash and hull them. Measure out the flaxseeds, chia seeds, and soy milk.
2. **Blend the Smoothie:** In a blender, combine the flaxseeds, chia seeds, tofu, strawberries, and soy milk.
3. **Process Until Smooth:** Blend on high speed until all ingredients are thoroughly mixed and the smoothie reaches a smooth consistency.
4. **Serve Fresh:** Divide the smoothie into two glasses and enjoy immediately for the best texture and flavor.

INGREDIENT SUBSTITUTIONS:

- **Flaxseeds and Chia Seeds:** Pumpkin or sunflower seeds ground up can be used as a substitute, maintaining high fiber and healthy fats.
- **Tofu:** Avocado can be used to maintain creaminess while providing similar fat content and increasing the fiber slightly.
- **Strawberries:** Blueberries or raspberries can be swapped for different flavors and antioxidant profiles without significantly altering the carbohydrate content.
- **Soy Milk:** Almond milk or coconut milk can be used as alternatives, altering the flavor slightly while keeping the carbohydrate levels comparable.

Almond Butter & Banana Smoothie

PREPARATION TIME: 5 minutes
COOKING TIME: 0 minutes
TOTAL TIME: 5 minutes
SERVING SIZE: 2 servings

INGREDIENTS:

- 2 tablespoons almond butter
- 1 medium banana
- 2 cups unsweetened oat milk

NUTRITION PER SERVING:

- **Total Calories:** 280 kcal
- **Total Carbohydrates:** 35 g
  - Dietary Fiber: 5 g
  - Sugars: 15 g
- **Protein:** 8 g
- **Total Fat:** 14 g
  - Saturated Fat: 1 g
  - Unsaturated Fat: 10 g
- **Sodium:** 95 mg

INSTRUCTIONS:

1. **Prepare Ingredients:** Peel the banana and measure out the almond butter and oat milk.
2. **Blend the Smoothie:** In a blender, combine the almond butter, banana, and oat milk.
3. **Process Until Smooth:** Blend on high speed until the mixture is smooth and creamy.
4. **Serve Immediately:** Pour the smoothie into two glasses and serve immediately to enjoy its fresh flavor and creamy texture.

INGREDIENT SUBSTITUTIONS:

- **Almond Butter:** Peanut butter or cashew butter can be used for a similar texture and nutritional profile while slightly altering the flavor.
- **Banana:** Avocado can substitute for banana to reduce sugar content and add healthy fats, changing the smoothie's texture to be even creamier.
- **Oat Milk:** Unsweetened almond milk or soy milk can replace oat milk, adjusting the overall flavor profile and nutritional content minimally while maintaining low sugar levels.

Cinnamon Spiced Coffee

PREPARATION TIME: 5 minutes
COOKING TIME: 5 minutes
TOTAL TIME: 10 minutes
SERVING SIZE: 2 servings

INGREDIENTS:

- 2 cups brewed coffee (preferably strong)
- 1/2 teaspoon ground cinnamon
- 2 tablespoons unsweetened almond milk

NUTRITION PER SERVING:

- **Total Calories:** 12 kcal
- **Total Carbohydrates:** 2 g
  - Dietary Fiber: 1 g
  - Sugars: 0 g
- **Protein:** 0.5 g
- **Total Fat:** 0.5 g
  - Saturated Fat: 0 g
  - Unsaturated Fat: 0.3 g
- **Sodium:** 5 mg

INSTRUCTIONS:

1. **Brew Coffee:** Prepare 2 cups of your preferred coffee using your usual method.
2. **Add Cinnamon:** Once brewed, stir in the ground cinnamon directly into the coffee pot or individual cups for even distribution.
3. **Add Almond Milk:** Pour the unsweetened almond milk into the cinnamon-spiced coffee and stir well.
4. **Serve Hot:** Serve the coffee hot, allowing the flavors to meld beautifully.

INGREDIENT SUBSTITUTIONS:

- **Cinnamon:** Nutmeg or pumpkin spice can be used as an alternative for a different but similarly warming spice flavor.
- **Unsweetened Almond Milk:** Coconut milk or cashew milk can replace almond milk to maintain a low carbohydrate content while slightly varying the flavor.

Vegetable Omelet

PREPARATION TIME: 10 minutes
COOKING TIME: 10 minutes
TOTAL TIME: 20 minutes
SERVING SIZE: 2 servings

INGREDIENTS:
- 4 large eggs
- 1/2 cup chopped spinach
- 1/4 cup diced bell peppers (assorted colors)
- 1/4 cup chopped onions
- 1/4 cup sliced mushrooms
- 2 tablespoons shredded low-fat cheese
- 1 tablespoon olive oil
- Salt and pepper to taste

NUTRITION PER SERVING:
- **Total Calories:** 220 kcal
- **Total Carbohydrates:** 6 g
  - Dietary Fiber: 1.5 g
  - Sugars: 3 g
- **Protein:** 15 g
- **Total Fat:** 15 g
  - Saturated Fat: 4 g
  - Unsaturated Fat: 9 g
- **Sodium:** 220 mg

INSTRUCTIONS:
1. **Prepare Vegetables:** Wash and chop the spinach, bell peppers, onions, and mushrooms.
2. **Beat Eggs:** In a bowl, beat the eggs until well mixed. Season with salt and pepper.
3. **Cook Vegetables:** Heat olive oil in a non-stick skillet over medium heat. Add onions and mushrooms; sauté until soft. Add bell peppers and spinach, cooking until the spinach is wilted.
4. **Add Eggs:** Pour the beaten eggs over the vegetables in the skillet, ensuring the vegetables are evenly covered.
5. **Cook Omelet:** Let the eggs cook undisturbed for about 3-4 minutes until the edges start to lift from the pan. Sprinkle the shredded cheese over the top.
6. **Fold and Serve:** Gently fold the omelet in half and let it cook for another 2 minutes. Serve hot.

INGREDIENT SUBSTITUTIONS:
- **Vegetables:** Try different combinations like zucchini, asparagus, or tomatoes to vary the flavor and nutritional content while maintaining a similar profile.
- **Cheese:** Switch out low-fat cheese for feta or goat cheese for a different flavor without significantly altering the fat content.

Spinach & Feta Egg Muffins

PREPARATION TIME: 10 minutes
COOKING TIME: 20 minutes
TOTAL TIME: 30 minutes
SERVING SIZE: 2 servings (6 muffins total, 3 per serving)

INGREDIENTS:
- 6 large eggs
- 1 cup fresh spinach, chopped
- 1/2 cup crumbled feta cheese
- 1/4 cup diced red onions
- Salt and pepper to taste
- Non-stick cooking spray

NUTRITION PER SERVING:
- **Total Calories:** 230 kcal
- **Total Carbohydrates:** 5 g
  - Dietary Fiber: 1 g
  - Sugars: 3 g
- **Protein:** 20 g
- **Total Fat:** 15 g
  - Saturated Fat: 6 g
  - Unsaturated Fat: 7 g
- **Sodium:** 450 mg

INSTRUCTIONS:
1. **Preheat Oven:** Preheat your oven to 350°F (175°C) and spray a muffin tin with non-stick cooking spray.
2. **Prepare Ingredients:** In a large bowl, whisk the eggs until smooth. Stir in the chopped spinach, crumbled feta, diced onions, and season with salt and pepper.
3. **Fill Muffin Tin:** Evenly distribute the egg mixture among 6 muffin cups in the prepared tin.
4. **Bake:** Place the muffin tin in the oven and bake for 20 minutes, or until the muffins are firm and the tops are slightly golden.
5. **Serve:** Remove from the oven and let cool for a few minutes before removing from the tin. Serve warm.

INGREDIENT SUBSTITUTIONS:
- **Spinach:** Substitute kale or arugula for a different flavor and texture.
- **Feta Cheese:** Swap for goat cheese or ricotta for a creamier texture while keeping the flavor profile and nutritional balance.

Turkish Menemen

PREPARATION TIME: 10 minutes
COOKING TIME: 15 minutes
TOTAL TIME: 25 minutes
SERVING SIZE: 2 servings

INGREDIENTS:
- 4 large eggs
- 2 medium tomatoes, finely chopped
- 1 green bell pepper, diced
- 1 small onion, finely chopped
- 2 cloves garlic, minced
- 1 tablespoon olive oil
- 1/2 teaspoon paprika
- Salt and pepper to taste
- Fresh parsley, chopped (for garnish)

NUTRITION PER SERVING:
- **Total Calories:** 285 kcal
- **Total Carbohydrates:** 15 g
  - Dietary Fiber: 3 g
  - Sugars: 9 g
- **Protein:** 14 g
- **Total Fat:** 20 g
  - Saturated Fat: 4 g
  - Unsaturated Fat: 13 g
- **Sodium:** 220 mg

INSTRUCTIONS:
1. **Prepare Ingredients:** Heat the olive oil in a large skillet over medium heat. Add the chopped onions and garlic, sautéing until translucent.
2. **Add Vegetables:** Stir in the diced green bell pepper and cook for 2-3 minutes until slightly softened. Add the chopped tomatoes and paprika, and season with salt and pepper. Cook for another 5 minutes until the tomatoes break down and form a thick sauce.
3. **Cook Eggs:** Reduce the heat to low. Crack the eggs directly over the tomato mixture, cover the skillet, and let the eggs cook for 5-7 minutes or until they are set to your liking.
4. **Garnish and Serve:** Garnish with fresh parsley before serving directly from the skillet.

INGREDIENT SUBSTITUTIONS:
- **Tomatoes:** Use canned no-salt-added diced tomatoes instead of fresh to save time without altering the nutritional content significantly.
- **Green Bell Pepper:** Substitute with red or yellow bell pepper for a sweeter taste or add chopped zucchini for a different texture.
- **Olive Oil:** Can be replaced with avocado oil for a similar nutritional profile.

Kale and Cheddar Scramble

PREPARATION TIME: 5 minutes
COOKING TIME: 10 minutes
TOTAL TIME: 15 minutes
SERVING SIZE: 2 servings

INGREDIENTS:
- 4 large eggs
- 1 cup chopped kale, stems removed
- 1/4 cup shredded cheddar cheese
- 1 tablespoon olive oil
- Salt and pepper to taste
- Optional: 1 tablespoon finely chopped onion for added flavor

NUTRITION PER SERVING:
- **Total Calories:** 310 kcal
- **Total Carbohydrates:** 4 g
  - Dietary Fiber: 1 g
  - Sugars: 1 g
- **Protein:** 20 g
- **Total Fat:** 24 g
  - Saturated Fat: 7 g
  - Unsaturated Fat: 14 g
- **Sodium:** 390 mg

INSTRUCTIONS:
1. **Prepare Ingredients:** In a bowl, whisk the eggs with salt and pepper until well blended. Set aside.
2. **Cook Kale:** Heat olive oil in a non-stick skillet over medium heat. Add the chopped onion (if using) and sauté until translucent. Add the kale and cook until it begins to wilt, about 3-4 minutes.
3. **Scramble Eggs:** Pour the beaten eggs over the kale. Let sit for a few moments without stirring to let the eggs begin to set around the edges. Sprinkle the shredded cheddar cheese evenly over the top. Stir gently to combine and cook until the eggs are fully set.
4. **Serve:** Divide the scramble between two plates. Serve immediately, optionally garnished with more fresh pepper or herbs.

INGREDIENT SUBSTITUTIONS:
- **Kale:** Spinach or Swiss chard can be used as a substitute for kale, providing similar nutritional benefits and a slightly different flavor.
- **Cheddar Cheese:** Swap for Swiss cheese to reduce fat content slightly or use a low-fat cheese option to further decrease the calories and fat.
- **Olive Oil:** Can be replaced with avocado oil, maintaining the healthy fat profile.

Avocado Baked Eggs

PREPARATION TIME: 5 minutes
COOKING TIME: 15 minutes
TOTAL TIME: 20 minutes
SERVING SIZE: 2 servings

INGREDIENTS:
- 2 ripe avocados
- 4 small eggs
- Salt and pepper, to taste
- Optional: 2 tablespoons chopped chives or parsley for garnish

NUTRITION PER SERVING:
- **Total Calories:** 470 kcal
- **Total Carbohydrates:** 17 g
  - Dietary Fiber: 13 g
  - Sugars: 1 g
- **Protein:** 19 g
- **Total Fat:** 40 g
  - Saturated Fat: 8 g
  - Unsaturated Fat: 27 g
- **Sodium:** 200 mg

INSTRUCTIONS:
1. **Preheat Oven:** Preheat your oven to 425°F (220°C).
2. **Prepare Avocados:** Slice the avocados in half and remove the pits. Scoop out a little more avocado to create space enough to accommodate an egg.
3. **Add Eggs:** Place the avocado halves on a baking tray, and carefully crack an egg into each avocado half. Season with salt and pepper.
4. **Bake:** Place in the oven and bake for about 15 minutes, or until the eggs are cooked to your liking.
5. **Serve:** Garnish with chopped chives or parsley before serving.

INGREDIENT SUBSTITUTIONS:
- **Avocado:** Although central to this dish, for a lower fat option, use small scooped tomatoes instead of avocados.
- **Eggs:** For those avoiding cholesterol, use egg whites instead of whole eggs.
- **Chives/Parsley:** Fresh dill or cilantro can be used as alternatives for a different herb flavor.

Steel-Cut Oats with Apple and Cinnamon

PREPARATION TIME: 5 minutes
COOKING TIME: 30 minutes
TOTAL TIME: 35 minutes
SERVING SIZE: 2 servings

INGREDIENTS:
- 1 cup steel-cut oats
- 3 cups water
- 1 medium apple, peeled and diced
- 1 teaspoon ground cinnamon
- 1 tablespoon ground flaxseed (optional)
- Sweetener of choice (e.g., stevia, erythritol), to taste

NUTRITION PER SERVING:
- **Total Calories:** 315 kcal
- **Total Carbohydrates:** 54 g
  - Dietary Fiber: 9 g
  - Sugars: 10 g
- **Protein:** 10 g
- **Total Fat:** 6 g
  - Saturated Fat: 1 g
  - Unsaturated Fat: 4 g
- **Sodium:** 10 mg

INSTRUCTIONS:
1. **Cook Oats:** In a medium saucepan, bring the water to a boil. Add the steel-cut oats and simmer on low heat for about 25-30 minutes, stirring occasionally, until the oats are cooked and have absorbed most of the water.
2. **Add Flavors:** During the last 5 minutes of cooking, add the diced apple, cinnamon, and ground flaxseed. Stir well and continue to cook until the apples are soft.
3. **Sweeten:** Remove from heat and sweeten to taste with your choice of a diabetes-friendly sweetener.
4. **Serve:** Divide the oatmeal into bowls, and serve warm.

INGREDIENT SUBSTITUTIONS:
- **Apple:** Substitute with pear or half a cup of fresh berries for a similar texture and fiber content but a different flavor profile.
- **Cinnamon:** Nutmeg or cardamom can be used as an alternative spice that complements the sweetness of the fruit.
- **Flaxseed:** Chia seeds can be used in place of flaxseed for a different source of omega-3 fatty acids and fiber, without significantly altering the nutritional profile.

Overnight Chia Oat Pudding

PREPARATION TIME: 10 minutes
CHILL TIME: Overnight
TOTAL TIME: 8 hours 10 minutes
SERVING SIZE: 2 servings

INGREDIENTS:
- 1/4 cup chia seeds
- 1/4 cup steel-cut oats
- 1 cup unsweetened almond milk
- 1/2 teaspoon vanilla extract
- 1 tablespoon almond butter
- 2 tablespoons sugar-free maple syrup or sweetener of choice
- Fresh berries for topping (optional)

NUTRITION PER SERVING:
- **Total Calories:** 280 kcal
- **Total Carbohydrates:** 34 g
  - Dietary Fiber: 10 g
  - Sugars: 1 g
- **Protein:** 9 g
- **Total Fat:** 14 g
  - Saturated Fat: 1 g
  - Unsaturated Fat: 9 g
- **Sodium:** 90 mg

INSTRUCTIONS:
1. **Combine Ingredients:** In a medium bowl, mix the chia seeds, steel-cut oats, almond milk, vanilla extract, almond butter, and sweetener until well combined.
2. **Refrigerate:** Cover the bowl with a lid or plastic wrap and refrigerate overnight, or at least 8 hours, allowing the chia seeds and oats to absorb the liquid and thicken into a pudding-like consistency.
3. **Serve:** Stir the pudding well before serving. Divide the mixture into bowls or jars and top with fresh berries if desired.

INGREDIENT SUBSTITUTIONS:
- **Almond Milk:** Coconut milk or soy milk can be used as a substitute for almond milk to maintain a similar nutritional profile while changing the flavor slightly.
- **Almond Butter:** Peanut butter or sunflower seed butter are great alternatives that provide similar healthy fats and protein content.
- **Sugar-Free Maple Syrup:** For those who prefer a different flavor, stevia or erythritol can be used to adjust the sweetness level without adding sugars.

Savory Quinoa Porridge

PREPARATION TIME: 10 minutes
COOKING TIME: 20 minutes
TOTAL TIME: 30 minutes
SERVING SIZE: 2 servings

INGREDIENTS:
- 1/2 cup quinoa, rinsed
- 1 cup low-sodium vegetable broth
- 1 small onion, finely chopped
- 1 clove garlic, minced
- 1/4 cup chopped red bell pepper
- 1/4 cup grated zucchini
- 1/2 teaspoon turmeric powder
- 1 tablespoon olive oil
- Salt and pepper, to taste
- 2 tablespoons chopped fresh parsley

NUTRITION PER SERVING:
- **Total Calories:** 260 kcal
- **Total Carbohydrates:** 35 g
  - Dietary Fiber: 5 g
  - Sugars: 4 g
- **Protein:** 8 g
- **Total Fat:** 10 g
  - Saturated Fat: 1.5 g
  - Unsaturated Fat: 7.5 g
- **Sodium:** 150 mg

INSTRUCTIONS:
1. **Cook Quinoa:** In a medium saucepan, heat the olive oil over medium heat. Add the onion and garlic, sautéing until translucent. Stir in the red bell pepper and zucchini, and cook for a few more minutes.
2. **Add Quinoa and Broth:** Add the rinsed quinoa to the saucepan, stir in turmeric powder, and season with salt and pepper. Pour in the vegetable broth and bring to a boil. Reduce heat to low, cover, and simmer for about 15 minutes, or until the quinoa is tender and the liquid is absorbed.
3. **Garnish and Serve:** Remove from heat and let sit covered for 5 minutes. Fluff with a fork, then divide between two bowls. Garnish with fresh parsley before serving.

INGREDIENT SUBSTITUTIONS:
- **Vegetable Broth:** Chicken or beef broth can be used for a different flavor profile while maintaining similar sodium levels if using low-sodium options.
- **Olive Oil:** Avocado oil or coconut oil can be substituted for olive oil to provide healthy fats with a slightly different taste.
- **Quinoa:** Couscous or bulgur wheat could be used as alternatives, keeping in mind that these substitutes may alter the glycemic index of the dish.

Buckwheat Porridge with Hazelnuts

PREPARATION TIME: 5 minutes
COOKING TIME: 15 minutes
TOTAL TIME: 20 minutes
SERVING SIZE: 2 servings

INGREDIENTS:
- 1/2 cup buckwheat groats
- 1 1/2 cups water
- 1/4 teaspoon salt
- 1/4 cup chopped hazelnuts, toasted
- 1/2 teaspoon cinnamon
- 1 tablespoon flaxseed meal
- 2 tablespoons sugar-free maple syrup or honey substitute

NUTRITION PER SERVING:
- **Total Calories:** 280 kcal
- **Total Carbohydrates:** 42 g
  - Dietary Fiber: 6 g
  - Sugars: 1 g
- **Protein:** 8 g
- **Total Fat:** 12 g
  - Saturated Fat: 1 g
  - Unsaturated Fat: 10 g
- **Sodium:** 300 mg

INSTRUCTIONS:
1. **Cook Buckwheat:** In a small saucepan, combine the buckwheat groats, water, and salt. Bring to a boil over high heat. Reduce heat to low, cover, and simmer for about 10-15 minutes, or until the groats are tender and the water is absorbed.
2. **Add Flavors:** Remove the cooked buckwheat from heat. Stir in the cinnamon and flaxseed meal. Drizzle with sugar-free maple syrup or honey substitute and mix well.
3. **Serve:** Divide the porridge into two bowls. Sprinkle each serving with toasted hazelnuts for crunch.

INGREDIENT SUBSTITUTIONS:
- **Hazelnuts:** Walnuts or almonds can be used as a substitute for hazelnuts to vary the flavor while maintaining similar nutritional benefits.
- **Buckwheat Groats:** Steel-cut oats or quinoa can be used in place of buckwheat for a different texture and flavor, keeping the glycemic index low.
- **Sugar-Free Maple Syrup:** For a different kind of sweetness, you can use stevia drops or a sugar-free honey alternative.

Barley Porridge with Blueberries

PREPARATION TIME: 5 minutes
COOKING TIME: 30 minutes
TOTAL TIME: 35 minutes
SERVING SIZE: 2 servings

INGREDIENTS:
- 1/2 cup hulled barley, rinsed
- 2 cups water
- Pinch of salt
- 1/2 cup fresh blueberries
- 1 teaspoon cinnamon
- 2 tablespoons ground flaxseed
- 1 tablespoon sugar-free syrup or a sweetener alternative

NUTRITION PER SERVING:
- **Total Calories:** 240 kcal
- **Total Carbohydrates:** 50 g
  - Dietary Fiber: 10 g
  - Sugars: 4 g
- **Protein:** 6 g
- **Total Fat:** 3 g
  - Saturated Fat: 0.5 g
  - Unsaturated Fat: 2 g
- **Sodium:** 80 mg

INSTRUCTIONS:
1. **Cook Barley:** In a medium saucepan, combine barley, water, and a pinch of salt. Bring to a boil, then reduce heat to low, cover, and simmer for about 25-30 minutes, or until the barley is tender and most of the water is absorbed.
2. **Finish Porridge:** Remove from heat. Stir in the cinnamon and ground flaxseed. Add the sugar-free syrup and mix until well combined.
3. **Serve with Blueberries:** Spoon the porridge into bowls and top each serving with fresh blueberries.

INGREDIENT SUBSTITUTIONS:
- **Blueberries:** Raspberries or blackberries can be used in place of blueberries for a similar low glycemic impact and antioxidant benefits.
- **Barley:** For a gluten-free option, replace barley with quinoa or buckwheat, which will maintain the high fiber content and nutritional profile.
- **Sugar-Free Syrup:** Honey or agave syrup can be used for natural sweetness, but these should be used sparingly due to their higher sugar content compared to the sugar-free alternative.

Almond Flour Pancakes

PREPARATION TIME: 10 minutes
COOKING TIME: 15 minutes
TOTAL TIME: 25 minutes
SERVING SIZE: 2 servings

INGREDIENTS:
- 1 cup almond flour
- 2 large eggs
- 1/3 cup unsweetened almond milk
- 1 tablespoon granulated erythritol or another sugar substitute
- 1 teaspoon baking powder
- 1/2 teaspoon vanilla extract
- Pinch of salt
- Cooking spray or butter for the pan

NUTRITION PER SERVING:
- **Total Calories:** 345 kcal
- **Total Carbohydrates:** 12 g
  - Dietary Fiber: 6 g
  - Sugars: 2 g
- **Protein:** 14 g
- **Total Fat:** 29 g
  - Saturated Fat: 3 g
  - Unsaturated Fat: 20 g
- **Sodium:** 236 mg

INSTRUCTIONS:
1. **Mix Ingredients:** In a mixing bowl, whisk together almond flour, baking powder, erythritol, and salt. In a separate bowl, beat the eggs with almond milk and vanilla extract. Combine the wet and dry ingredients until a smooth batter forms.
2. **Prepare Pan:** Heat a non-stick skillet over medium heat and lightly grease with cooking spray or a small amount of butter.
3. **Cook Pancakes:** Pour small batches of the batter onto the hot skillet. Cook for about 2-3 minutes on one side or until bubbles form on the surface. Flip and cook for an additional 2 minutes on the other side or until golden brown.
4. **Serve:** Serve hot with a diabetic-friendly syrup or fresh berries.

INGREDIENT SUBSTITUTIONS:
- **Almond Milk:** Coconut milk can be used in place of almond milk for a different flavor while maintaining the low carbohydrate profile.
- **Erythritol:** Stevia or monk fruit sweetener can be substituted for erythritol, adjusting the quantity according to taste as these sweeteners vary in sweetness intensity.
- **Almond Flour:** Coconut flour can be used, but keep in mind it absorbs more liquid, so you may need to adjust the amount of almond milk slightly.

Coconut Flour Waffles

PREPARATION TIME: 10 minutes
COOKING TIME: 15 minutes
SERVING SIZE: 2 servings

INGREDIENTS:
- 1/2 cup coconut flour
- 4 large eggs
- 1/4 cup unsweetened almond milk
- 2 tablespoons coconut oil, melted
- 1 tablespoon erythritol or another sugar substitute
- 1 teaspoon baking powder
- 1/2 teaspoon vanilla extract
- Pinch of salt
- Cooking spray for the waffle iron

NUTRITION PER SERVING:
- **Total Calories:** 310 kcal
- **Total Carbohydrates:** 18 g
  - Dietary Fiber: 10 g
  - Sugars: 3 g
- **Protein:** 14 g
- **Total Fat:** 22 g
  - Saturated Fat: 15 g
  - Unsaturated Fat: 5 g
- **Sodium:** 308 mg

INSTRUCTIONS:
1. **Mix Ingredients:** In a large bowl, combine coconut flour, baking powder, and salt. In another bowl, whisk together eggs, almond milk, melted coconut oil, erythritol, and vanilla extract.
2. **Prepare Waffle Iron:** Preheat your waffle iron according to the manufacturer's instructions and lightly grease it with cooking spray.
3. **Cook Waffles:** Pour the batter into the preheated waffle iron, spreading evenly. Close the lid and cook until the waffle is golden and crispy, about 3-5 minutes.
4. **Serve:** Serve the waffles hot with toppings of your choice, such as a sugar-free syrup or fresh berries.

INGREDIENT SUBSTITUTIONS:
- **Almond Milk:** Swap out almond milk for coconut milk for a richer flavor and creamier texture while keeping the carbohydrate content low.
- **Coconut Oil:** Butter can be used in place of coconut oil if preferred, which will add a richer flavor to the waffles.
- **Erythritol:** You can substitute erythritol with monk fruit sweetener or a small amount of stevia, adjusting to taste.

Cottage Cheese Pancakes

PREPARATION TIME: 10 minutes
COOKING TIME: 10 minutes
TOTAL TIME: 20 minutes
SERVING SIZE: 2 servings

INGREDIENTS:
- 1 cup low-fat cottage cheese
- 2 large eggs
- 1/4 cup almond flour
- 2 tablespoons ground flaxseed
- 1/2 teaspoon baking powder
- 1 teaspoon vanilla extract
- 1 tablespoon olive oil (for cooking)

NUTRITION PER SERVING:
- **Total Calories:** 325 kcal
- **Total Carbohydrates:** 12 g
  - Dietary Fiber: 4 g
  - Sugars: 4 g
- **Protein:** 26 g
- **Total Fat:** 20 g
  - Saturated Fat: 4 g
  - Unsaturated Fat: 12 g
- **Sodium:** 560 mg

INSTRUCTIONS:
1. **Blend Ingredients:** In a blender, combine cottage cheese, eggs, almond flour, flaxseed, baking powder, and vanilla extract. Blend until smooth.
2. **Heat Skillet:** Heat olive oil in a non-stick skillet over medium heat.
3. **Cook Pancakes:** Pour 1/4 cup of batter for each pancake into the skillet. Cook until the edges are set and bubbles form on the surface, about 2-3 minutes. Flip and cook for another 2 minutes until golden brown.
4. **Serve:** Serve the pancakes warm with a topping of your choice, such as fresh berries or a drizzle of sugar-free syrup.

INGREDIENT SUBSTITUTIONS:
- **Almond Flour:** Coconut flour can be used as a substitute for almond flour to maintain a low carbohydrate profile while adding a slight coconut flavor.
- **Low-Fat Cottage Cheese:** Ricotta cheese can replace cottage cheese for a creamier texture while keeping the protein content high.
- **Ground Flaxseed:** Chia seeds can be used in place of flaxseed to provide a similar texture and nutritional profile, enhancing the omega-3 fatty acids.

Flaxseed and Walnut Pancakes

PREPARATION TIME: 15 minutes
COOKING TIME: 10 minutes
TOTAL TIME: 25 minutes
SERVING SIZE: 2 servings

INGREDIENTS:
- 1/2 cup ground flaxseed
- 1/4 cup crushed walnuts
- 1/4 cup whole wheat flour
- 1 teaspoon baking powder
- 1/2 teaspoon cinnamon
- 1 cup unsweetened almond milk
- 1 egg
- 1 tablespoon olive oil (for cooking)
- Optional: 1 teaspoon vanilla extract for added flavor

NUTRITION PER SERVING:
- **Total Calories:** 310 kcal
- **Total Carbohydrates:** 18 g
  - Dietary Fiber: 8 g
  - Sugars: 1 g
- **Protein:** 12 g
- **Total Fat:** 24 g
  - Saturated Fat: 3 g
  - Unsaturated Fat: 15 g
- **Sodium:** 300 mg

INSTRUCTIONS:
1. **Mix Dry Ingredients:** In a large bowl, mix ground flaxseed, crushed walnuts, whole wheat flour, baking powder, and cinnamon.
2. **Add Wet Ingredients:** Beat the egg and almond milk together in a separate bowl. Add the vanilla extract if using. Pour the wet ingredients into the dry ingredients and stir until well combined.
3. **Heat Pan:** Heat olive oil in a non-stick skillet over medium heat.
4. **Cook Pancakes:** Pour 1/4 cup of batter for each pancake into the skillet. Cook for about 2-3 minutes on each side or until pancakes are golden brown and cooked through.
5. **Serve:** Serve hot with your choice of diabetic-friendly toppings, such as sugar-free maple syrup or fresh berries.

INGREDIENT SUBSTITUTIONS:
- **Whole Wheat Flour:** Coconut flour can be used instead of whole wheat flour to reduce the carbohydrate content and add a mild coconut flavor.
- **Unsweetened Almond Milk:** Soy milk can be used as an alternative to almond milk for a different flavor and higher protein content.
- **Crushed Walnuts:** Almonds or pecans can be substituted for walnuts, providing a similar texture and maintaining the healthy fats.

Banana Yogurt Pancakes

PREPARATION TIME: 10 minutes
COOKING TIME: 15 minutes
TOTAL TIME: 25 minutes
SERVING SIZE: 2 servings

INGREDIENTS:
- 1 medium ripe banana
- 1/2 cup Greek yogurt, plain and unsweetened
- 1/2 cup oat flour
- 2 large eggs
- 1/2 teaspoon baking powder
- 1/4 teaspoon cinnamon
- Olive oil or cooking spray (for cooking)

NUTRITION PER SERVING:
- **Total Calories:** 280 kcal
- **Total Carbohydrates:** 33 g
  - Dietary Fiber: 4 g
  - Sugars: 8 g
- **Protein:** 15 g
- **Total Fat:** 10 g
  - Saturated Fat: 3 g
  - Unsaturated Fat: 5 g
- **Sodium:** 180 mg

INSTRUCTIONS:
1. **Mash the Banana:** In a mixing bowl, mash the banana until smooth.
2. **Combine Ingredients:** Add the Greek yogurt, oat flour, eggs, baking powder, and cinnamon to the mashed banana. Stir until well combined and the batter is somewhat smooth.
3. **Prepare the Skillet:** Heat a non-stick skillet over medium heat and lightly grease with olive oil or cooking spray.
4. **Cook Pancakes:** Pour 1/4 cup of batter for each pancake onto the hot skillet. Cook for 2-3 minutes on each side or until pancakes are golden and cooked through.
5. **Serve:** Serve the pancakes warm with diabetic-friendly toppings like a dollop of Greek yogurt or fresh berries.

INGREDIENT SUBSTITUTIONS:
- **Banana:** Applesauce can be used in place of banana for a different flavor and lower glycemic index.
- **Greek Yogurt:** For a dairy-free version, use unsweetened almond or coconut yogurt.
- **Oat Flour:** Almond flour can be substituted to lower carbohydrate content and provide a richer flavor.

Avocado Toast on Sprouted Grain Bread

PREPARATION TIME: 5 minutes
COOKING TIME: 2 minutes
TOTAL TIME: 7 minutes
SERVING SIZE: 2 servings

INGREDIENTS:
- 2 slices of sprouted grain bread
- 1 ripe avocado
- Juice of 1/2 a lemon
- Salt and pepper, to taste
- Optional toppings: sliced radishes, cherry tomatoes, or a sprinkle of flaxseeds

NUTRITION PER SERVING:
- **Total Calories:** 250 kcal
- **Total Carbohydrates:** 27 g
  - Dietary Fiber: 10 g
  - Sugars: 3 g
- **Protein:** 9 g
- **Total Fat:** 14 g
  - Saturated Fat: 2 g
  - Unsaturated Fat: 10 g
- **Sodium:** 200 mg

INSTRUCTIONS:
1. **Toast the Bread:** Lightly toast the sprouted grain bread slices until golden and crispy.
2. **Prepare the Avocado:** While the bread is toasting, halve the avocado, remove the pit, and scoop the flesh into a bowl.
3. **Mash and Season:** Add lemon juice, salt, and pepper to the avocado. Mash the mixture until it's creamy but still has some texture.
4. **Assemble the Toast:** Spread the mashed avocado evenly over each slice of toasted bread.
5. **Add Toppings:** Garnish with optional toppings such as sliced radishes, cherry tomatoes, or a sprinkle of flaxseeds for extra flavor and nutrition.
6. **Serve:** Enjoy immediately for the best texture and flavor.

INGREDIENT SUBSTITUTIONS:
- **Sprouted Grain Bread:** For a gluten-free option, use a high-fiber, gluten-free bread that mimics the nutritional profile of sprouted grain.
- **Lemon Juice:** Lime juice can be used as a citrus alternative, offering a slightly different tartness.
- **Toppings:** For variety, try topping with alfalfa sprouts, cucumber slices, or a sprinkle of chia seeds to maintain similar nutritional benefits.

Smoked Salmon and Cream Cheese Bagel

PREPARATION TIME: 10 minutes
COOKING TIME: 0 minutes
TOTAL TIME: 10 minutes
SERVING SIZE: 2 servings

INGREDIENTS:
- 2 whole grain bagels
- 4 oz smoked salmon
- 2 tablespoons light cream cheese
- Fresh dill, chopped (for garnish)
- Capers, for topping (optional)
- Red onion slices (optional)

NUTRITION PER SERVING:
- **Total Calories:** 320 kcal
- **Total Carbohydrates:** 37 g
  - Dietary Fiber: 6 g
  - Sugars: 5 g
- **Protein:** 24 g
- **Total Fat:** 12 g
  - Saturated Fat: 3 g
  - Unsaturated Fat: 6 g
- **Sodium:** 860 mg

INSTRUCTIONS:
1. **Prepare the Bagels:** Slice the bagels in half and toast them until they are lightly browned and crispy.
2. **Spread Cream Cheese:** Spread 1 tablespoon of light cream cheese on each half of the bagel.
3. **Add Smoked Salmon:** Lay slices of smoked salmon evenly over the cream cheese on each bagel half.
4. **Garnish:** Sprinkle chopped dill, capers, and thin slices of red onion on top of the smoked salmon, if using.
5. **Serve:** Serve immediately to enjoy the crispiness of the bagels with the creamy and savory toppings.

INGREDIENT SUBSTITUTIONS:
- **Whole Grain Bagels:** Substitute with gluten-free bagels to accommodate those with gluten sensitivities while maintaining a similar fiber content.
- **Light Cream Cheese:** Neufchâtel cheese or a plant-based cream cheese alternative can be used to lower fat content or for those avoiding dairy.
- **Smoked Salmon:** For a vegetarian alternative, replace the smoked salmon with thinly sliced tomato and a sprinkle of sea salt, though this will change the protein content.

Ricotta and Tomato Basil Toast

PREPARATION TIME: 10 minutes
COOKING TIME: 5 minutes
TOTAL TIME: 15 minutes
SERVING SIZE: 2 servings

INGREDIENTS:
- 2 slices of whole grain bread
- 1/2 cup part-skim ricotta cheese
- 1 medium tomato, sliced
- Fresh basil leaves, chopped
- Salt and pepper to taste
- Drizzle of extra virgin olive oil (optional)

NUTRITION PER SERVING:
- **Total Calories:** 220 kcal
- **Total Carbohydrates:** 28 g
  - Dietary Fiber: 5 g
  - Sugars: 4 g
- **Protein:** 12 g
- **Total Fat:** 8 g
  - Saturated Fat: 3 g
  - Unsaturated Fat: 4 g
- **Sodium:** 180 mg

INSTRUCTIONS:
1. **Toast the Bread:** Toast the whole grain bread slices until golden and crispy.
2. **Prepare Ricotta:** Spread the part-skim ricotta cheese evenly over each slice of toasted bread.
3. **Add Toppings:** Arrange the tomato slices over the ricotta. Sprinkle with fresh basil, salt, and pepper to taste. Drizzle with a little olive oil if desired.
4. **Serve:** Serve immediately, enjoying the creamy texture of ricotta with the fresh flavors of tomato and basil.

INGREDIENT SUBSTITUTIONS:
- **Whole Grain Bread:** Substitute with sprouted grain bread for an even lower glycemic index and higher fiber content.
- **Part-Skim Ricotta:** Use low-fat cottage cheese or a dairy-free ricotta alternative to accommodate dietary restrictions or preferences.
- **Tomato and Basil:** For a different flavor profile, try swapping tomato and basil with sliced cucumber and dill, maintaining a similar calorie and carbohydrate content.

Peanut Butter and Strawberry Open Sandwich

PREPARATION TIME: 5 minutes
COOKING TIME: 0 minutes
TOTAL TIME: 5 minutes
SERVING SIZE: 2 servings

INGREDIENTS:
- 2 slices of whole grain bread
- 2 tablespoons natural peanut butter (unsweetened)
- 1/2 cup fresh strawberries, sliced
- A sprinkle of chia seeds (optional)

NUTRITION PER SERVING:
- **Total Calories:** 280 kcal
- **Total Carbohydrates:** 30 g
  - Dietary Fiber: 6 g
  - Sugars: 8 g
- **Protein:** 10 g
- **Total Fat:** 15 g
  - Saturated Fat: 3 g
  - Unsaturated Fat: 9 g
- **Sodium:** 200 mg

INSTRUCTIONS:
1. **Prepare the Bread:** Toast the whole grain bread slices to your preferred level of crispiness.
2. **Spread Peanut Butter:** Evenly spread one tablespoon of natural peanut butter on each slice of toasted bread.
3. **Add Strawberries:** Top each slice with sliced strawberries, arranging them evenly over the peanut butter.
4. **Garnish:** Sprinkle chia seeds over the strawberries for an added boost of fiber and omega-3 fatty acids.
5. **Serve:** Enjoy immediately for a fresh, nutritious start to your day or as a satisfying snack.

INGREDIENT SUBSTITUTIONS:
- **Whole Grain Bread:** Can be substituted with low-carb almond flour bread to further reduce carbohydrate content and enhance the fiber content.
- **Natural Peanut Butter:** Almond butter or sunflower seed butter can be used as alternatives for those with peanut allergies or preferences.
- **Strawberries:** Blueberries or thinly sliced apples can replace strawberries, offering similar nutritional benefits and maintaining a low glycemic index.

Egg Spinach and Feta Wrap

PREPARATION TIME: 10 minutes
COOKING TIME: 5 minutes
TOTAL TIME: 15 minutes
SERVING SIZE: 2 servings

INGREDIENTS:
- 4 large eggs
- 1 cup fresh spinach, chopped
- 1/4 cup feta cheese, crumbled
- 2 whole grain tortillas
- 1 tablespoon olive oil
- Salt and pepper to taste

NUTRITION PER SERVING:
- **Total Calories:** 340 kcal
- **Total Carbohydrates:** 28 g
  - Dietary Fiber: 5 g
  - Sugars: 3 g
- **Protein:** 20 g
- **Total Fat:** 18 g
  - Saturated Fat: 6 g
  - Unsaturated Fat: 9 g
- **Sodium:** 540 mg

INSTRUCTIONS:
1. **Heat the Pan:** Heat olive oil in a non-stick skillet over medium heat.
2. **Scramble the Eggs:** In a bowl, whisk the eggs with salt and pepper. Pour into the skillet and gently scramble until they begin to set.
3. **Add Spinach and Feta:** Stir in the chopped spinach and cook until the spinach wilts and the eggs are fully cooked. Sprinkle feta cheese over the eggs and let it slightly melt.
4. **Prepare the Wraps:** Warm the whole grain tortillas for a few seconds on each side in the skillet or in the microwave.
5. **Assemble the Wraps:** Divide the egg mixture evenly among the tortillas. Fold the sides of the tortilla over the filling, then roll up tightly.
6. **Serve:** Cut each wrap in half and serve warm.

INGREDIENT SUBSTITUTIONS:
- **Eggs:** Use egg whites to reduce the fat content; two egg whites per one whole egg is a good ratio.
- **Feta Cheese:** Substitute with goat cheese or a low-fat mozzarella for a different flavor profile while maintaining a similar texture and reducing saturated fat.
- **Whole Grain Tortillas:** Swap for low-carb or gluten-free tortillas depending on dietary needs or preferences.

Lunch Recipes

Grilled Chicken Salad

PREPARATION TIME: 20 minutes
COOKING TIME: 10 minutes
TOTAL TIME: 30 minutes
SERVINGS: 2

INGREDIENTS:
- 2 boneless, skinless chicken breasts (approximately 6 ounces each)
- 4 cups mixed salad greens (such as romaine, arugula, and spinach)
- 1 cup cherry tomatoes, halved
- 1/2 cucumber, sliced
- 1/4 red onion, thinly sliced
- 2 tablespoons olive oil (for dressing)
- 1 tablespoon balsamic vinegar
- Salt and pepper to taste
- 1 teaspoon dried Italian herbs or fresh herbs like basil or parsley

NUTRITION PER SERVING:
- **Total Calories:** 350
- **Total Carbohydrates:** 10g
    - Dietary Fiber: 3g
    - Sugars: 4g
- **Protein:** 38g
- **Total Fat:** 17 g
    - Saturated Fat: 2g
    - Unsaturated Fat: 7g
- **Sodium:** 200mg

INSTRUCTIONS:
1. **Preheat Grill:** Preheat your grill to medium-high heat.
2. **Season Chicken:** Brush the chicken breasts with 1 tablespoon of olive oil, then season with salt, pepper, and dried Italian herbs.
3. **Grill Chicken:** Grill the chicken for about 5 minutes on each side, or until the internal temperature reaches 165°F (74°C). Remove from the grill and let rest for a few minutes before slicing.
4. **Prepare Salad:** In a large bowl, combine the mixed greens, cherry tomatoes, cucumber, and red onion.
5. **Make Dressing:** Whisk together the remaining olive oil, balsamic vinegar, salt, and pepper.
6. **Combine:** Slice the grilled chicken and add it to the salad. Drizzle with the dressing and toss everything to coat.
7. **Serve:** Divide the salad between two plates and serve immediately.

INGREDIENT SUBSTITUTIONS:
- **Chicken:** Substitute grilled tofu or tempeh for a vegetarian version without significantly altering the macronutrients.
- **Olive Oil:** Use avocado oil for a similar fat profile with a different flavor.
- **Balsamic Vinegar:** Apple cider vinegar can be used for a different tangy taste while maintaining the health benefits.

Turkey and Avocado Wrap

PREPARATION TIME: 10 minutes
COOKING TIME: 0 minutes
TOTAL TIME: 10 minutes
SERVINGS: 2

INGREDIENTS:
- 4 whole grain or low-carb tortillas
- 8 slices of deli turkey breast (low sodium)
- 1 ripe avocado, sliced
- 1/2 cup shredded lettuce
- 1 tomato, sliced
- 1 small red onion, thinly sliced
- 2 tablespoons mustard
- 2 tablespoons Greek yogurt
- Salt and pepper to taste

NUTRITION PER SERVING:
- **Total Calories:** 370
- **Total Carbohydrates:** 34g
  - Dietary Fiber: 8g
  - Sugars: 4g
- **Protein:** 25g
- **Total Fat:** 15 g
  - Saturated Fat: 3g
  - Unsaturated Fat: 10g
- **Sodium:** 400mg

INSTRUCTIONS:
1. **Prepare Wraps:** Lay out the tortillas on a flat surface.
2. **Spread Condiments:** Mix the mustard and Greek yogurt together and spread evenly across each tortilla.
3. **Add Fillings:** On each tortilla, layer two slices of turkey, a few slices of avocado, shredded lettuce, tomato slices, and a few rings of red onion.
4. **Season:** Sprinkle a little salt and pepper over the fillings to taste.
5. **Wrap:** Carefully roll up the tortillas tightly to enclose the fillings. If necessary, secure with a toothpick.
6. **Serve:** Cut each wrap in half and serve immediately or wrap in parchment paper for an on-the-go meal.

INGREDIENT SUBSTITUTIONS:
- **Turkey:** Substitute with grilled chicken or smoked salmon for different flavors and similar protein content.
- **Avocado:** For a less creamy texture but similar health benefits, use thin slices of cucumber.
- **Greek Yogurt:** Plain low-fat yogurt can be used in place of Greek yogurt for a similar consistency and nutrient profile, but slightly less protein.

Vegetable Stir-Fry with Tofu

PREPARATION TIME: 15 minutes
COOKING TIME: 10 minutes
SERVINGS: 2

INGREDIENTS:
- 200g firm tofu, cubed
- 1 bell pepper, sliced
- 1 carrot, julienned
- 1 cup broccoli florets
- 1 zucchini, sliced
- 2 cloves garlic, minced
- 1 tablespoon ginger, grated
- 2 tablespoons low-sodium soy sauce
- 1 tablespoon sesame oil
- 1 teaspoon chili flakes (optional)
- Fresh coriander, for garnish

NUTRITION PER SERVING:
- **Total Calories:** 280
- **Total Carbohydrates:** 18g
  - Dietary Fiber: 5g
  - Sugars: 6g
- **Protein:** 16g
- **Total Fat:** 15 g
  - Saturated Fat: 2g
  - Unsaturated Fat: 8g
- **Sodium:** 420mg

INSTRUCTIONS:
1. **Prepare Ingredients:** Press tofu to remove excess water and then cube. Prepare all vegetables as noted.
2. **Heat Oil:** In a large skillet or wok, heat sesame oil over medium heat.
3. **Cook Tofu:** Add tofu to the skillet and stir-fry until golden brown on all sides, about 5-7 minutes. Remove tofu and set aside.
4. **Stir-Fry Vegetables:** In the same skillet, add garlic and ginger, sauté for a minute, then add all the vegetables. Stir-fry for about 5 minutes or until vegetables are just tender.
5. **Combine and Season:** Return the tofu to the skillet, add soy sauce and chili flakes if using, and toss everything together until well combined and heated through.
6. **Garnish and Serve:** Garnish with fresh coriander before serving.

INGREDIENT SUBSTITUTIONS:
- **Tofu:** Can be replaced with tempeh or chicken breast for those who prefer a different protein source while maintaining a similar nutrient profile.
- **Sesame Oil:** Use olive oil or avocado oil as a substitute; both offer heart-healthy fats and a high smoke point suitable for stir-frying.
- **Vegetables:** Feel free to swap in or add other vegetables like snap peas, mushrooms, or spinach.

Beef and Broccoli

PREPARATION TIME: 10 minutes
COOKING TIME: 15 minutes
TOTAL TIME: 25 minutes
SERVINGS: 2

INGREDIENTS:
- 200g lean beef, thinly sliced
- 2 cups broccoli florets
- 1 tablespoon olive oil
- 2 cloves garlic, minced
- 1 teaspoon ginger, grated
- 3 tablespoons low-sodium soy sauce
- 1 tablespoon oyster sauce
- 1 teaspoon cornstarch (dissolved in 2 tablespoons water)
- 1/2 teaspoon sesame oil

NUTRITION PER SERVING:
- **Total Calories:** 300
- **Total Carbohydrates:** 12g
  - Dietary Fiber: 3g
  - Sugars: 2g
- **Protein:** 28g
- **Total Fat:** 14 g
  - Saturated Fat: 3g
  - Unsaturated Fat: 5g
- **Sodium:** 530mg

INSTRUCTIONS:
1. **Prepare Beef:** Slice the beef thinly against the grain to ensure tenderness.
2. **Blanch Broccoli:** In a pot of boiling water, blanch the broccoli florets for about 2 minutes, then drain and set aside.
3. **Heat Oil:** In a large skillet or wok, heat olive oil over medium-high heat.
4. **Cook Beef:** Add the garlic and ginger to the skillet and sauté until fragrant. Add the beef slices and stir-fry until they start to brown, about 3-4 minutes.
5. **Add Sauces:** Pour in the soy sauce and oyster sauce, stirring to coat the beef well.
6. **Thicken Sauce:** Stir in the dissolved cornstarch to thicken the sauce slightly.
7. **Combine with Broccoli:** Add the blanched broccoli to the skillet and toss everything together until the broccoli is heated through and coated with the sauce.
8. **Finish with Sesame Oil:** Drizzle sesame oil over the dish just before serving to enhance the flavor.

INGREDIENT SUBSTITUTIONS:
- **Beef:** Substitute with chicken or tofu for a leaner or vegetarian option, maintaining protein.
- **Oyster Sauce:** Replace with hoisin sauce or a mix of soy sauce and honey for similar umami flavor.
- **Broccoli:** Use cauliflower or green beans for comparable nutritional benefits with a flavor variation.

Shrimp and Arugula Salad

PREPARATION TIME: 10 minutes
COOKING TIME: 5 minutes
SERVINGS: 2

INGREDIENTS:
- 200g shrimp, peeled and deveined
- 4 cups arugula, washed
- 1/2 cup cherry tomatoes, halved
- 1/4 cup cucumber, sliced
- 1 tablespoon olive oil
- 1 lemon, juiced
- 1 clove garlic, minced
- Salt and pepper to taste
- 1 tablespoon Parmesan cheese, grated

NUTRITION PER SERVING:
- **Total Calories:** 240
- **Total Carbohydrates:** 8g
  - Dietary Fiber: 2g
  - Sugars: 3g
- **Protein:** 24g
- **Total Fat:** 12 g
  - Saturated Fat: 2g
  - Unsaturated Fat: 6g
- **Sodium:** 350mg

INSTRUCTIONS:
1. **Cook Shrimp:** Heat a skillet over medium heat and add a splash of olive oil. Add garlic and sauté until fragrant. Add shrimp and cook for 2-3 minutes on each side or until pink and opaque.
2. **Prepare Salad:** In a large bowl, combine arugula, cherry tomatoes, and cucumber.
3. **Dressing:** In a small bowl, whisk together lemon juice, the remaining olive oil, salt, and pepper.
4. **Combine:** Add the cooked shrimp to the salad. Drizzle with the dressing and toss gently to combine.
5. **Serve:** Divide the salad into two servings, sprinkle with grated Parmesan cheese if desired, and serve immediately.

INGREDIENT SUBSTITUTIONS:
- **Shrimp:** Can be substituted with grilled chicken or tofu for those who prefer a non-seafood option while maintaining a high protein content.
- **Arugula:** Spinach or mixed greens can replace arugula for a different but equally nutritious base.
- **Parmesan Cheese:** Nutritional yeast or a vegan cheese alternative can be used for a dairy-free version, providing a similar cheesy flavor with fewer calories.

Lentil and Barley Soup

IMPORTANT NOTE

This recipe, and others that will follow, features ingredients like lentils and barley, making it rich in carbohydrates. Although the glycemic index is moderate, individuals with diabetes should diligently monitor their blood glucose levels after consuming this meal. Given that reactions to foods can differ from person to person, it may be necessary to adjust the portion size to align with specific dietary needs and ensure stable blood sugar levels. Consulting a healthcare professional or dietitian can also be advantageous to further tailor this meal to meet individual health requirements effectively.

PREPARATION TIME: 10 minutes
COOKING TIME: 45 minutes
TOTAL TIME: 55 minutes
SERVINGS: 2

INGREDIENTS:

- 1/2 cup dried lentils, rinsed
- 1/4 cup pearl barley, rinsed
- 1 small onion, diced
- 1 carrot, diced
- 1 celery stalk, diced
- 2 cloves garlic, minced
- 4 cups low-sodium vegetable broth
- 1 teaspoon olive oil
- 1/2 teaspoon dried thyme
- Salt and pepper to taste
- 2 tablespoons fresh parsley, chopped for garnish

NUTRITION PER SERVING:

- **Total Calories:** 320
- **Total Carbohydrates:** 55g
  - Dietary Fiber: 15g
  - Sugars: 4g
- **Protein:** 14g
- **Total Fat:** 4.5 g
  - Saturated Fat: 0.5g
  - Unsaturated Fat: 2g
- **Sodium:** 300mg

INSTRUCTIONS:

1. **Sauté Vegetables:** In a large pot, heat olive oil over medium heat. Add onion, carrot, celery, and garlic. Sauté until vegetables are softened, about 5 minutes.
2. **Add Lentils and Barley:** Stir in lentils and barley until well combined with the vegetables.
3. **Add Broth and Seasonings:** Pour in vegetable broth, add thyme, and season with salt and pepper. Bring to a boil.
4. **Simmer:** Reduce heat to low and let simmer for about 40 minutes, or until lentils and barley are tender.
5. **Serve:** Adjust seasoning if necessary. Serve hot, garnished with fresh parsley.

INGREDIENT SUBSTITUTIONS:

- **Lentils:** Chickpeas or black beans can be used as alternatives to lentils, offering a similar nutritional profile and adding variety in texture and flavor.
- **Pearl Barley:** Quinoa or brown rice can replace barley for a gluten-free option while still providing high fiber and essential nutrients.
- **Vegetable Broth:** Chicken broth can be used for a non-vegetarian version, enhancing the soup's flavor profile without significantly altering the nutritional content.

Chickpea and Farro Soup

PREPARATION TIME: 10 minutes
COOKING TIME: 30 minutes
SERVINGS: 2

INGREDIENTS:
- 1/2 cup dry farro, rinsed
- 1 cup canned chickpeas, drained and rinsed
- 1 small onion, chopped
- 2 cloves garlic, minced
- 1 carrot, peeled and diced
- 1 celery stalk, diced
- 4 cups low-sodium vegetable broth
- 1 teaspoon olive oil
- 1/2 teaspoon dried rosemary
- Salt and pepper to taste
- Fresh parsley, chopped (for garnish)

NUTRITION PER SERVING:
- **Total Calories:** 340
- **Total Carbohydrates:** 60g
  - Dietary Fiber: 12g; Sugars: 7g
- **Protein:** 12g
- **Total Fat:** 5.5 g
  - Saturated Fat: 0.5g
  - Unsaturated Fat: 2.5g
- **Sodium:** 480mg

INSTRUCTIONS:
1. **Sauté Vegetables:** In a large pot, heat the olive oil over medium heat. Add the onion, carrot, and celery, and sauté until the vegetables are softened, about 5 minutes. Add the minced garlic and sauté for another minute until fragrant.
2. **Cook Soup:** Stir in the farro, chickpeas, rosemary, and vegetable broth. Bring to a boil, then reduce heat to a simmer, cover, and let cook for about 25 minutes, or until the farro is tender.
3. **Season and Serve:** Season the soup with salt and pepper to taste. Serve hot, garnished with fresh parsley.

INGREDIENT SUBSTITUTIONS:
- **Farro:** Brown rice or bulgur can be used as substitutes for farro, offering a similar texture and whole-grain nutrients while keeping the dish gluten-free if necessary.
- **Chickpeas:** Navy beans or lentils are excellent alternatives, providing comparable nutritional benefits and a slight variation in flavor and texture.
- **Vegetable Broth:** For a non-vegetarian version, chicken broth can be used to add depth to the flavor.

White Bean and Quinoa Soup

PREPARATION TIME: 10 minutes
COOKING TIME: 25 minutes
SERVINGS: 2

INGREDIENTS:
- 1/2 cup quinoa, rinsed
- 1 cup canned white beans, drained and rinsed
- 1 small onion, chopped
- 2 cloves garlic, minced
- 1 carrot, peeled and diced
- 1 celery stalk, diced
- 4 cups low-sodium vegetable broth
- 1 teaspoon olive oil
- 1/2 teaspoon dried thyme
- Salt and pepper to taste
- Fresh basil, chopped (for garnish)

NUTRITION PER SERVING:
- **Total Calories:** 320
- **Total Carbohydrates:** 54g
  - Dietary Fiber: 11g
  - Sugars: 4g
- **Protein:** 16g
- **Total Fat:** 4.5 g
  - Saturated Fat: 0.5g
  - Unsaturated Fat: 2g
- **Sodium:** 400mg

INSTRUCTIONS:
1. **Sauté Vegetables:** In a large pot, heat the olive oil over medium heat. Add the onion, carrot, and celery, and sauté until the vegetables are softened, about 5 minutes. Add the minced garlic and cook for another minute until fragrant.
2. **Cook Soup:** Stir in the quinoa, white beans, thyme, and vegetable broth. Bring to a boil, then reduce heat to a simmer, cover, and let cook for about 20 minutes, or until the quinoa is fully cooked.
3. **Season and Serve:** Season the soup with salt and pepper to taste. Serve hot, garnished with fresh basil.

INGREDIENT SUBSTITUTIONS:
- **Quinoa:** Millet or brown rice can be substituted for quinoa, offering a similar texture while maintaining the gluten-free status and providing whole-grain benefits.
- **White Beans:** Cannellini beans or great northern beans are excellent alternatives, offering similar flavors and health benefits.
- **Vegetable Broth:** Chicken or beef broth can be used for non-vegetarian options, adding additional flavor depth.

Mediterranean Vegetable and Bulgur Soup

PREPARATION TIME: 15 minutes
COOKING TIME: 30 minutes
SERVINGS: 2

INGREDIENTS:
- 1/2 cup bulgur, rinsed
- 1 small zucchini, diced
- 1 red bell pepper, diced
- 1 small onion, chopped
- 2 cloves garlic, minced
- 1 medium tomato, diced
- 3 cups low-sodium vegetable broth
- 2 tablespoons olive oil
- 1 teaspoon dried oregano
- Salt and pepper to taste
- Fresh parsley, chopped (for garnish)
- Lemon wedges (for serving)

NUTRITION PER SERVING:
- **Total Calories:** 290
- **Total Carbohydrates:** 45g
  - Dietary Fiber: 9g; Sugars: 6g
- **Protein:** 8g
- **Total Fat:** 8.5g
  - Saturated Fat: 1g;
  - Unsaturated Fat: 5g
- **Sodium:** 300mg

INSTRUCTIONS:
1. **Sauté Vegetables:** In a large pot, heat the olive oil over medium heat. Add the onion and bell pepper, and sauté until they begin to soften, about 5 minutes. Add the garlic and cook for another minute until fragrant.
2. **Add Bulgur and Broth:** Stir in the bulgur, chopped tomato, zucchini, oregano, and vegetable broth. Bring the mixture to a boil.
3. **Simmer:** Reduce heat to low, cover, and simmer for about 20 minutes, or until the bulgur is tender and the vegetables are cooked through.
4. **Season and Garnish:** Season with salt and pepper to taste. Serve hot, garnished with fresh parsley and a squeeze of lemon juice for extra flavor.

INGREDIENT SUBSTITUTIONS:
- **Bulgur:** Couscous or quinoa can be used as an alternative to bulgur, offering a different texture but still providing a healthy, whole-grain base.
- **Zucchini:** Eggplant or summer squash can replace zucchini, maintaining the Mediterranean flavor profile and similar nutritional content.
- **Vegetable Broth:** For a non-vegetarian option, low-sodium chicken broth can be used, adding depth to the flavor while keeping the dish health-conscious.

Split Pea and Rice Soup

PREPARATION TIME: 10 minutes
COOKING TIME: 60 minutes
SERVINGS: 2

INGREDIENTS:
- 1/2 cup dried split peas, rinsed
- 1/4 cup brown rice, rinsed
- 1 carrot, diced
- 1 celery stalk, diced
- 1 small onion, diced
- 2 cloves garlic, minced
- 4 cups low-sodium vegetable broth
- 1 bay leaf
- 1 teaspoon dried thyme
- Salt and pepper to taste
- 1 tablespoon olive oil

NUTRITION PER SERVING:
- **Total Calories:** 320
- **Total Carbohydrates:** 55g
  - Dietary Fiber: 14g; Sugars: 5g
- **Protein:** 15g
- **Total Fat:** 4.5g
  - Saturated Fat: 1g
  - Unsaturated Fat: 3g
- **Sodium:** 300mg

INSTRUCTIONS:
1. **Sauté Vegetables:** In a large pot, heat the olive oil over medium heat. Add the onion, carrot, and celery, and sauté until the vegetables are soft, about 5 minutes. Add the garlic and cook for another minute until fragrant.
2. **Add Peas and Rice:** Add the split peas, brown rice, vegetable broth, bay leaf, and thyme to the pot. Stir to combine.
3. **Simmer:** Bring the mixture to a boil, then reduce heat to low. Cover and simmer for about 50 minutes, or until the split peas and rice are tender.
4. **Season:** Remove the bay leaf, and season the soup with salt and pepper to taste. If the soup is too thick, add more broth or water until desired consistency is reached.
5. **Serve:** Ladle the soup into bowls and serve hot.

INGREDIENT SUBSTITUTIONS:
- **Split Peas:** Lentils can be used instead of split peas, offering a similar texture and nutritional profile with a slight variation in cooking time.
- **Brown Rice:** Barley or farro can replace brown rice, both of which will add a chewy texture and rich flavor to the soup.
- **Vegetable Broth:** Chicken broth can be used for a non-vegetarian version, enhancing the soup's flavor while still keeping it healthy.

Chickpea Curry with Brown Rice

PREPARATION TIME: 15 minutes
COOKING TIME: 35 minutes
SERVINGS: 2

INGREDIENTS:

- 1 cup cooked brown rice
- 1 can (15 oz) chickpeas, drained and rinsed
- 1 tablespoon olive oil
- 1 medium onion, finely chopped
- 2 cloves garlic, minced
- 1 teaspoon grated ginger
- 1 medium tomato, diced
- 1 teaspoon turmeric
- 1 teaspoon cumin
- 1 teaspoon coriander
- 1/2 teaspoon chili powder (adjust to taste)
- 1 cup low-sodium vegetable broth
- 1/4 cup coconut milk
- Salt to taste
- Fresh cilantro for garnish

NUTRITION PER SERVING:

- **Total Calories:** 485
- **Total Carbohydrates:** 75g
  - Dietary Fiber: 15g; Sugars: 10g
- **Protein:** 15g
- **Total Fat:** 14g
  - Saturated Fat: 3g; Unsaturated Fat: 5g
- **Sodium:** 400mg

INSTRUCTIONS:

1. **Prepare Rice:** Cook brown rice according to package instructions.
2. **Sauté Onion and Spices:** In a large skillet, heat olive oil over medium heat. Add onion and sauté until translucent, about 5 minutes. Add garlic and ginger, cooking for another minute until fragrant.
3. **Add Spices and Tomato:** Stir in turmeric, cumin, coriander, and chili powder. Add diced tomato and cook until tomatoes soften, about 3 minutes.
4. **Simmer Chickpeas:** Add chickpeas and vegetable broth to the skillet. Simmer on low heat for 20 minutes, allowing the flavors to meld.
5. **Add Coconut Milk:** Stir in coconut milk and simmer for another 10 minutes. Adjust seasoning with salt.
6. **Serve:** Serve the curry over the cooked brown rice and garnish with fresh cilantro.

INGREDIENT SUBSTITUTIONS:

- **Chickpeas:** Can be substituted with lentils or black beans for a different protein source while maintaining similar texture and nutritional values.
- **Brown Rice:** Quinoa or millet can be used in place of brown rice, offering a different set of nutrients but similar fiber content.
- **Coconut Milk:** For a less rich option, light coconut milk or plain yogurt can be used, adjusting the curry's creaminess and calorie content.

Mexican Chicken Salad

PREPARATION TIME: 15 minutes
COOKING TIME: 10 minutes
SERVINGS: 2

INGREDIENTS:

- 2 boneless, skinless chicken breasts
- 1 tablespoon olive oil
- 1 teaspoon chili powder
- 1/2 teaspoon ground cumin
- Salt and pepper to taste
- 4 cups mixed greens (romaine, arugula, spinach)
- 1/2 cup cherry tomatoes, halved
- 1/4 cup diced red onion
- 1/4 cup chopped fresh cilantro
- 1/2 avocado, sliced
- 1 lime, juiced
- 1/4 cup low-fat Greek yogurt

NUTRITION PER SERVING:

- **Total Calories:** 350
- **Total Carbohydrates:** 15g
  - Dietary Fiber: 6g; Sugars: 5g
- **Protein:** 36g
- **Total Fat:** 16g
  - Saturated Fat: 3g; Unsaturated Fat: 7g
- **Sodium:** 250mg

INSTRUCTIONS:

1. **Marinate Chicken:** Season chicken breasts with chili powder, cumin, salt, and pepper. Drizzle with olive oil.
2. **Cook Chicken:** Heat a grill pan over medium-high heat. Grill chicken until thoroughly cooked and charred, about 5 minutes per side. Let it rest for a few minutes before slicing.
3. **Prepare Salad:** In a large bowl, combine mixed greens, cherry tomatoes, red onion, and cilantro.
4. **Assemble Salad:** Add sliced chicken to the salad. Top with avocado slices.
5. **Dressing:** In a small bowl, mix Greek yogurt and lime juice. Drizzle over the salad.
6. **Serve:** Toss everything together and serve immediately.

INGREDIENT SUBSTITUTIONS:

- **Chicken:** Substitute grilled tofu or tempeh for a vegetarian protein option while keeping similar macro profiles.
- **Greek Yogurt:** Use low-fat sour cream or a dairy-free yogurt to adjust the creaminess and fat content without significant changes to the overall flavor profile.
- **Avocado:** If unavailable, consider adding diced cucumber for a similar texture and refreshing taste.

Greek Salad with Grilled Salmon

PREPARATION TIME: 10 minutes
COOKING TIME: 10 minutes
TOTAL TIME: 20 minutes
SERVINGS: 2

INGREDIENTS:

- 2 salmon fillets (about 6 ounces each)
- 1 tablespoon olive oil
- Salt and pepper to taste
- 4 cups mixed salad greens (such as romaine and arugula)
- 1/2 cup cherry tomatoes, halved
- 1/4 cup sliced cucumbers
- 1/4 cup red onion, thinly sliced
- 1/4 cup Kalamata olives, pitted and halved
- 1/4 cup feta cheese, crumbled
- 2 tablespoons red wine vinegar

NUTRITION PER SERVING:

- **Total Calories:** 420
- **Total Carbohydrates:** 12g
  - Dietary Fiber: 3g; Sugars: 4g
- **Protein:** 35g
- **Total Fat:** 19g
  - Saturated Fat: 5g; Unsaturated Fat: 12g
- **Sodium:** 480mg

INSTRUCTIONS:

1. **Preheat Grill:** Heat a grill or grill pan to medium-high heat.
2. **Prepare Salmon:** Brush salmon fillets with olive oil and season with salt and pepper.
3. **Grill Salmon:** Grill salmon for about 4-5 minutes on each side or until cooked through and easily flakes with a fork.
4. **Assemble Salad:** In a large bowl, combine salad greens, cherry tomatoes, cucumbers, red onion, and Kalamata olives.
5. **Add Dressing:** Drizzle red wine vinegar over the salad and toss to combine.
6. **Serve:** Divide the salad among plates, top each with a grilled salmon fillet, and sprinkle with crumbled feta cheese.

INGREDIENT SUBSTITUTIONS:

- **Salmon:** Replace salmon with grilled chicken breast or tofu for a different protein choice with comparable nutritional value.
- **Feta Cheese:** Use reduced-fat feta or goat cheese for a lower fat option while maintaining a similar flavor.
- **Olives:** Swap Kalamata olives with black olives for a milder taste while keeping the heart-healthy fats.

Japanese Soba Noodle Bowl

PREPARATION TIME: 15 minutes
COOKING TIME: 10 minutes
SERVINGS: 2

INGREDIENTS:
- 4 ounces soba noodles (buckwheat noodles)
- 2 cups vegetable broth (low-sodium)
- 1/2 cup shiitake mushrooms, sliced
- 1 small carrot, julienned
- 1/2 red bell pepper, julienned
- 1/2 cup snap peas, trimmed
- 2 green onions, chopped
- 1 tablespoon soy sauce (low sodium)
- 1 teaspoon sesame oil
- 1 teaspoon grated ginger
- 1 garlic clove, minced
- 1 tablespoon toasted sesame seeds
- Fresh cilantro for garnish

NUTRITION PER SERVING:
- **Total Calories:** 320
- **Total Carbohydrates:** 52g
  - Dietary Fiber: 6g; Sugars: 5g
- **Protein:** 12g
- **Total Fat:** 7g
  - Saturated Fat: 1g; Unsaturated Fat: 4g
- **Sodium:** 480mg

INSTRUCTIONS:
1. **Cook Noodles:** Cook soba noodles according to package instructions, drain and rinse under cold water to stop cooking.
2. **Prepare Broth:** In a large pot, bring vegetable broth to a simmer. Add soy sauce, sesame oil, ginger, and garlic.
3. **Add Vegetables:** Add mushrooms, carrots, bell pepper, and snap peas to the broth. Simmer for about 5 minutes or until vegetables are tender.
4. **Combine:** Add cooked soba noodles to the pot and heat through.
5. **Serve:** Divide the noodle bowl into two servings, garnish with green onions, sesame seeds, and fresh cilantro.

INGREDIENT SUBSTITUTIONS:
- **Soba Noodles:** Replace soba noodles with whole wheat spaghetti or zucchini noodles for a lower carbohydrate option.
- **Soy Sauce:** Use tamari for a gluten-free alternative while maintaining a similar flavor profile.
- **Sesame Oil:** Substitute with extra virgin olive oil if desired, although it will slightly alter the traditional flavor.

Mediterranean Tuna Salad

PREPARATION TIME: 15 minutes
COOKING TIME: 0 minutes
SERVINGS: 2

INGREDIENTS:
- 1 can (5 ounces) tuna in water, drained
- 1/2 cup cherry tomatoes, halved
- 1/4 cup red onion, finely chopped
- 1/4 cup cucumber, chopped
- 1/4 cup black olives, sliced
- 2 tablespoons feta cheese, crumbled
- 1 tablespoon extra virgin olive oil
- 1 tablespoon lemon juice
- 1/2 teaspoon dried oregano
- Salt and pepper to taste
- Fresh parsley, chopped (for garnish)

NUTRITION PER SERVING:
- **Total Calories:** 210
- **Total Carbohydrates:** 8g
  - Dietary Fiber: 2g; Sugars: 3g
- **Protein:** 18g
- **Total Fat:** 12g
  - Saturated Fat: 3g; Unsaturated Fat: 9g
- **Sodium:** 580mg

INSTRUCTIONS:
1. **Mix Ingredients:** In a large bowl, combine the drained tuna, cherry tomatoes, red onion, cucumber, and black olives.
2. **Dress Salad:** Add olive oil, lemon juice, oregano, salt, and pepper. Toss well to coat all ingredients evenly.
3. **Add Cheese:** Sprinkle feta cheese over the salad and gently mix.
4. **Serve:** Divide the salad into two portions, garnish with fresh parsley, and serve chilled or at room temperature.

INGREDIENT SUBSTITUTIONS:
- **Tuna:** Swap out canned tuna for canned salmon or chicken for a different protein source with a similar nutritional profile.
- **Feta Cheese:** Replace feta with diced avocado to maintain the creaminess but alter the flavor profile slightly.
- **Black Olives:** Substitute with capers or green olives for a variation in flavor while keeping the Mediterranean essence.

Turkey Club Sandwich

PREPARATION TIME: 10 minutes
COOKING TIME: 0 minutes
TOTAL TIME: 10 minutes
SERVINGS: 2

INGREDIENTS:
- 4 slices whole grain bread, toasted
- 6 ounces sliced turkey breast (low sodium)
- 4 lettuce leaves
- 2 slices of tomato
- 2 teaspoons mayonnaise, low-fat
- 4 slices cooked bacon (turkey or low-sodium)
- Salt and pepper to taste

NUTRITION PER SERVING:
- **Total Calories:** 320
- **Total Carbohydrates:** 28g
  - Dietary Fiber: 5g
  - Sugars: 4g
- **Protein:** 28g
- **Total Fat:** 10.5g
  - Saturated Fat: 2g
  - Unsaturated Fat: 5g
- **Sodium:** 720mg

INSTRUCTIONS:
1. **Assemble the Sandwich:** Spread 1/2 teaspoon of low-fat mayonnaise on each slice of toasted whole grain bread.
2. **Layer Ingredients:** On two slices of bread, layer three ounces of turkey, two slices of bacon, one lettuce leaf, and one tomato slice. Season with salt and pepper.
3. **Top and Serve:** Place the remaining slices of bread on top to form sandwiches. Cut each sandwich in half and serve immediately.

INGREDIENT SUBSTITUTIONS:
- **Turkey Breast:** Substitute with grilled chicken breast for a similar protein content with a different flavor.
- **Mayonnaise:** Use mashed avocado as a healthier fat alternative that provides creaminess.
- **Bacon:** Opt for turkey bacon or even a plant-based bacon to reduce fat and sodium content.

Egg Salad on Rye

PREPARATION TIME: 15 minutes
COOKING TIME: 10 minutes
TOTAL TIME: 25 minutes
SERVINGS: 2

INGREDIENTS:
- 4 large eggs, hard-boiled
- 4 slices of rye bread
- 2 tablespoons Greek yogurt, plain
- 1 tablespoon mustard
- Salt and pepper to taste
- 1/4 cup chopped celery
- 1 tablespoon chopped chives

NUTRITION PER SERVING:
- **Total Calories:** 350
- **Total Carbohydrates:** 30g
  - Dietary Fiber: 5g
  - Sugars: 3g
- **Protein:** 20g
- **Total Fat:** 16g
  - Saturated Fat: 3g
  - Unsaturated Fat: 5g
- **Sodium:** 450mg

INSTRUCTIONS:
1. **Prepare the Eggs:** Peel the hard-boiled eggs and chop them coarsely.
2. **Make Egg Salad:** In a mixing bowl, combine chopped eggs, Greek yogurt, mustard, chopped celery, and chives. Season with salt and pepper to taste. Stir until all ingredients are well mixed.
3. **Assemble:** Evenly distribute the egg salad mixture onto two slices of rye bread. Top each with another slice of rye bread.
4. **Serve:** Cut each sandwich in half and serve.

INGREDIENT SUBSTITUTIONS:
- **Greek Yogurt:** Substitute with low-fat mayonnaise or mashed avocado for a different texture and taste while maintaining a similar nutritional profile.
- **Rye Bread:** Switch to whole grain or sprouted bread for an alternative with potentially lower glycemic index.
- **Mustard:** Try a different type of mustard or a small amount of horseradish for a flavor twist.

Caprese Sandwich

PREPARATION TIME: 10 minutes
COOKING TIME: 0 minutes
TOTAL TIME: 10 minutes
SERVINGS: 2
INGREDIENTS:
- 4 slices of whole grain bread
- 2 medium tomatoes, sliced
- 4 ounces fresh mozzarella cheese, sliced
- Fresh basil leaves
- 1 tablespoon extra virgin olive oil
- Balsamic vinegar reduction for drizzling
- Salt and pepper to taste

NUTRITION PER SERVING:
- **Total Calories:** 400
- **Total Carbohydrates:** 35g
  - Dietary Fiber: 6g
  - Sugars: 5g
- **Protein:** 18g
- **Total Fat:** 21g
  - Saturated Fat: 7g
  - Unsaturated Fat: 10g
- **Sodium:** 420mg

INSTRUCTIONS:
1. **Prepare Ingredients:** Slice the tomatoes and mozzarella cheese.
2. **Assemble Sandwiches:** Lay out two slices of bread. On each slice, layer fresh mozzarella slices, tomato slices, and basil leaves. Drizzle with olive oil and balsamic reduction. Season with salt and pepper to taste.
3. **Complete the Sandwich:** Top with the remaining slices of bread.
4. **Serve:** Cut each sandwich in half and serve immediately.

INGREDIENT SUBSTITUTIONS:
- **Whole Grain Bread:** Substitute with gluten-free bread if necessary, aiming for a variety with similar fiber content.
- **Mozzarella Cheese:** Try low-fat mozzarella to reduce the fat content while keeping the creamy texture.
- **Extra Virgin Olive Oil:** Avocado oil can be used for its similar monounsaturated fat profile and mild flavor.

Mediterranean Chicken Wrap

PREPARATION TIME: 20 minutes
COOKING TIME: 10 minutes
TOTAL TIME: 30 minutes
SERVINGS: 2
INGREDIENTS:
- 2 whole grain tortillas
- 1 cup cooked chicken breast, sliced or shredded
- 1/4 cup tzatziki sauce
- 1/2 cup chopped romaine lettuce
- 1/4 cup diced tomatoes
- 1/4 cup cucumber, diced
- 2 tablespoons red onion, finely chopped
- 2 tablespoons feta cheese, crumbled
- 1/4 cup roasted red peppers, sliced
- 2 tablespoons black olives, sliced
- Salt and pepper to taste

NUTRITION PER SERVING:
- **Total Calories:** 350
- **Total Carbohydrates:** 38g
  - Dietary Fiber: 6g
  - Sugars: 4g
- **Protein:** 28g
- **Total Fat:** 9g
  - Saturated Fat: 3g
  - Unsaturated Fat: 4g
- **Sodium:** 550mg

INSTRUCTIONS:
1. **Prepare Ingredients:** Cook the chicken breast if not already prepared. Slice or shred it into bite-sized pieces. Dice the tomatoes, cucumber, and red onion. Slice the roasted red peppers and olives.
2. **Assemble Wraps:** Lay out the whole grain tortillas on a flat surface. Spread the tzatziki sauce evenly over each tortilla.
3. **Add Fillings:** Layer the romaine lettuce, chicken, tomatoes, cucumber, red onion, roasted red peppers, black olives, and feta cheese evenly among the tortillas. Season with salt and pepper.
4. **Roll the Wraps:** Fold in the sides of each tortilla, then roll tightly to enclose the fillings. Cut in half diagonally.
5. **Serve:** Enjoy immediately, or wrap in foil to keep fresh for a packed lunch.

INGREDIENT SUBSTITUTIONS:
- **Chicken:** Swap for grilled tofu or chickpeas for a vegetarian option, maintaining high protein and lower fat content.
- **Tzatziki Sauce:** Use a hummus or avocado spread if tzatziki is not preferred or available.
- **Feta Cheese:** Omit or replace with a dairy-free cheese alternative to cater to vegan or lactose-intolerant diets.

Roast Beef and Horseradish Cream on Whole Grain Roll

PREPARATION TIME: 15 minutes
COOKING TIME: 0 minutes (assuming roast beef is pre-cooked)
TOTAL TIME: 15 minutes
SERVINGS: 2

INGREDIENTS:
- 2 whole grain rolls, halved
- 6 ounces thinly sliced roast beef
- 1/4 cup horseradish cream sauce
- 1/2 cup arugula
- 2 tablespoons red onion, thinly sliced

NUTRITION PER SERVING:
- **Total Calories:** 390
- **Total Carbohydrates:** 40g
  - Dietary Fiber: 5g
  - Sugars: 3g
- **Protein:** 25g
- **Total Fat:** 14g
  - Saturated Fat: 2g
  - Unsaturated Fat: 3g
- **Sodium:** 610mg

INSTRUCTIONS:
1. **Prepare Ingredients:** If not already done, thinly slice the roast beef and red onion. Wash and dry the arugula.
2. **Assemble Sandwiches:** Spread each half of the whole grain rolls with horseradish cream sauce. Layer the roast beef slices evenly among the rolls. Top with arugula and red onion slices.
3. **Serve:** Put the top half of each roll on and press lightly. Serve immediately, or wrap for a grab-and-go meal.

INGREDIENT SUBSTITUTIONS:
- **Roast Beef:** Can be substituted with grilled chicken or turkey for a leaner protein option, maintaining a similar nutritional profile.
- **Horseradish Cream Sauce:** Plain Greek yogurt mixed with prepared horseradish can be used as a lower-fat alternative to traditional horseradish cream sauce.
- **Whole Grain Roll:** For those who prefer a lower-carb option, swap the whole grain roll for a low-carb wrap or serve the ingredients over a bed of mixed greens.

Cucumber Boat with Tuna Salad

PREPARATION TIME: 10 minutes
COOKING TIME: 0 minutes
TOTAL TIME: 10 minutes
SERVINGS: 2

INGREDIENTS:
- 2 large cucumbers
- 1 can (6 ounces) tuna in water, drained
- 1/4 cup Greek yogurt
- 1 tablespoon lemon juice
- 2 tablespoons red onion, finely chopped
- 2 tablespoons celery, finely chopped
- Salt and pepper to taste
- Fresh dill or parsley for garnish (optional)

NUTRITION PER SERVING:
- **Total Calories:** 180
- **Total Carbohydrates:** 10g
  - Dietary Fiber: 2g
  - Sugars: 5g
- **Protein:** 20g
- **Total Fat:** 7g
  - Saturated Fat: 1g
  - Unsaturated Fat: 1g
- **Sodium:** 400mg

INSTRUCTIONS:
1. **Prepare the Cucumbers:** Cut the cucumbers in half lengthwise. Using a spoon, scoop out the seeds to create a hollow boat.
2. **Make Tuna Salad:** In a mixing bowl, combine the drained tuna, Greek yogurt, lemon juice, red onion, and celery. Stir until well mixed. Season with salt and pepper to taste.
3. **Fill Cucumber Boats:** Spoon the tuna salad evenly into the hollowed-out cucumber halves.
4. **Garnish and Serve:** Garnish with fresh dill or parsley if desired. Serve chilled as a refreshing and light meal.

INGREDIENT SUBSTITUTIONS:
- **Tuna:** Swap with canned salmon or chicken for a different flavor but similar nutritional values.
- **Greek Yogurt:** May be replaced with low-fat mayonnaise or sour cream depending on preference and dietary restrictions.
- **Cucumbers:** For a different texture, use bell peppers cut in half as an alternative "boat."

Kale and Quinoa Salad

PREPARATION TIME: 15 minutes
COOKING TIME: 20 minutes
TOTAL TIME: 35 minutes
SERVINGS: 2

INGREDIENTS:

- 1/2 cup quinoa, uncooked
- 1 cup water
- 2 cups chopped kale, stems removed
- 1/2 cup cherry tomatoes, halved
- 1/4 cup diced cucumber
- 1/4 cup red onion, finely chopped
- 2 tablespoons olive oil
- 2 tablespoons lemon juice
- Salt and pepper to taste
- 2 tablespoons crumbled feta cheese (optional)

NUTRITION PER SERVING:

- **Total Calories:** 280
- **Total Carbohydrates:** 35g
  - Dietary Fiber: 5g; Sugars: 3g
- **Protein:** 8g
- **Total Fat:** 12g
  - Saturated Fat: 3g
  - Unsaturated Fat: 7g
- **Sodium:** 150mg

INSTRUCTIONS:

1. **Cook Quinoa:** Rinse the quinoa under cold water. In a small saucepan, bring 1 cup of water to a boil. Add the quinoa, reduce heat to low, cover, and simmer for 15-20 minutes, or until all water is absorbed. Remove from heat and let stand covered for 5 minutes. Fluff with a fork and allow to cool.
2. **Prepare the Kale:** While the quinoa is cooking, place chopped kale in a large bowl. Add a pinch of salt and massage the kale with your hands for about 2 minutes to soften the leaves.
3. **Combine Ingredients:** Add the cooked and cooled quinoa to the kale along with cherry tomatoes, cucumber, and red onion.
4. **Dressing:** In a small bowl, whisk together olive oil and lemon juice, season with salt and pepper. Pour the dressing over the salad and toss to combine.
5. **Serve:** Divide the salad into two portions, sprinkle with feta cheese if using, and serve immediately.

INGREDIENT SUBSTITUTIONS:

- **Quinoa:** Substitute with farro or bulgur for a different texture and similar nutritional content.
- **Kale:** Spinach or arugula can be used as an alternative green for a different flavor profile.
- **Feta Cheese:** Omit for a dairy-free option or replace with diced avocado.

Broccoli and Chicken Pasta Salad

PREPARATION TIME: 15 minutes
COOKING TIME: 20 minutes
SERVINGS: 2

INGREDIENTS:

- 1 cup whole wheat pasta, uncooked
- 1 cup broccoli florets
- 1/2 cup cooked and shredded chicken breast
- 1/4 cup red bell pepper, diced
- 1/4 cup low-fat Greek yogurt
- 1 tablespoon olive oil
- 1 tablespoon white wine vinegar
- 1/2 teaspoon Dijon mustard
- Salt and pepper to taste
- 2 tablespoons chopped fresh parsley

NUTRITION PER SERVING:

- **Total Calories:** 350
- **Total Carbohydrates:** 42g
  - Dietary Fiber: 7g; Sugars: 3g
- **Protein:** 24g
- **Total Fat:** 9g
  - Saturated Fat: 2g
  - Unsaturated Fat: 5g
- **Sodium:** 190mg

INSTRUCTIONS:

1. **Cook Pasta:** Bring a large pot of water to a boil. Add the whole wheat pasta and cook according to package instructions until al dente. Drain and rinse under cold water to cool.
2. **Steam Broccoli:** While the pasta is cooking, steam the broccoli florets for about 3-4 minutes until tender but still crisp. Rinse under cold water to stop the cooking process.
3. **Prepare Dressing:** In a small bowl, whisk together Greek yogurt, olive oil, white wine vinegar, Dijon mustard, salt, and pepper until smooth.
4. **Combine Ingredients:** In a large bowl, combine the cooked pasta, steamed broccoli, shredded chicken, and red bell pepper. Pour the dressing over the salad and toss to coat evenly.
5. **Serve:** Sprinkle chopped parsley over the salad before serving.

INGREDIENT SUBSTITUTIONS:

- **Whole Wheat Pasta:** Substitute with chickpea pasta or lentil pasta for a gluten-free option and to increase protein content.
- **Chicken Breast:** Canned tuna or grilled tofu can be used as a substitute to vary protein sources without affecting the overall nutritional balance.
- **Greek Yogurt:** For a dairy-free alternative, use a plant-based yogurt like almond or soy yogurt.

Balsamic Glazed Salmon

PREPARATION TIME: 10 minutes
COOKING TIME: 15 minutes
TOTAL TIME: 25 minutes
SERVINGS: 2

INGREDIENTS:
- 2 salmon fillets (about 6 ounces each)
- 2 tablespoons balsamic vinegar
- 1 tablespoon olive oil
- 1 teaspoon honey (or a sweetener suitable for diabetics, like stevia equivalent)
- 1 clove garlic, minced
- Salt and pepper to taste
- Fresh herbs (like dill or parsley), for garnish

NUTRITION PER SERVING:
- **Total Calories:** 300
- **Total Carbohydrates:** 6g
  - Dietary Fiber: 0g
  - Sugars: 5g
- **Protein:** 23g
- **Total Fat:** 20g
  - Saturated Fat: 1.5g
  - Unsaturated Fat: 9g
- **Sodium:** 180mg

INSTRUCTIONS:
1. **Preheat Oven:** Preheat your oven to 400°F (200°C).
2. **Prepare Glaze:** In a small bowl, mix together balsamic vinegar, olive oil, honey (or stevia), and minced garlic.
3. **Season Salmon:** Place the salmon fillets on a baking tray lined with parchment paper. Brush the balsamic glaze over the salmon fillets. Season with salt and pepper.
4. **Bake:** Place the salmon in the oven and bake for 12-15 minutes, or until the salmon is cooked through and flakes easily with a fork.
5. **Garnish and Serve:** Remove from the oven and garnish with fresh herbs before serving.

INGREDIENT SUBSTITUTIONS:
- **Honey:** Use stevia or another low-glycemic sweetener to reduce the sugar content while maintaining the slight sweetness of the glaze.
- **Salmon:** Can be substituted with other fatty fish like mackerel or trout, which also provide healthy omega-3 fatty acids.
- **Balsamic Vinegar:** For a different flavor profile, apple cider vinegar or red wine vinegar can be used, which may alter the taste but keep the nutritional values similar.

Cucumber and Avocado Salad with Lemon Dressing

PREPARATION TIME: 10 minutes
COOKING TIME: 0 minutes
TOTAL TIME: 10 minutes
SERVINGS: 2

INGREDIENTS:
- 2 medium cucumbers, peeled and thinly sliced
- 1 ripe avocado, diced
- 1/4 cup diced red onion
- 2 tablespoons chopped fresh dill
- 2 tablespoons lemon juice
- 1 tablespoon olive oil
- Salt and pepper to taste

NUTRITION PER SERVING:
- **Total Calories:** 240
- **Total Carbohydrates:** 15g
  - Dietary Fiber: 7g
  - Sugars: 4g
- **Protein:** 3g
- **Total Fat:** 19g
  - Saturated Fat: 2g
  - Unsaturated Fat: 10g
- **Sodium:** 10mg

INSTRUCTIONS:
1. **Prepare the Salad:** In a large bowl, combine the sliced cucumbers, diced avocado, and red onion.
2. **Make the Dressing:** In a small bowl, whisk together lemon juice, olive oil, salt, and pepper.
3. **Combine and Serve:** Drizzle the dressing over the salad ingredients and gently toss to combine. Sprinkle chopped dill on top and serve immediately to prevent the avocado from browning.

INGREDIENT SUBSTITUTIONS:
- **Cucumber:** Zucchini or celery can be used for a different texture but similar fresh, crisp taste.
- **Avocado:** Cubed mozzarella or tofu cubes can replace avocado for those looking for a less fatty option but still wanting some creaminess.
- **Lemon Juice:** Apple cider vinegar or lime juice can be used as a substitute for a different acidic touch, maintaining the light and refreshing quality of the dressing.

Dinner Recipes

Zucchini Lasagna

SERVINGS: 2
PREPARATION TIME: 30 minutes
COOKING TIME: 45 minutes
TOTAL TIME: 1 hour 15 minutes

INGREDIENTS:

- 2 large zucchinis, sliced lengthwise into thin strips
- 200 grams lean ground turkey
- 1 cup low-carb marinara sauce
- 1/2 cup ricotta cheese
- 1/4 cup shredded mozzarella cheese (part-skim)
- 2 tablespoons grated Parmesan cheese
- 1 small onion, finely chopped
- 2 cloves garlic, minced
- 1 teaspoon olive oil
- 1/2 teaspoon dried basil
- 1/2 teaspoon dried oregano
- Salt and pepper to taste

NUTRITION PER SERVING:

- **Total Calories:** 350
- **Total Carbohydrates:** 14g
  - Dietary Fiber: 4g
  - Sugars: 8g
- **Protein:** 28g
- **Total Fat:** 20g
  - Saturated Fat: 8g
  - Unsaturated Fat: 10g
- **Sodium:** 480mg

INSTRUCTIONS:

1. **Preheat and Prep:** Preheat the oven to 375°F (190°C).
2. **Sauté Onions and Garlic:** In a skillet, heat the olive oil over medium heat. Add the chopped onion and minced garlic, sautéing until translucent.
3. **Brown the Meat:** Add the ground turkey, breaking it up with a spoon. Cook until browned. Season with salt, pepper, basil, and oregano.
4. **Simmer the Sauce:** Stir in the marinara sauce and simmer for about 10 minutes to blend the flavors.
5. **Assemble the First Layer:** In a baking dish, layer the zucchini slices to cover the bottom. Spread half of the meat sauce over the zucchini. Dot with half of the ricotta cheese.
6. **Add the Second Layer:** Repeat with another layer of zucchini, the remaining meat sauce, and ricotta cheese.
7. **Top and Bake:** Top with shredded mozzarella and grated Parmesan. Cover with foil and bake for 30 minutes.
8. **Final Baking:** Remove the foil and bake for an additional 15 minutes or until the cheese is golden and bubbly.
9. **Rest and Serve:** Let rest for 10 minutes before serving to allow the layers to set.

INGREDIENT SUBSTITUTIONS:

- **Ground Turkey:** Substitute with ground chicken or tofu for a similar protein profile.
- **Ricotta Cheese:** Use cottage cheese for a different texture but similar flavor.
- **Marinara Sauce:** Opt for diced tomatoes mixed with Italian herbs if low-carb marinara is unavailable.

Stuffed Bell Peppers

SERVINGS: 2
PREPARATION TIME: 15 minutes
COOKING TIME: 45 minutes

INGREDIENTS:
- 2 large bell peppers, any color
- 150 grams ground turkey (lean)
- 1/2 cup cooked quinoa
- 1/4 cup chopped onions
- 1 clove garlic, minced
- 1/2 cup chopped tomatoes
- 1/4 cup low-sodium chicken broth
- 2 tablespoons chopped fresh parsley
- 1/4 teaspoon salt
- 1/4 teaspoon black pepper
- 1/4 teaspoon smoked paprika
- 2 tablespoons shredded part-skim mozzarella cheese

NUTRITION PER SERVING:
- **Total Calories:** 320
- **Total Carbohydrates:** 23g
  - Dietary Fiber: 5g; Sugars: 7g
- **Protein:** 25g
- **Total Fat:** 15g
  - Saturated Fat: 5g; Unsaturated Fat: 8g
- **Sodium:** 340mg

INSTRUCTIONS:
1. **Prepare the Peppers:** Preheat the oven to 350°F (175°C). Cut the tops off the bell peppers and remove the seeds and membranes. Set aside.
2. **Cook the Filling:** Heat a skillet over medium heat. Add the ground turkey, onion, and garlic, cooking until the meat is browned and the onions are soft.
3. **Mix Ingredients:** Stir in the tomatoes, cooked quinoa, chicken broth, parsley, salt, pepper, and paprika. Cook until everything is heated through and slightly reduced, about 5 minutes.
4. **Stuff the Peppers:** Spoon the filling into the hollowed-out bell peppers. Place the stuffed peppers upright in a baking dish.
5. **Bake:** Cover with foil and bake for 30 minutes. Uncover, top each pepper with mozzarella, and bake for another 15 minutes or until the cheese is melted and bubbly.
6. **Serve:** Allow to cool slightly before serving.

INGREDIENT SUBSTITUTIONS:
- **Ground Turkey:** Can be substituted with ground chicken or crumbled tofu for a similar nutritional profile.
- **Quinoa:** Brown rice or bulgur wheat can be used as alternatives, adjusting the cooking time as necessary.
- **Mozzarella Cheese:** Try using feta cheese for a tangier flavor or vegan cheese to make it dairy-free.

Spinach and Mushroom Stuffed Chicken Breast

SERVINGS: 2
PREPARATION TIME: 20 minutes
COOKING TIME: 30 minutes

INGREDIENTS:
- 2 boneless, skinless chicken breasts
- 1 cup fresh spinach, chopped
- 1/2 cup mushrooms, finely chopped
- 1 clove garlic, minced
- 2 tablespoons low-fat cream cheese
- 1 tablespoon olive oil
- 1/4 teaspoon salt
- 1/4 teaspoon black pepper
- 1/2 teaspoon dried thyme

NUTRITION PER SERVING:
- **Total Calories:** 295
- **Total Carbohydrates:** 4g
  - Dietary Fiber: 1g; Sugars: 1g
- **Protein:** 31g
- **Total Fat:** 16g
  - Saturated Fat: 4g
  - Unsaturated Fat: 10g
- **Sodium:** 370mg

INSTRUCTIONS:
1. **Prepare the Chicken:** Preheat the oven to 375°F (190°C). Using a sharp knife, slice each chicken breast horizontally to create a pocket, being careful not to cut all the way through.
2. **Cook the Filling:** Heat olive oil in a pan over medium heat. Add garlic, mushrooms, and spinach. Sauté until the mushrooms are soft and the spinach has wilted. Remove from heat and let cool slightly. Mix in the cream cheese, salt, pepper, and thyme.
3. **Stuff the Chicken:** Spoon the spinach and mushroom mixture into each chicken breast pocket. Secure with toothpicks if necessary.
4. **Cook the Chicken:** Bake the stuffed chicken breasts in a preheated oven for 25-30 minutes until cooked through and juices run clear.
5. **Serve:** Remove the toothpicks and serve hot.

INGREDIENT SUBSTITUTIONS:
- **Low-fat Cream Cheese:** Use Greek yogurt or ricotta cheese for a different texture and slightly altered flavor profile but maintaining a similar nutritional content.
- **Mushrooms:** Portobello or shiitake mushrooms can replace the regular mushrooms for a richer flavor.
- **Spinach:** Kale or Swiss chard are excellent alternatives with similar nutritional benefits.

Eggplant Parmesan

SERVINGS: 2
PREPARATION TIME: 15 minutes
COOKING TIME: 45 minutes
INGREDIENTS:
- 1 large eggplant, sliced into 1/2-inch thick rounds
- 1 cup crushed tomatoes
- 1 clove garlic, minced
- 1/2 cup shredded mozzarella cheese (low-fat)
- 2 tablespoons grated Parmesan cheese
- 1 teaspoon olive oil
- 1/2 teaspoon dried oregano
- 1/2 teaspoon dried basil
- Salt and pepper, to taste
- Fresh basil leaves, for garnish

NUTRITION PER SERVING:
- **Total Calories:** 220
- **Total Carbohydrates:** 20g
  - Dietary Fiber: 6g; Sugars: 12g
- **Protein:** 12g
- **Total Fat:** 10g
  - Saturated Fat: 3g
  - Unsaturated Fat: 5g
- **Sodium:** 450mg

INSTRUCTIONS:
1. **Prepare the Eggplant:** Preheat the oven to 375°F (190°C). Lightly salt the eggplant slices and let them sit for 10 minutes. Pat dry with paper towels to remove excess moisture.
2. **Sauté Garlic:** In a small saucepan, heat olive oil over medium heat. Add garlic and sauté until fragrant, about 1 minute.
3. **Prepare the Tomato Sauce:** Add crushed tomatoes, oregano, and dried basil to the saucepan. Season with salt and pepper. Simmer for 10 minutes until slightly thickened.
4. **Assemble the Eggplant Parmesan:** In a baking dish, layer half of the eggplant slices. Spoon half of the tomato sauce over the slices and sprinkle with half of the mozzarella. Repeat with the remaining eggplant, sauce, and mozzarella. Top with Parmesan cheese.
5. **Bake:** Bake in the preheated oven for 25-30 minutes, or until the cheese is bubbly and golden brown.
6. **Serve:** Garnish with fresh basil leaves before serving.

INGREDIENT SUBSTITUTIONS:
- **Mozzarella Cheese:** Opt for vegan cheese to reduce cholesterol and fat, maintaining a similar mouthfeel and melting quality.
- **Crushed Tomatoes:** Freshly chopped tomatoes can be used for a fresher taste; adjust cooking time accordingly.
- **Eggplant:** Zucchini can be used as a lower carbohydrate alternative, altering texture but keeping a similar flavor profile.

Cauliflower Mac and Cheese

SERVINGS: 2
PREPARATION TIME: 10 minutes
COOKING TIME: 20 minutes
INGREDIENTS:
- 1 large head of cauliflower, cut into small florets
- 1 cup shredded cheddar cheese (low-fat)
- 1/4 cup grated Parmesan cheese
- 1/2 cup unsweetened almond milk
- 1 tablespoon cream cheese (low-fat)
- 1/2 teaspoon garlic powder
- 1/2 teaspoon onion powder
- 1/2 teaspoon mustard powder
- Salt and pepper, to taste
- Fresh parsley, chopped, for garnish

NUTRITION PER SERVING:
- **Total Calories:** 290
- **Total Carbohydrates:** 18g
  - Dietary Fiber: 5g; Sugars: 8g
- **Protein:** 18g
- **Total Fat:** 18g
  - Saturated Fat: 9g
  - Unsaturated Fat: 6g
- **Sodium:** 450mg

INSTRUCTIONS:
1. **Precook Cauliflower:** Bring a large pot of water to a boil. Add the cauliflower florets and cook for 5-7 minutes until tender but still firm. Drain well.
2. **Prepare the Cheese Sauce:** In a saucepan, heat the almond milk over medium heat. Whisk in the cream cheese until smooth. Add garlic powder, onion powder, and mustard powder. Season with salt and pepper.
3. **Combine Ingredients:** Add the drained cauliflower to the saucepan with the cheese sauce. Stir in the cheddar cheese and Parmesan until the cheeses are melted and the cauliflower is well coated.
4. **Broil for Finish:** Transfer the cauliflower and cheese mixture to a baking dish. Place under a broiler for 2-3 minutes or until the top is golden and bubbly.
5. **Garnish and Serve:** Sprinkle chopped parsley over the top before serving.

INGREDIENT SUBSTITUTIONS:
- **Cheddar Cheese:** Use vegan or dairy-free cheese to lower cholesterol and lactose content.
- **Almond Milk:** Coconut milk can be substituted for a different flavor profile.
- **Cauliflower:** Broccoli can be used instead of cauliflower for a variation in flavor and texture.

Garlic Lemon Butter Salmon

SERVINGS: 2
PREPARATION TIME: 5 minutes
COOKING TIME: 15 minutes
TOTAL TIME: 20 minutes
INGREDIENTS:

- 2 salmon fillets (6 ounces each)
- 2 tablespoons unsalted butter
- 1 tablespoon olive oil
- 2 garlic cloves, minced
- Juice of 1 lemon
- 1 teaspoon lemon zest
- Salt and pepper, to taste
- Fresh parsley, chopped, for garnish

NUTRITION PER SERVING:

- **Total Calories:** 350
- **Total Carbohydrates:** 3g
  - Dietary Fiber: 0.5g
  - Sugars: 0.5g
- **Protein:** 34g
- **Total Fat:** 23g
  - Saturated Fat: 8g
  - Unsaturated Fat: 12g
- **Sodium:** 110mg

INSTRUCTIONS:

1. **Preheat the Pan:** Heat the olive oil in a large skillet over medium heat.
2. **Prepare the Salmon:** Season the salmon fillets with salt and pepper on both sides. Place them skin side down in the skillet. Cook for 5 minutes.
3. **Make the Garlic Lemon Butter:** In a small saucepan, melt the butter. Add the minced garlic and cook until fragrant, about 1 minute. Remove from heat and stir in the lemon juice and zest.
4. **Flip and Finish:** Flip the salmon in the skillet and pour the garlic lemon butter over the fillets. Cook for another 5-7 minutes, or until the salmon is fully cooked and flakes easily with a fork.
5. **Garnish and Serve:** Remove from heat, garnish with chopped parsley, and serve immediately.

INGREDIENT SUBSTITUTIONS:

- **Salmon:** Trout or mackerel can be used instead of salmon to provide a similar fatty acid profile and flaky texture.
- **Butter:** Use a low-fat or plant-based butter alternative to reduce saturated fat content.
- **Lemon Juice:** Lime juice can be substituted for a slightly different citrus profile without significantly affecting the dish's flavor or carbohydrate content.

Lemon Garlic Herb Tilapia

SERVINGS: 2
PREPARATION TIME: 10 minutes
COOKING TIME: 15 minutes
TOTAL TIME: 25 minutes
INGREDIENTS:

- 2 tilapia fillets (about 6 ounces each)
- 2 tablespoons olive oil
- 2 cloves garlic, finely minced
- 1 tablespoon fresh lemon juice
- 1 teaspoon dried herbs (such as thyme, parsley, or dill)
- Salt and pepper, to taste
- Lemon slices and fresh herbs, for garnish

NUTRITION PER SERVING:

- **Total Calories:** 290
- **Total Carbohydrates:** 2g
  - Dietary Fiber: 0.5g
  - Sugars: 0.5g
- **Protein:** 34g
- **Total Fat:** 16g
  - Saturated Fat: 2.5g
  - Unsaturated Fat: 10g
- **Sodium:** 125mg

INSTRUCTIONS:

1. **Preheat the Oven:** Preheat your oven to 375 degrees Fahrenheit.
2. **Prepare the Marinade:** In a small bowl, mix together olive oil, minced garlic, lemon juice, dried herbs, salt, and pepper.
3. **Marinate the Fish:** Place the tilapia fillets in a shallow baking dish. Pour the marinade over the fillets, making sure they are well-coated. Let them marinate for about 5 minutes.
4. **Bake:** Place the dish in the oven and bake for 10-12 minutes, or until the fish flakes easily with a fork.
5. **Serve:** Remove from the oven and garnish with fresh lemon slices and additional herbs. Serve immediately.

INGREDIENT SUBSTITUTIONS:

- **Tilapia:** If you prefer a different type of fish, try cod or halibut as they both adapt well to this cooking method.
- **Lemon Juice:** For a different citrus twist, replace lemon juice with orange or lime juice.
- **Herbs:** Depending on what's available or your preference, you can use fresh herbs instead of dried for a more vibrant flavor.

Grilled Tuna Steaks with Olive Tapenade

SERVINGS: 2
PREPARATION TIME: 10 minutes
COOKING TIME: 10 minutes
TOTAL TIME: 20 minutes
INGREDIENTS:
- 2 tuna steaks (about 6 ounces each)
- 2 tablespoons olive oil
- Salt and pepper, to taste
- 1/4 cup pitted Kalamata olives
- 1 tablespoon capers
- 2 cloves garlic
- 1 tablespoon lemon juice
- 2 tablespoons chopped fresh parsley

NUTRITION PER SERVING:
- **Total Calories:** 350
- **Total Carbohydrates:** 4g
  - Dietary Fiber: 2g
  - Sugars: 1g
- **Protein:** 34g
- **Total Fat:** 22g
  - Saturated Fat: 3g
  - Unsaturated Fat: 15g
- **Sodium:** 400mg

INSTRUCTIONS:
1. **Preheat the Grill:** Preheat your grill to medium-high heat.
2. **Prepare the Tuna:** Brush the tuna steaks lightly with one tablespoon of olive oil and season with salt and pepper.
3. **Make the Tapenade:** In a food processor, combine the Kalamata olives, capers, garlic, remaining olive oil, lemon juice, and parsley. Pulse until the mixture is coarsely chopped but not pureed.
4. **Grill the Tuna:** Place the tuna steaks on the hot grill and cook for about 4-5 minutes on each side or until desired doneness is reached.
5. **Serve:** Top each grilled tuna steak with half of the olive tapenade and serve immediately.

INGREDIENT SUBSTITUTIONS:
- **Tuna Steaks:** If you prefer a different type of fish, try salmon or swordfish steaks as good alternatives that grill well.
- **Kalamata Olives:** Green olives or black olives can be used instead, depending on your preference or availability.
- **Capers:** If you're not a fan of capers, chopped pickles or a small amount of chopped anchovy can add a similar briny flavor.

Cod in Parchment with Asparagus

SERVINGS: 2
PREPARATION TIME: 10 minutes
COOKING TIME: 20 minutes
TOTAL TIME: 30 minutes
INGREDIENTS:
- 2 cod fillets (6 ounces each)
- 1 bunch asparagus, trimmed
- 1 lemon, thinly sliced
- 2 tablespoons olive oil
- Salt and pepper, to taste
- Fresh herbs (such as dill or parsley), chopped

NUTRITION PER SERVING:
- **Total Calories:** 295
- **Total Carbohydrates:** 6g
  - Dietary Fiber: 3g
  - Sugars: 2g
- **Protein:** 34g
- **Total Fat:** 14g
  - Saturated Fat: 2g
  - Unsaturated Fat: 10g
- **Sodium:** 200mg

INSTRUCTIONS:
1. **Preheat the Oven:** Preheat your oven to 400°F (200°C).
2. **Prepare the Parchment:** Cut two large pieces of parchment paper, enough to wrap each fillet and its accompaniments.
3. **Assemble the Packets:** Place half of the asparagus in the middle of each piece of parchment. Top with a cod fillet. Drizzle each with one tablespoon of olive oil and season with salt and pepper. Place a few lemon slices and sprinkle fresh herbs over the top.
4. **Fold the Parchment:** Bring the edges of the parchment paper together and fold over several times to seal. Tuck in the ends to form a sealed packet.
5. **Bake:** Place the packets on a baking sheet and bake in the preheated oven for about 20 minutes or until the fish is cooked through and vegetables are tender.
6. **Serve:** Carefully open the packets (watch for steam), and serve immediately.

INGREDIENT SUBSTITUTIONS:
- **Cod:** If cod is not available, any white fish like halibut or tilapia can be used as a substitute.
- **Asparagus:** Green beans or thinly sliced zucchini are great alternatives to asparagus and cook in a similar time.
- **Lemon:** Orange slices can be used for a slightly sweeter citrus flavor.

Seafood Paella with Brown Rice

SERVINGS: 2
PREPARATION TIME: 15 minutes
COOKING TIME: 40 minutes
TOTAL TIME: 55 minutes
INGREDIENTS:

- 1 cup brown rice, uncooked
- 2 cups low-sodium chicken or vegetable broth
- 1 small onion, finely chopped
- 2 cloves garlic, minced
- 1/2 cup diced tomatoes, canned or fresh
- 1/2 teaspoon saffron threads
- 1/2 teaspoon smoked paprika
- 4 ounces shrimp, peeled and deveined
- 4 ounces scallops
- 4 ounces mussels, cleaned and debearded
- 1/2 cup frozen peas, thawed
- 1 lemon, cut into wedges
- 2 tablespoons olive oil
- Salt and pepper, to taste
- Fresh parsley, chopped (for garnish)

NUTRITION PER SERVING:

- **Total Calories:** 510
- **Total Carbohydrates:** 68g
  - Dietary Fiber: 8g
  - Sugars: 4g
- **Protein:** 33g
- **Total Fat:** 15g
  - Saturated Fat: 2g
  - Unsaturated Fat: 10g
- **Sodium:** 460mg

INSTRUCTIONS:

1. **Prepare the Rice:** In a large skillet or paella pan, heat 1 tablespoon olive oil over medium heat. Add the onion and garlic, sautéing until onion is translucent. Stir in the rice, saffron, smoked paprika, and diced tomatoes. Cook for a couple of minutes.
2. **Add Broth and Simmer:** Pour in the broth and bring to a boil. Reduce heat to low, cover, and simmer for about 30 minutes, or until the rice is almost tender.
3. **Cook the Seafood:** In a separate pan, heat the remaining olive oil over medium heat. Add the shrimp, scallops, and mussels, cooking until the seafood is just done (shrimp should be pink, and mussels should open).
4. **Combine Ingredients:** Add the cooked seafood, including any juices, to the rice. Add the peas and gently mix to combine everything. Cover and cook for an additional 10 minutes.
5. **Garnish and Serve:** Remove from heat. Season with salt and pepper to taste. Garnish with fresh parsley and serve with lemon wedges.

INGREDIENT SUBSTITUTIONS:

- **Brown Rice:** Quinoa can be used for a higher protein alternative with a similar nutty flavor.
- **Seafood:** Chicken or firm tofu can be used as alternatives for a different type of protein if seafood is not preferred.

Chickpea Vegetable Curry

SERVINGS: 2
PREPARATION TIME: 10 minutes
COOKING TIME: 25 minutes
INGREDIENTS:

- 1 can (15 oz) chickpeas, drained and rinsed
- 1 medium onion, chopped
- 2 cloves garlic, minced
- 1 tablespoon ginger, minced
- 1 medium carrot, diced
- 1 small bell pepper, chopped
- 1 medium zucchini, chopped
- 2 tablespoons tomato paste
- 1 can (14 oz) coconut milk, light
- 1 tablespoon curry powder
- 1/2 teaspoon turmeric powder
- 1/2 teaspoon cumin
- Salt and pepper, to taste
- 2 tablespoons olive oil
- Fresh cilantro, chopped (for garnish)

NUTRITION PER SERVING:

- **Total Calories:** 380
- **Total Carbohydrates:** 45g
  - Dietary Fiber: 10g; Sugars: 8g
- **Protein:** 12g
- **Total Fat:** 18g
  - Saturated Fat: 8g; Unsaturated Fat: 7g
- **Sodium:** 480mg

INSTRUCTIONS:

1. **Sauté Aromatics:** In a large skillet or saucepan, heat olive oil over medium heat. Add onion, garlic, and ginger, sautéing until onion is translucent.
2. **Add Vegetables:** Stir in the carrot, bell pepper, and zucchini. Cook for about 5 minutes, or until vegetables start to soften.
3. **Mix in Spices and Tomato Paste:** Add curry powder, turmeric, cumin, and tomato paste to the pan, stirring to coat the vegetables well.
4. **Combine with Chickpeas and Coconut Milk:** Add the chickpeas and coconut milk to the pan. Bring the mixture to a simmer, then reduce heat and let cook for 15 minutes, stirring occasionally.
5. **Season and Garnish:** Season the curry with salt and pepper to taste. Remove from heat and garnish with chopped cilantro.

INGREDIENT SUBSTITUTIONS:

- **Chickpeas:** Lentils can be used as a high-protein alternative with similar textural benefits.
- **Coconut Milk:** For a creamier texture with reduced fat, unsweetened almond milk mixed with a teaspoon of cornstarch can be used.

Tofu Stir-Fry with Broccoli and Bell Pepper

SERVINGS: 2
PREPARATION TIME: 10 minutes
COOKING TIME: 15 minutes
INGREDIENTS:

- 8 oz firm tofu, drained and cubed
- 1 large head of broccoli, cut into florets
- 1 red bell pepper, sliced
- 2 cloves garlic, minced
- 2 tablespoons low-sodium soy sauce
- 1 tablespoon sesame oil
- 1 teaspoon ginger, grated
- Olive oil for cooking
- Sesame seeds for garnish

NUTRITION PER SERVING:

- **Total Calories:** 280
- **Total Carbohydrates:** 20g
  - Dietary Fiber: 5g; Sugars: 5g
- **Protein:** 16g
- **Total Fat:** 18g
  - Saturated Fat: 2g;
  - Unsaturated Fat: 12g
- **Sodium:** 350mg

INSTRUCTIONS:

1. **Prepare Tofu:** Pat the tofu dry and cut into cubes.
2. **Heat Oil:** In a large skillet or wok, heat a drizzle of olive oil over medium heat.
3. **Cook Tofu:** Add tofu to the skillet and sauté until golden brown on all sides, about 5-7 minutes. Remove tofu and set aside.
4. **Sauté Vegetables:** In the same skillet, add a little more olive oil if needed, then add the garlic, ginger, broccoli, and bell pepper. Stir-fry for about 5 minutes, or until the vegetables are tender-crisp.
5. **Combine and Season:** Return the tofu to the skillet, add soy sauce and sesame oil, and stir well to combine. Cook for another 2 minutes to let flavors meld.
6. **Garnish:** Sprinkle with sesame seeds before serving.

INGREDIENT SUBSTITUTIONS:

- **Tofu:** Cubed chicken or shrimp can be used for a non-vegetarian protein option.
- **Soy Sauce:** Tamari or coconut aminos can be used as a gluten-free or lower sodium alternative.
- **Sesame Oil:** Flaxseed oil or another omega-rich oil can be used for a different flavor profile.

Butternut Squash Barley Risotto

SERVINGS: 2
PREPARATION TIME: 10 minutes
COOKING TIME: 55 minutes
INGREDIENTS:

- 1 cup peeled and diced butternut squash
- 3/4 cup pearl barley, rinsed
- 1 small onion, finely chopped
- 2 cloves garlic, minced
- 4 cups low-sodium vegetable broth, warmed
- 1/2 cup dry white wine (optional)
- 2 tablespoons olive oil
- 1/4 cup grated Parmesan cheese (optional)
- Salt and pepper to taste
- Fresh parsley, chopped (for garnish)

NUTRITION PER SERVING:

- **Total Calories:** 410
- **Total Carbohydrates:** 70g
  - Dietary Fiber: 15g
  - Sugars: 5g
- **Protein:** 12g
- **Total Fat:** 12g
  - Saturated Fat: 2g
  - Unsaturated Fat: 8g
- **Sodium:** 180mg

INSTRUCTIONS:

1. **Prepare Ingredients:** Heat 1 tablespoon of olive oil in a large skillet over medium heat. Add the diced butternut squash and sauté until slightly tender and golden, about 8-10 minutes. Remove from the skillet and set aside.
2. **Cook Barley:** In the same skillet, add another tablespoon of olive oil. Sauté the onion and garlic until the onion becomes translucent, about 3-4 minutes. Stir in the pearl barley and toast lightly for 2 minutes.
3. **Deglaze:** Pour in the white wine (if using) and let it simmer until the liquid has almost evaporated.
4. **Simmer:** Gradually add the warm vegetable broth, one cup at a time, stirring frequently. Allow the barley to absorb most of the broth before adding the next cup. Continue this process until the barley is creamy and al dente, about 40-45 minutes.
5. **Combine:** Return the cooked butternut squash to the skillet with the barley. Stir well to combine. Season with salt and pepper.
6. **Add Cheese:** If using Parmesan, stir it in until melted and incorporated.
7. **Serve:** Garnish with fresh parsley before serving.

INGREDIENT SUBSTITUTIONS:

- **Butternut Squash:** Can be substituted with pumpkin or sweet potatoes for a similar texture and flavor profile.
- **Pearl Barley:** For a gluten-free option, consider using quinoa or brown rice, noting that cooking times may vary.
- **Parmesan Cheese:** To make this recipe vegan, omit the cheese or use a vegan cheese alternative.

Portobello Mushroom Pizzas

SERVINGS: 2
PREPARATION TIME: 10 minutes
COOKING TIME: 20 minutes
INGREDIENTS:

- 4 large Portobello mushrooms, stems and gills removed
- 1/2 cup tomato sauce, no added sugar
- 1/2 cup shredded mozzarella cheese
- 1/4 cup chopped bell peppers
- 1/4 cup sliced black olives
- 1/4 cup finely chopped red onion
- 2 tablespoons olive oil
- Salt and pepper to taste
- Fresh basil leaves for garnish

NUTRITION PER SERVING:

- **Total Calories:** 250
- **Total Carbohydrates:** 15g
  - Dietary Fiber: 4g
  - Sugars: 6g
- **Protein:** 12g
- **Total Fat:** 18g
  - Saturated Fat: 4g
  - Unsaturated Fat: 12g
- **Sodium:** 400mg

INSTRUCTIONS:

1. **Preheat Oven:** Preheat your oven to 375°F (190°C).
2. **Prepare Mushrooms:** Brush the mushrooms with olive oil and season with salt and pepper. Place them on a baking sheet, gill-side up.
3. **Bake:** Place the mushrooms in the oven and bake for 10 minutes to release some of their moisture.
4. **Add Toppings:** Remove the mushrooms from the oven. Spread each mushroom with tomato sauce, then top with mozzarella, bell peppers, olives, and red onion.
5. **Bake Again:** Return the mushrooms to the oven and bake for another 10 minutes, or until the cheese is melted and bubbly.
6. **Garnish and Serve:** Garnish with fresh basil leaves before serving.

INGREDIENT SUBSTITUTIONS:

- **Tomato Sauce:** Use pesto or a low-carbohydrate marinara sauce for a different flavor.
- **Mozzarella Cheese:** Can be substituted with any cheese of your choice, such as feta for a tangier flavor or vegan cheese to make it dairy-free.
- **Toppings:** Feel free to swap out or add other vegetables like spinach or diced tomatoes, or add cooked ground turkey or chicken for extra protein.

Lentil Tacos with Homemade Salsa

SERVINGS: 2
PREPARATION TIME: 15 minutes
COOKING TIME: 20 minutes
INGREDIENTS:

- 1 cup cooked lentils
- 4 whole wheat or low-carb tortillas
- 1/2 cup diced tomatoes
- 1/4 cup diced red onion
- 1 small jalapeño, finely chopped (optional)
- 1/4 cup chopped fresh cilantro
- Juice of 1 lime
- 1 avocado, diced
- Salt and pepper to taste
- 1 teaspoon olive oil
- 1 teaspoon ground cumin
- 1/2 teaspoon chili powder

NUTRITION PER SERVING:

- **Total Calories:** 400
- **Total Carbohydrates:** 50g
  - Dietary Fiber: 15g; Sugars: 5g
- **Protein:** 20g
- **Total Fat:** 15g
  - Saturated Fat: 2g
  - Unsaturated Fat: 10g
- **Sodium:** 300mg

INSTRUCTIONS:

1. **Prepare the Salsa:** In a bowl, combine the tomatoes, red onion, jalapeño (if using), cilantro, half of the lime juice, and a pinch of salt. Mix well and set aside to let the flavors meld.
2. **Cook Lentils:** Heat olive oil in a pan over medium heat. Add cooked lentils, ground cumin, chili powder, and a pinch of salt and pepper. Cook for 5-7 minutes, stirring occasionally until the lentils are heated through and flavorful.
3. **Prepare Tortillas:** Warm the tortillas in a dry skillet over medium heat for about 30 seconds on each side or until they are pliable.
4. **Assemble Tacos:** Spoon an even amount of the lentil mixture onto each tortilla. Top with homemade salsa and diced avocado. Drizzle the remaining lime juice over the tacos.
5. **Serve:** Serve immediately, garnished with additional cilantro if desired.

INGREDIENT SUBSTITUTIONS:

- **Lentils:** Substitute with ground turkey or black beans for a different protein base.
- **Whole Wheat Tortillas:** Use corn tortillas for a gluten-free option or additional low-carb tortillas to further reduce carbohydrate intake.

Thai Basil Chicken

SERVINGS: 2
PREPARATION TIME: 10 minutes
COOKING TIME: 20 minutes
INGREDIENTS:

- 300 grams chicken breast, thinly sliced
- 1 tablespoon olive oil
- 2 cloves garlic, minced
- 1 small red bell pepper, sliced
- 1 medium onion, sliced
- 1 chili (optional), finely sliced
- 1 cup fresh basil leaves, preferably Thai basil
- 2 tablespoons low-sodium soy sauce
- 1 tablespoon fish sauce
- 1 teaspoon sweetener (such as stevia or a diabetic-friendly alternative)
- 1/2 teaspoon ground black pepper

NUTRITION PER SERVING:

- **Total Calories:** 290
- **Total Carbohydrates:** 10g
  - Dietary Fiber: 2g; Sugars: 4g
- **Protein:** 35g
- **Total Fat:** 12g
  - Saturated Fat: 2g; Unsaturated Fat: 8g
- **Sodium:** 600mg

INSTRUCTIONS:

1. **Prepare the Ingredients:** Mince the garlic, slice the bell pepper, onion, and chili. Set aside.
2. **Cook the Chicken:** Heat olive oil in a large skillet over medium-high heat. Add the chicken and stir-fry until it starts to brown, about 5-7 minutes.
3. **Add Vegetables:** Add the garlic, bell pepper, onion, and chili to the skillet. Cook for another 3-5 minutes until the vegetables are slightly tender.
4. **Season:** Lower the heat to medium. Add soy sauce, fish sauce, sweetener, and black pepper to the skillet. Stir well to combine all the ingredients.
5. **Finish with Basil:** Add the basil leaves, stir for another minute until the basil is wilted and the chicken is well-coated with the sauce.
6. **Serve:** Remove from heat and divide the mixture between two plates. Serve immediately.

INGREDIENT SUBSTITUTIONS:

- **Chicken Breast:** Substitute with tofu for a vegetarian version or turkey for a different flavor profile, keeping the protein content high.
- **Thai Basil:** If unavailable, substitute with regular basil for a slightly different but still delicious taste.
- **Soy Sauce:** Use tamari for a gluten-free option.

Indian Spiced Cauliflower and Chickpeas

SERVINGS: 2
PREPARATION TIME: 10 minutes
COOKING TIME: 25 minutes
INGREDIENTS:

- 1 medium cauliflower, cut into florets
- 1 can (15 oz) chickpeas, drained and rinsed
- 1 tablespoon olive oil
- 1 teaspoon cumin seeds
- 1 teaspoon turmeric powder
- 1/2 teaspoon coriander powder
- 1/2 teaspoon garam masala
- 1/4 teaspoon chili powder (adjust to taste)
- Salt to taste
- Fresh cilantro, chopped, for garnish

NUTRITION PER SERVING:

- **Total Calories:** 295
- **Total Carbohydrates:** 45g
  - Dietary Fiber: 12g
  - Sugars: 8g
- **Protein:** 14g
- **Total Fat:** 8g
  - Saturated Fat: 1g
  - Unsaturated Fat: 6g
- **Sodium:** 400mg

INSTRUCTIONS:

1. **Roast Cauliflower:** Preheat oven to 400°F (200°C). Toss cauliflower florets with half the olive oil, turmeric, coriander, and salt. Spread on a baking sheet and roast for 20 minutes, until tender and golden.
2. **Spice the Chickpeas:** While cauliflower roasts, heat the remaining olive oil in a skillet over medium heat. Add cumin seeds and let them sizzle for a few seconds. Add chickpeas, garam masala, and chili powder. Cook for 5 minutes, stirring frequently until chickpeas are golden and fragrant.
3. **Combine:** Mix roasted cauliflower with spiced chickpeas in the skillet. Adjust seasoning as needed.
4. **Garnish and Serve:** Garnish with fresh cilantro before serving.

INGREDIENT SUBSTITUTIONS:

- **Chickpeas:** Can be substituted with cooked lentils for a different texture but similar nutritional profile.
- **Cauliflower:** Broccoli can be used as an alternative, offering a different flavor but maintaining a similar texture and nutritional benefits.
- **Olive Oil:** For a variation in flavor, coconut oil may be used; it has a higher smoke point and a subtly sweet flavor that pairs well with Indian spices.

Moroccan Vegetable Tagine

SERVINGS: 2
PREPARATION TIME: 15 minutes
COOKING TIME: 40 minutes

INGREDIENTS:

- 1 tablespoon olive oil
- 1 small onion, chopped
- 2 cloves garlic, minced
- 1 teaspoon ground cumin
- 1 teaspoon ground coriander
- 1/2 teaspoon cinnamon
- 1/2 teaspoon turmeric
- 1 large carrot, peeled and sliced
- 1 sweet potato, peeled and cubed
- 1 zucchini, cubed
- 1 bell pepper, any color, chopped
- 1 cup chickpeas, drained and rinsed
- 1 cup diced tomatoes, canned or fresh
- 1 cup vegetable broth, low sodium
- 2 tablespoons raisins
- Salt and pepper to taste
- Fresh cilantro, chopped, for garnish

NUTRITION PER SERVING:

- **Total Calories:** 330
- **Total Carbohydrates:** 55g
  - Dietary Fiber: 12g
  - Sugars: 18g
- **Protein:** 9g
- **Total Fat:** 7g
  - Saturated Fat: 1g
  - Unsaturated Fat: 5g
- **Sodium:** 300mg

INSTRUCTIONS:

1. **Sauté Aromatics:** In a large pot or tagine, heat olive oil over medium heat. Add onion and garlic, sautéing until onions are translucent, about 5 minutes.
2. **Spice it Up:** Stir in cumin, coriander, cinnamon, and turmeric, cooking for another minute until fragrant.
3. **Add Vegetables:** Add carrots, sweet potatoes, zucchini, and bell pepper to the pot, stirring to coat the vegetables with the spices.
4. **Simmer:** Add chickpeas, diced tomatoes, and vegetable broth. Bring to a simmer, then reduce heat and cover. Cook for about 30 minutes, or until vegetables are tender.
5. **Finish with Raisins:** Stir in raisins and season with salt and pepper. Cook for an additional 5 minutes.
6. **Serve:** Garnish with fresh cilantro before serving.

INGREDIENT SUBSTITUTIONS:

- **Sweet Potato:** Substitute with butternut squash for a similar texture and flavor.
- **Chickpeas:** Can be replaced with lentils for a different kind of protein and texture.
- **Raisins:** Try dried apricots or dates, chopped, for a variation in sweetness and nutrients.

Korean Beef Bowl with Vegetables

SERVINGS: 2
PREPARATION TIME: 15 minutes
COOKING TIME: 20 minutes
INGREDIENTS:

- 1/2 lb lean ground beef (90% lean)
- 2 cups mixed vegetables (carrots, bell peppers, and spinach)
- 1 tablespoon sesame oil
- 2 cloves garlic, minced
- 1 tablespoon fresh ginger, minced
- 2 tablespoons low-sodium soy sauce
- 1 tablespoon rice vinegar
- 1 teaspoon chili paste (adjust to taste)
- 2 green onions, thinly sliced
- 1 teaspoon sesame seeds
- 1/2 cup brown rice, cooked

NUTRITION PER SERVING:

- **Total Calories:** 460
- **Total Carbohydrates:** 38g
  - Dietary Fiber: 5g; Sugars: 5g
- **Protein:** 26g
- **Total Fat:** 22g
  - Saturated Fat: 5g
  - Unsaturated Fat: 14g
- **Sodium:** 480mg

INSTRUCTIONS:
1. **Cook Rice:** Prepare brown rice according to package instructions. Set aside.
2. **Sauté Vegetables:** In a large skillet, heat sesame oil over medium heat. Add garlic and ginger, sautéing until fragrant. Add the mixed vegetables and stir-fry until just tender, about 5-7 minutes. Remove vegetables and set aside.
3. **Cook Beef:** In the same skillet, add ground beef, breaking it apart with a spoon. Cook until browned and no longer pink.
4. **Combine Flavors:** Return vegetables to the skillet with the beef. Add soy sauce, rice vinegar, and chili paste. Stir well to combine and cook for another 5 minutes, allowing flavors to meld.
5. **Serve:** Divide cooked brown rice between two bowls. Top with the beef and vegetable mixture. Garnish with green onions and sesame seeds.

INGREDIENT SUBSTITUTIONS:
- **Ground Beef:** Substitute with ground turkey or ground chicken for a leaner option with similar protein content.
- **Brown Rice:** Quinoa can be used in place of brown rice to increase protein and fiber content while maintaining a low glycemic index.
- **Soy Sauce:** Coconut aminos can be used as a lower sodium alternative to soy sauce.

Italian Chicken Skillet with Fresh Herbs

SERVINGS: 2
PREPARATION TIME: 10 minutes
COOKING TIME: 20 minutes
INGREDIENTS:

- 2 boneless, skinless chicken breasts
- 1 tablespoon olive oil
- 1/2 cup cherry tomatoes, halved
- 1/2 cup bell peppers, sliced
- 2 cloves garlic, minced
- 1/4 cup low-sodium chicken broth
- 1/4 cup chopped fresh basil
- 1 tablespoon chopped fresh oregano
- 1 teaspoon chopped fresh thyme
- Salt and pepper to taste
- Fresh parsley, chopped for garnish

NUTRITION PER SERVING:

- **Total Calories:** 295
- **Total Carbohydrates:** 8g
  - Dietary Fiber: 2g; Sugars: 4g
- **Protein:** 28g
- **Total Fat:** 16g
  - Saturated Fat: 2.5g
  - Unsaturated Fat: 12g
- **Sodium:** 170mg

INSTRUCTIONS:
1. **Prepare Ingredients:** Pat the chicken breasts dry and season with salt and pepper.
2. **Cook Chicken:** Heat olive oil in a large skillet over medium heat. Add chicken breasts and cook until golden brown on each side, about 5-7 minutes per side. Remove chicken from the skillet and set aside.
3. **Sauté Vegetables:** In the same skillet, add garlic, cherry tomatoes, and bell peppers. Sauté until vegetables are just soft, about 5 minutes.
4. **Simmer with Herbs:** Return the chicken to the skillet. Add chicken broth, basil, oregano, and thyme. Cover and simmer over low heat until the chicken is cooked through, about 10 minutes.
5. **Garnish and Serve:** Garnish with fresh parsley before serving.

INGREDIENT SUBSTITUTIONS:
- **Chicken Breast:** Swap with turkey breast or tofu for a variation in protein while maintaining similar nutritional values.
- **Olive Oil:** Avocado oil can be used as an alternative with a similar profile of healthy fats.
- **Chicken Broth:** Use vegetable broth to keep it lighter and for a vegetarian option, if using tofu instead of chicken.

Grilled Pork Chops with Apple Slaw

SERVINGS: 2
PREPARATION TIME: 15 minutes
COOKING TIME: 15 minutes
INGREDIENTS:

- 2 bone-in pork chops, about 1-inch thick
- 1 tablespoon olive oil
- Salt and pepper to taste
- 1 medium apple, julienned (preferably a tart variety like Granny Smith)
- 1 cup shredded cabbage
- 1 medium carrot, julienned
- 2 tablespoons apple cider vinegar
- 1 teaspoon Dijon mustard
- 1 tablespoon extra virgin olive oil
- A pinch of stevia or other non-caloric sweetener

NUTRITION PER SERVING:

- **Total Calories:** 350
- **Total Carbohydrates:** 15g
  - Dietary Fiber: 4g
  - Sugars: 9g
- **Protein:** 28g
- **Total Fat:** 20g
  - Saturated Fat: 4g
  - Unsaturated Fat: 14g
- **Sodium:** 240mg

INSTRUCTIONS:

1. **Prep the Pork:** Brush the pork chops with olive oil and season both sides with salt and pepper.
2. **Grill the Pork:** Preheat the grill to medium-high heat. Grill the pork chops for about 6-7 minutes on each side, or until they reach an internal temperature of 145°F (63°C). Remove from the grill and let rest.
3. **Make Apple Slaw:** In a mixing bowl, combine the julienned apple, shredded cabbage, and carrot. In a small bowl, whisk together the apple cider vinegar, Dijon mustard, extra virgin olive oil, and a pinch of sweetener to make the dressing. Toss the slaw with the dressing until well coated.
4. **Serve:** Plate each pork chop and top with a generous serving of apple slaw.

INGREDIENT SUBSTITUTIONS:

- **Pork Chops:** For a lighter option, replace pork with chicken breasts or for a vegetarian option, use thick-cut grilled tempeh.
- **Apple Cider Vinegar:** White wine vinegar can substitute for a milder tang.
- **Olive Oil:** Can be swapped with avocado oil, which has a similar profile of healthy monounsaturated fats.

Herb Roasted Turkey Breast with Roasted Vegetables

SERVINGS: 2
PREPARATION TIME: 20 minutes
COOKING TIME: 60 minutes
INGREDIENTS:

- 2 turkey breast cutlets (about 6 ounces each)
- 2 tablespoons olive oil
- 1 teaspoon dried rosemary
- 1 teaspoon dried thyme
- Salt and pepper to taste
- 1 medium zucchini, sliced into half-moons
- 1 red bell pepper, cut into 1-inch pieces
- 1 small red onion, sliced
- 1/2 head of cauliflower, cut into florets

NUTRITION PER SERVING:

- **Total Calories:** 390
- **Total Carbohydrates:** 15g
  - Dietary Fiber: 4g; Sugars: 6g
- **Protein:** 45g
- **Total Fat:** 18g
  - Saturated Fat: 3g
  - Unsaturated Fat: 13g
- **Sodium:** 190mg

INSTRUCTIONS:

1. **Preheat the Oven:** Preheat your oven to 375°F (190°C).
2. **Season the Turkey:** Rub each turkey breast cutlet with one tablespoon of olive oil, then season with rosemary, thyme, salt, and pepper.
3. **Prepare the Vegetables:** In a large bowl, toss the zucchini, bell pepper, onion, and cauliflower with the remaining tablespoon of olive oil, and season with salt and pepper.
4. **Roast:** Place the seasoned turkey breasts on a roasting tray. Spread the vegetables around the turkey in the tray. Roast in the preheated oven for about 50-60 minutes, or until the turkey is cooked through and the vegetables are tender and lightly caramelized.
5. **Rest and Serve:** Let the turkey rest for a few minutes after removing from the oven, then slice and serve with the roasted vegetables.

INGREDIENT SUBSTITUTIONS:

- **Turkey Breast:** Chicken breasts can be used as an alternative if turkey is not available.
- **Olive Oil:** Can be substituted with avocado oil for similar health benefits.
- **Vegetables:** Any seasonal non-starchy vegetables can be used.

Steak and Arugula Salad

SERVINGS: 2
PREPARATION TIME: 15 minutes
COOKING TIME: 10 minutes

INGREDIENTS:

- 2 beef steaks (6 ounces each, such as sirloin or flank steak)
- 2 cups arugula, washed and dried
- 1/2 cup cherry tomatoes, halved
- 1/4 cup shaved Parmesan cheese
- 2 tablespoons balsamic vinegar
- 1 tablespoon olive oil
- Salt and pepper to taste
- 1 teaspoon Dijon mustard

NUTRITION PER SERVING:

- **Total Calories:** 320
- **Total Carbohydrates:** 6g
  - Dietary Fiber: 2g
  - Sugars: 3g
- **Protein:** 35g
- **Total Fat:** 18g
  - Saturated Fat: 6g
  - Unsaturated Fat: 10g
- **Sodium:** 320mg

INSTRUCTIONS:

1. **Preheat the Grill:** Heat a grill or grill pan over medium-high heat.
2. **Prepare the Steak:** Season the steaks with salt and pepper. Grill the steaks for about 4-5 minutes on each side for medium-rare, or until desired doneness is reached. Remove from heat and let rest for 5 minutes.
3. **Mix the Dressing:** In a small bowl, whisk together the balsamic vinegar, olive oil, Dijon mustard, salt, and pepper to create the dressing.
4. **Assemble the Salad:** Slice the steak into thin strips. In a large salad bowl, toss the arugula, cherry tomatoes, and sliced steak. Drizzle with the dressing and toss again to combine. Top with shaved Parmesan cheese.
5. **Serve:** Divide the salad between two plates and serve immediately.

INGREDIENT SUBSTITUTIONS:

- **Steak:** Can be substituted with grilled chicken breast or tofu for a lower-fat option.
- **Arugula:** Baby spinach or mixed greens can be used as alternatives.
- **Balsamic Vinegar:** Red wine vinegar or apple cider vinegar can be used for a different acidic note.
- **Parmesan Cheese:** Nutritional yeast or vegan cheese can be used for a dairy-free version.

Grilled Veggie Platter with Tzatziki Sauce

SERVINGS: 2
PREPARATION TIME: 15 minutes
COOKING TIME: 10 minutes
INGREDIENTS:

- 1 medium zucchini, sliced into 1/2-inch rounds
- 1 red bell pepper, seeded and cut into wide strips
- 1 yellow bell pepper, seeded and cut into wide strips
- 1 small eggplant, sliced into 1/2-inch rounds
- 1 tablespoon olive oil
- Salt and pepper to taste
- Fresh herbs (like dill or parsley), for garnish

FOR THE TZATZIKI SAUCE:

- 1 cup Greek yogurt, unsweetened
- 1/2 cucumber, grated and excess water squeezed out
- 2 cloves garlic, minced
- 1 tablespoon lemon juice
- 1 tablespoon chopped fresh dill
- Salt and pepper to taste

NUTRITION PER SERVING:

- **Total Calories:** 220
- **Total Carbohydrates:** 24g
  - Dietary Fiber: 8g
  - Sugars: 14g
- **Protein:** 10g
- **Total Fat:** 10g
  - Saturated Fat: 2g
  - Unsaturated Fat: 7g
- **Sodium:** 180mg

INSTRUCTIONS:

1. **Preheat the Grill:** Preheat your grill or grill pan to medium-high heat.
2. **Prepare the Vegetables:** Toss zucchini, bell peppers, and eggplant slices in olive oil, salt, and pepper.
3. **Grill the Vegetables:** Arrange the vegetables on the grill and cook for about 4-5 minutes on each side, until charred and tender.
4. **Make the Tzatziki Sauce:** While the vegetables are grilling, combine Greek yogurt, grated cucumber, minced garlic, lemon juice, and dill in a bowl. Season with salt and pepper to taste and mix well.
5. **Serve:** Arrange the grilled vegetables on a platter and serve with a bowl of tzatziki sauce. Garnish with fresh herbs.

INGREDIENT SUBSTITUTIONS:

- **Greek Yogurt:** Use coconut yogurt for a dairy-free version.
- **Vegetables:** Swap out any of the vegetables for others like mushrooms, asparagus, or cauliflower based on availability and preference.
- **Olive Oil:** Avocado oil can be used as an alternative for a different monounsaturated fat source.

Roasted Chicken with Ratatouille

SERVINGS: 2
PREPARATION TIME: 20 minutes
COOKING TIME: 50 minutes
INGREDIENTS:

- 2 boneless, skinless chicken breasts (about 6 ounces each)
- 1 tablespoon olive oil
- 1/2 teaspoon salt
- 1/4 teaspoon black pepper
- 1 small eggplant, cubed
- 1 zucchini, cubed
- 1 yellow squash, cubed
- 1 red bell pepper, seeded and cubed
- 1 onion, chopped
- 2 cloves garlic, minced
- 1 cup chopped tomatoes
- 1 tablespoon fresh thyme leaves
- 1 tablespoon fresh basil, chopped

NUTRITION PER SERVING:

- **Total Calories:** 360
- **Total Carbohydrates:** 22g
  - Dietary Fiber: 8g
  - Sugars: 12g
- **Protein:** 38g
- **Total Fat:** 14g
  - Saturated Fat: 2g
  - Unsaturated Fat: 10g
- **Sodium:** 620mg

INSTRUCTIONS:

1. **Preheat the Oven:** Preheat your oven to 375°F (190°C).
2. **Prepare the Chicken:** Season the chicken breasts with half the olive oil, salt, and pepper. Place in a roasting pan.
3. **Roast the Chicken:** Put the chicken in the oven and roast for about 25 minutes, or until fully cooked (internal temperature should reach 165°F).
4. **Prepare the Ratatouille:** While the chicken is roasting, heat the remaining olive oil in a large skillet over medium heat. Add the eggplant, zucchini, yellow squash, and bell pepper. Cook for about 10 minutes, stirring occasionally.
5. **Add Aromatics:** Add the onion and garlic to the skillet and cook until the vegetables are tender and the onion is translucent, about 10 more minutes.
6. **Add Tomatoes and Herbs:** Stir in the chopped tomatoes, thyme, and basil. Season with salt and pepper to taste. Cook for an additional 10 minutes, until the mixture is saucy.
7. **Combine and Serve:** Once the chicken is cooked, serve each breast with a generous portion of the ratatouille.

INGREDIENT SUBSTITUTIONS:

- **Chicken:** Turkey breast can be used as a leaner alternative with similar protein content.
- **Olive Oil:** Can be substituted with avocado oil for similar monounsaturated fat benefits.
- **Herbs:** Rosemary or marjoram can be used instead of thyme or basil for a different flavor profile.

Snack Recipes

Turkey Cucumber Roll-Ups

SERVINGS: 2
PREPARATION TIME: 5 minutes
COOKING TIME: No cooking required
INGREDIENTS:

- 4 large slices of turkey breast (deli-style, low sodium)
- 1 large cucumber, peeled and cut into thin strips
- 2 tablespoons cream cheese, low-fat
- Fresh herbs (like dill or parsley), finely chopped
- Salt and pepper, to taste

NUTRITION PER SERVING:

- **Total Calories:** 120
- **Total Carbohydrates:** 4 g
  - Dietary Fiber: 1 g
  - Sugars: 2 g
- **Protein:** 15 g
- **Total Fat:** 5 g
  - Saturated Fat: 2 g
  - Unsaturated Fat: 2 g
- **Sodium:** 670 mg

PREPARATION:

1. **Prepare Ingredients**: Lay out turkey slices on a clean surface. Spread each slice with a thin layer of cream cheese.
2. **Add Flavor**: Sprinkle the fresh herbs, salt, and pepper over the cream cheese.
3. **Roll Them Up**: Place a few strips of cucumber on the narrow end of each turkey slice. Roll the turkey tightly around the cucumber into a neat roll.
4. **Serve**: Cut each roll into bite-sized pieces if desired and serve immediately.

INGREDIENT SUBSTITUTIONS:

- **Cream Cheese**: Substitute with hummus or Greek yogurt for a different taste while maintaining a creamy texture.
- **Turkey**: Chicken breast or smoked salmon can be used as alternatives for a different protein choice without significantly altering the nutritional profile.
- **Cucumber**: Bell peppers or carrot strips can offer a crunchy texture and sweet flavor if preferred.

Hummus and Veggie Pita Pocket

SERVINGS: 2
PREPARATION TIME: 5 minutes
COOKING TIME: No cooking required
INGREDIENTS:

- 2 whole grain pita breads, cut in half
- 1/2 cup hummus (low-fat, low-sodium)
- 1/2 cucumber, thinly sliced
- 1 small carrot, shredded
- 1/2 bell pepper, thinly sliced
- 1/4 cup red onion, thinly sliced
- 1/2 cup fresh spinach leaves
- 2 tablespoons feta cheese, crumbled (optional)

NUTRITION PER SERVING:

- **Total Calories:** 280
- **Total Carbohydrates:** 42 g
  - Dietary Fiber: 8 g
  - Sugars: 5 g
- **Protein:** 12 g
- **Total Fat:** 9 g
  - Saturated Fat: 2 g
  - Unsaturated Fat: 4 g
- **Sodium:** 450 mg

PREPARATION:

1. **Prepare the Pita**: Warm the pita bread slightly in a microwave or oven to make it more pliable.
2. **Fill the Pockets**: Open each pita half to form a pocket. Spread a generous layer of hummus inside each pita half.
3. **Add Vegetables**: Stuff the pita pockets with cucumber, carrot, bell pepper, red onion, and spinach.
4. **Add Cheese**: Sprinkle crumbled feta cheese into each pita pocket for added flavor, if using.
5. **Serve**: Serve the pita pockets immediately, or wrap them up for a convenient, portable snack.

INGREDIENT SUBSTITUTIONS:

- **Hummus**: Try avocado mash or bean spread for a creamy texture with different flavors.
- **Feta Cheese**: Omit or substitute with diced avocado for a dairy-free, creamy addition.
- **Pita Bread**: Use lettuce wraps or collard greens as low-carb, gluten-free alternatives.

Chicken Salad Lettuce Wraps

SERVINGS: 2
PREPARATION TIME: 5 minutes
COOKING TIME: No cooking required
INGREDIENTS:

- 1 cup cooked chicken breast, shredded
- 1/4 cup Greek yogurt, unsweetened
- 1 tablespoon Dijon mustard
- 1/4 cup celery, finely chopped
- 2 tablespoons red onion, finely chopped
- 1/4 cup apple, chopped (optional)
- 1/4 teaspoon black pepper
- 6 large lettuce leaves (Romaine or Iceberg)

NUTRITION PER SERVING:

- **Total Calories:** 180
- **Total Carbohydrates:** 6 g
  - Dietary Fiber: 2 g
  - Sugars: 3 g
- **Protein:** 27 g
- **Total Fat:** 5 g
  - Saturated Fat: 1 g
  - Unsaturated Fat: 3 g
- **Sodium:** 200 mg

PREPARATION:

1. **Mix Chicken Salad**: In a mixing bowl, combine the shredded chicken, Greek yogurt, Dijon mustard, celery, red onion, and apple (if using). Season with black pepper to taste.
2. **Prepare Lettuce Leaves**: Wash and dry the lettuce leaves, ensuring they are intact to hold the filling.
3. **Assemble Wraps**: Spoon an equal amount of chicken salad into each lettuce leaf. Fold or wrap the lettuce around the filling to form a wrap.
4. **Serve Chilled**: Chill the wraps for about 10 minutes before serving for enhanced flavors.

INGREDIENT SUBSTITUTIONS:

- **Greek Yogurt**: Substitute with low-fat mayonnaise or avocado puree for a different creamy base.
- **Chicken**: Tofu or chickpeas can be used as a vegetarian protein source.
- **Apple**: Add grapes or dried cranberries for a touch of sweetness with a different texture.

Roast Beef and Spinach Roll-Up

SERVINGS: 2
PREPARATION TIME: 5 minutes
COOKING TIME: No cooking required
INGREDIENTS:

- 4 slices of lean roast beef (about 4 ounces)
- 1 cup fresh spinach leaves
- 2 tablespoons low-fat cream cheese
- 1/4 teaspoon garlic powder
- 1/4 teaspoon black pepper
- 2 whole wheat tortillas (8-inch)

NUTRITION PER SERVING:

- **Total Calories:** 230
- **Total Carbohydrates:** 18 g
  - Dietary Fiber: 3 g
  - Sugars: 2 g
- **Protein:** 20 g
- **Total Fat:** 9 g
  - Saturated Fat: 3 g
  - Unsaturated Fat: 4 g
- **Sodium:** 480 mg

PREPARATION:

1. **Prepare Spread**: In a small bowl, mix the low-fat cream cheese with garlic powder and black pepper until smooth.
2. **Assemble Roll-Ups**: Lay out the whole wheat tortillas. Spread each tortilla evenly with the cream cheese mixture.
3. **Layer Ingredients**: Arrange two slices of roast beef on each tortilla and top with a layer of fresh spinach leaves.
4. **Roll and Serve**: Roll up the tortillas tightly, slice in half, and serve immediately or wrap in cling film to chill in the refrigerator before serving.

INGREDIENT SUBSTITUTIONS:

- **Roast Beef**: Substitute with turkey or cooked chicken for a different protein choice.
- **Cream Cheese**: Use hummus or mashed avocado for a dairy-free or lower-fat option.
- **Spinach**: Arugula or kale can be used as an alternative green for a different flavor and nutrient profile.

Salmon Salad on Cucumber Slices

SERVINGS: 2
PREPARATION TIME: 5 minutes
COOKING TIME: No cooking required
INGREDIENTS:

- 4 ounces canned salmon, drained and flaked
- 1 tablespoon Greek yogurt
- 1 tablespoon chopped fresh dill
- 1 teaspoon lemon juice
- 1/4 teaspoon black pepper
- 1 large cucumber, sliced into 1/4 inch thick rounds

NUTRITION PER SERVING:

- **Total Calories:** 120
- **Total Carbohydrates:** 4 g
  - Dietary Fiber: 1 g
  - Sugars: 2 g
- **Protein:** 15 g
- **Total Fat:** 5 g
  - Saturated Fat: 1 g
  - Unsaturated Fat: 2 g
- **Sodium:** 220 mg

PREPARATION:

1. **Make Salmon Salad**: In a bowl, combine the flaked salmon, Greek yogurt, chopped dill, lemon juice, and black pepper. Mix well until all ingredients are incorporated.
2. **Prepare Cucumbers**: Wash the cucumber and slice it into thick rounds.
3. **Assemble**: Spoon a small amount of salmon salad onto each cucumber slice. Arrange on a platter and serve chilled.

INGREDIENT SUBSTITUTIONS:

- **Salmon**: Substitute with canned tuna or chicken for a different protein option while keeping similar nutritional values.
- **Greek Yogurt**: Use a dairy-free yogurt or light mayonnaise if preferred.
- **Dill**: Fresh parsley or chives can be used as an alternative herb for variety in flavor.

Ricotta and Roasted Pepper Toast

SERVINGS: 2
PREPARATION TIME: 5 minutes
COOKING TIME: No cooking required
INGREDIENTS:

- 2 slices of whole grain bread
- 1/2 cup ricotta cheese (low-fat)
- 1 roasted red bell pepper, sliced
- 1 tablespoon chopped basil
- 1/4 teaspoon black pepper
- Drizzle of balsamic glaze (optional)

NUTRITION PER SERVING:

- **Total Calories:** 180
- **Total Carbohydrates:** 22 g
  - Dietary Fiber: 4 g
  - Sugars: 4 g
- **Protein:** 10 g
- **Total Fat:** 6 g
  - Saturated Fat: 3 g
  - Unsaturated Fat: 2 g
- **Sodium:** 200 mg

PREPARATION:

1. **Prepare the Toast**: Toast the whole grain bread slices to your desired crispness.
2. **Mix Ricotta**: In a small bowl, mix the ricotta cheese with chopped basil and black pepper.
3. **Assemble the Toast**: Spread the ricotta mixture evenly over the toasted bread slices. Top with sliced roasted red peppers.
4. **Add Final Touches**: Drizzle a small amount of balsamic glaze over each toast for added flavor.

INGREDIENT SUBSTITUTIONS:

- **Ricotta Cheese**: Substitute with low-fat cottage cheese or tofu for a lower fat content while maintaining a similar texture.
- **Whole Grain Bread**: Gluten-free bread can be used for those with gluten sensitivities.
- **Roasted Red Pepper**: Freshly sliced tomatoes or cucumber can be used as a refreshing alternative.

Cottage Cheese and Tomato Toast

SERVINGS: 2
PREPARATION TIME: 5 minutes
COOKING TIME: No cooking required
INGREDIENTS:

- 2 slices of whole grain bread
- 1/2 cup low-fat cottage cheese
- 1 large tomato, sliced
- Fresh basil leaves, for garnish
- Salt and pepper to taste
- Drizzle of extra virgin olive oil (optional)

NUTRITION PER SERVING:

- **Total Calories:** 200
- **Total Carbohydrates:** 27 g
  - Dietary Fiber: 5 g
  - Sugars: 6 g
- **Protein:** 14 g
- **Total Fat:** 5 g
  - Saturated Fat: 2 g
  - Unsaturated Fat: 2 g
- **Sodium:** 310 mg

PREPARATION:

1. **Toast Preparation**: Toast the bread slices to desired crispness.
2. **Prepare Toppings**: Spread the cottage cheese evenly over each slice of toasted bread.
3. **Add Tomatoes**: Top each slice with fresh tomato slices. Season with salt and pepper.
4. **Garnish and Serve**: Add fresh basil leaves on top for flavor and a drizzle of olive oil if desired.

INGREDIENT SUBSTITUTIONS:

- **Cottage Cheese**: Substitute with ricotta or mashed avocado for a different texture or fat content while keeping a similar creamy base.
- **Whole Grain Bread**: Use gluten-free bread or a low-carb alternative like almond flour bread for those with dietary restrictions.
- **Tomatoes**: Switch out for cucumber slices or radish for a crunchier texture or to vary the flavor profile.

Almond Butter and Pear Toast

SERVINGS: 2
PREPARATION TIME: 5 minutes
COOKING TIME: No cooking required
INGREDIENTS:

- 2 slices of whole grain bread
- 2 tablespoons almond butter
- 1 medium pear, thinly sliced
- A sprinkle of cinnamon (optional)
- A drizzle of honey (optional, for those who can accommodate a slight increase in sugars)

NUTRITION PER SERVING:

- **Total Calories:** 280
- **Total Carbohydrates:** 38 g
  - Dietary Fiber: 7 g
  - Sugars: 16 g
- **Protein:** 8 g
- **Total Fat:** 12 g
  - Saturated Fat: 1 g
  - Unsaturated Fat: 9 g
- **Sodium:** 150 mg

PREPARATION:

1. **Toast the Bread**: Lightly toast the bread slices until they are golden and crispy.
2. **Spread Almond Butter**: Evenly spread the almond butter over each slice of toasted bread.
3. **Add Pear Slices**: Arrange the thinly sliced pear on top of the almond butter.
4. **Add Flavors**: Sprinkle a light dusting of cinnamon and a tiny drizzle of honey over the pear slices, if using.

INGREDIENT SUBSTITUTIONS:

- **Almond Butter**: Swap with cashew butter or sunflower seed butter for a similar texture and nutritional profile but a different flavor.
- **Whole Grain Bread**: For a gluten-free option, substitute with your preferred gluten-free bread that aligns with diabetic dietary needs.
- **Pears**: Can be replaced with apple slices or fresh figs for a variation in taste while maintaining a similar texture and sweetness.

Avocado and Radish Toast

SERVINGS: 2
PREPARATION TIME: 5 minutes
COOKING TIME: No cooking required
INGREDIENTS:

- 2 slices of whole grain bread
- 1 ripe avocado, mashed
- 4-5 radishes, thinly sliced
- Fresh lemon juice
- Salt and pepper to taste
- Fresh dill or parsley for garnish (optional)

NUTRITION PER SERVING:

- **Total Calories:** 250
- **Total Carbohydrates:** 27 g
  - Dietary Fiber: 9 g
  - Sugars: 3 g
- **Protein:** 6 g
- **Total Fat:** 14 g
  - Saturated Fat: 2 g
  - Unsaturated Fat: 10 g
- **Sodium:** 200 mg

PREPARATION:

1. **Toast the Bread**: Toast the bread slices to your preferred level of crispiness.
2. **Prepare the Avocado**: In a small bowl, mash the avocado with a fork until creamy. Add a squeeze of fresh lemon juice, and salt and pepper to taste.
3. **Assemble the Toast**: Spread the mashed avocado evenly over the toasted bread slices. Arrange the thinly sliced radishes on top.
4. **Add Garnish**: Sprinkle with fresh dill or parsley for an additional layer of flavor, if desired.

INGREDIENT SUBSTITUTIONS:

- **Whole Grain Bread**: Can be substituted with keto bread for those watching carbohydrate intake more strictly.
- **Avocado**: For a different texture and flavor, use hummus or a low-fat cream cheese spread.
- **Radishes**: Substitute with thin cucumber slices or shredded carrot for a different crunch and nutritional content.

Tuna and Olive Tapenade on Crispbread

SERVINGS: 2
PREPARATION TIME: 5 minutes
COOKING TIME: No cooking required
INGREDIENTS:

- 4 pieces of whole grain crispbread
- 1 can (5 ounces) of tuna in water, drained
- 1/4 cup olive tapenade
- Fresh lemon juice
- Fresh parsley, chopped (optional for garnish)

NUTRITION PER SERVING:

- **Total Calories:** 210
- **Total Carbohydrates:** 18 g
  - Dietary Fiber: 5 g
  - Sugars: 1 g
- **Protein:** 15 g
- **Total Fat:** 9 g
  - Saturated Fat: 1.5 g
  - Unsaturated Fat: 7 g
- **Sodium:** 550 mg

PREPARATION:

1. **Prepare the Tuna**: In a small bowl, mix the drained tuna with a squeeze of fresh lemon juice, breaking it into flakes.
2. **Spread Olive Tapenade**: Spread the olive tapenade evenly across the crispbread slices.
3. **Add Tuna**: Top each piece of crispbread with the lemon-flavored tuna.
4. **Garnish and Serve**: Garnish with chopped parsley if desired before serving.

INGREDIENT SUBSTITUTIONS:

- **Whole Grain Crispbread**: Can be substituted with gluten-free crispbread for those with gluten intolerance.
- **Tuna in Water**: For a vegetarian version, substitute with chickpea salad mixed with a little mayo and celery.
- **Olive Tapenade**: For a less salty option, use a homemade blend of olives, capers, and olive oil, adjusting the salt content according to dietary needs.

Mango Coconut Yogurt

SERVINGS: 2
PREPARATION TIME: 5 minutes
COOKING TIME: No cooking required
INGREDIENTS:
- 1 cup Greek yogurt, unsweetened
- 1 fresh mango, peeled and cubed
- 2 tablespoons unsweetened coconut flakes

NUTRITION PER SERVING:
- **Total Calories:** 190
- **Total Carbohydrates:** 28 g
  - Dietary Fiber: 3 g
  - Sugars: 24 g
- **Protein:** 12 g
- **Total Fat:** 5 g
  - Saturated Fat: 4 g
  - Unsaturated Fat: 1 g
- **Sodium:** 45 mg

PREPARATION:
1. **Prepare Mango**: Peel the mango and cut it into small cubes.
2. **Mix Ingredients**: In a bowl, combine the Greek yogurt with the cubed mango.
3. **Add Coconut**: Sprinkle the unsweetened coconut flakes over the top.
4. **Chill and Serve**: For best flavor, chill the mixture for about 30 minutes before serving, or serve immediately if desired.

INGREDIENT SUBSTITUTIONS:
- **Greek Yogurt**: Use a dairy-free yogurt alternative like coconut yogurt or almond milk yogurt if you're avoiding dairy.
- **Mango**: Can be substituted with peaches or nectarines for a similar texture and sweetness.
- **Unsweetened Coconut Flakes**: Try sliced almonds or chopped walnuts for a crunch without changing the carbohydrate profile significantly.

Peach Ginger Smoothie

SERVINGS: 2
PREPARATION TIME: 5 minutes
COOKING TIME: No cooking required
INGREDIENTS:
- 2 medium peaches, pitted and sliced
- 1/2 inch fresh ginger, peeled and grated
- 1 cup unsweetened almond milk
- 1/2 cup Greek yogurt, unsweetened
- Ice cubes (optional)

NUTRITION PER SERVING:
- **Total Calories:** 120
- **Total Carbohydrates:** 18 g
  - Dietary Fiber: 3 g
  - Sugars: 15 g
- **Protein:** 6 g
- **Total Fat:** 3 g
  - Saturated Fat: 0 g
  - Unsaturated Fat: 2 g
- **Sodium:** 55 mg

PREPARATION:
1. **Prepare Ingredients**: Pit and slice the peaches, and peel and grate the ginger.
2. **Blend**: Combine peaches, ginger, almond milk, and Greek yogurt in a blender. Add a handful of ice cubes if a colder or thicker smoothie is desired.
3. **Process Until Smooth**: Blend on high until smooth and creamy.
4. **Serve Immediately**: Pour into glasses and serve immediately for the freshest taste.

INGREDIENT SUBSTITUTIONS:
- **Peaches**: Can be substituted with nectarines for a similar flavor profile or with frozen peaches to make the smoothie colder and thicker without ice.
- **Ginger**: Adjust the amount of ginger according to taste preference or substitute with a small amount of ground ginger if fresh is unavailable.
- **Almond Milk**: Any other unsweetened non-dairy milk like soy or coconut milk can be used.
- **Greek Yogurt**: Use any plain, unsweetened plant-based yogurt to make this recipe dairy-free.

Mixed Berry Yogurt Parfait

SERVINGS: 2
PREPARATION TIME: 5 minutes
COOKING TIME: No cooking required
INGREDIENTS:

- 1 cup Greek yogurt, unsweetened
- 1/2 cup fresh strawberries, sliced
- 1/2 cup fresh blueberries
- 1/4 cup fresh raspberries
- 2 tablespoons chopped nuts (almonds or walnuts)
- A drizzle of honey (optional, for those who can include a bit more sugar in their diet)

NUTRITION PER SERVING:

- **Total Calories:** 180
- **Total Carbohydrates:** 24 g
  - Dietary Fiber: 4 g
  - Sugars: 16 g
- **Protein:** 12 g
- **Total Fat:** 6 g
  - Saturated Fat: 1 g
  - Unsaturated Fat: 4 g
- **Sodium:** 50 mg

PREPARATION:

1. **Layer the Parfait**: Begin with a layer of Greek yogurt at the bottom of two glasses or parfait cups.
2. **Add Berries**: Add a layer of mixed berries (strawberries, blueberries, and raspberries).
3. **Repeat Layers**: Repeat the layers of yogurt and berries until the cups are full.
4. **Top with Nuts**: Sprinkle chopped nuts on top for added texture and a boost of healthy fats.
5. **Drizzle Honey (optional)**: Drizzle a small amount of honey over the top for a touch of sweetness.

INGREDIENT SUBSTITUTIONS:

- **Greek Yogurt**: Use any plain, unsweetened plant-based yogurt if a dairy-free option is needed.
- **Mixed Berries**: Any combination of low GI berries can be used. Frozen berries can be a good off-season choice.
- **Nuts**: Any type of nuts or seeds can be used, such as chia seeds or flaxseeds, to maintain similar nutritional benefits.
- **Honey**: For those strictly managing sugar intake, substitute with a drizzle of agave syrup or skip the sweetener altogether.

Avocado and Cocoa Smoothie

SERVINGS: 2
PREPARATION TIME: 5 minutes
COOKING TIME: No cooking required
INGREDIENTS:

- 1 ripe avocado, peeled and pitted
- 2 tablespoons unsweetened cocoa powder
- 1 cup unsweetened almond milk
- 1/2 teaspoon vanilla extract
- 1 tablespoon chia seeds
- Ice cubes (optional, for a thicker smoothie)
- Sweetener of choice (stevia or a suitable sugar substitute), to taste

NUTRITION PER SERVING:

- **Total Calories:** 230
- **Total Carbohydrates:** 15 g
  - Dietary Fiber: 9 g
  - Sugars: 2 g
- **Protein:** 5 g
- **Total Fat:** 18 g
  - Saturated Fat: 3 g
  - Unsaturated Fat: 12 g
- **Sodium:** 90 mg

PREPARATION:

1. **Blend Ingredients**: In a blender, combine the avocado, cocoa powder, almond milk, vanilla extract, and chia seeds. Add ice cubes if a thicker consistency is desired.
2. **Sweeten to Taste**: Add sweetener according to your dietary needs and blend until the mixture is smooth.
3. **Serve Immediately**: Pour the smoothie into two glasses and serve immediately for the freshest taste.

INGREDIENT SUBSTITUTIONS:

- **Almond Milk**: Can be replaced with any other plant-based milk like coconut milk or soy milk to maintain a similar nutritional profile.
- **Cocoa Powder**: Use carob powder for a caffeine-free alternative.
- **Sweetener**: Adjust or substitute with monk fruit sweetener or erythritol for different sweetness levels without affecting blood sugar significantly.

Carrot and Orange Smoothie

SERVINGS: 2
PREPARATION TIME: 5 minutes
COOKING TIME: No cooking required
INGREDIENTS:

- 2 large carrots, peeled and chopped
- 1 large orange, peeled and deseeded
- 1/2 inch piece of ginger, peeled
- 1 tablespoon flaxseeds
- 1 cup unsweetened almond milk
- Ice cubes (optional)
- Sweetener of choice (such as stevia), to taste

NUTRITION PER SERVING:

- **Total Calories:** 120
- **Total Carbohydrates:** 18 g
  - Dietary Fiber: 5 g
  - Sugars: 10 g
- **Protein:** 3 g
- **Total Fat:** 4 g
  - Saturated Fat: 0.5 g
  - Unsaturated Fat: 2.5 g
- **Sodium:** 85 mg

PREPARATION:

1. **Combine Ingredients**: In a blender, combine the chopped carrots, orange segments, ginger, flax-seeds, and almond milk. Add a few ice cubes if a colder or thicker smoothie is preferred.
2. **Blend Until Smooth**: Blend all the ingredients until smooth. Taste and add sweetener if desired, blending again to mix thoroughly.
3. **Serve Fresh**: Pour the smoothie into two glasses and serve immediately to enjoy its vibrant flavor and nutrients.

INGREDIENT SUBSTITUTIONS:

- **Almond Milk**: Substitute with coconut water or soy milk for a different flavor and similar nutritional benefits.
- **Orange**: Replace with grapefruit for a less sweet, more tangy flavor while maintaining a good vitamin C content.
- **Sweetener**: Adjust the type and amount of sweetener based on dietary needs, using monk fruit sweetener or erythritol as alternatives.

Strawberry Basil Yogurt

SERVINGS: 2
PREPARATION TIME: 5 minutes
COOKING TIME: No cooking required
INGREDIENTS:

- 1 cup plain Greek yogurt (low-fat)
- 1 cup fresh strawberries, chopped
- 4-6 fresh basil leaves, finely chopped
- Optional sweetener: 1 teaspoon honey or stevia (to taste)

NUTRITION PER SERVING:

- **Total Calories**: 90 kcal
- **Total Carbohydrates**: 12 g
  - Dietary Fiber: 2 g
  - Sugars: 8 g
- **Protein**: 10 g
- **Total Fat**: 1 g
  - Saturated Fat: 0.5 g
  - Unsaturated Fat: 0.5 g
- **Sodium**: 30 mg

INSTRUCTIONS:

1. **Mix Ingredients**: In a medium bowl, combine the Greek yogurt with the chopped strawberries and finely chopped basil leaves. If a sweeter taste is desired, add honey or stevia to taste and mix well.
2. **Serve**: Divide the yogurt mixture into two servings and garnish with a few small basil leaves or additional strawberry slices for presentation.

INGREDIENT SUBSTITUTIONS:

- **Fruit Variation**: Substitute strawberries with blueberries or raspberries for a different taste while maintaining a similar nutritional profile.
- **Herb Variation**: Mint can be used instead of basil for a fresh, peppery flavor that complements the sweetness of the fruit.
- **Yogurt Alternative**: For a dairy-free version, use unsweetened coconut yogurt or almond yogurt instead of Greek yogurt. Adjust the sweetness as needed.

Pineapple Coconut Smoothie

SERVINGS: 2
PREPARATION TIME: 5 minutes
COOKING TIME: No cooking required
INGREDIENTS:
- 1 cup fresh pineapple chunks
- 1/2 cup unsweetened coconut milk
- 1/2 cup Greek yogurt (low-fat, plain)
- 1 tablespoon chia seeds
- Ice cubes (optional for a thicker smoothie)

NUTRITION PER SERVING:
- **Total Calories**: 150 kcal
- **Total Carbohydrates**: 18 g
  - Dietary Fiber: 3 g
  - Sugars: 12 g
- **Protein**: 6 g
- **Total Fat**: 7 g
  - Saturated Fat: 5 g
  - Unsaturated Fat: 2 g
- **Sodium**: 30 mg

INSTRUCTIONS:
1. **Blend Ingredients**: In a blender, combine the pineapple chunks, unsweetened coconut milk, Greek yogurt, and chia seeds. Add a few ice cubes if a thicker consistency is desired.
2. **Process Until Smooth**: Blend on high speed until smooth and creamy.
3. **Serve Immediately**: Pour the smoothie into two glasses and serve immediately for the freshest taste.

INGREDIENT SUBSTITUTIONS:
- **Fruit Variation**: Mango can replace pineapple for a similar tropical flavor with comparable nutritional values.
- **Yogurt Alternative**: For a dairy-free version, use a plant-based yogurt such as almond or soy yogurt.
- **Chia Seeds Alternative**: Flaxseeds can be used in place of chia seeds for a similar nutritional boost with a slightly different texture.

Apple Cinnamon Yogurt Parfait

SERVINGS: 2
PREPARATION TIME: 10 minutes
COOKING TIME: No cooking required
INGREDIENTS:
- 1 large apple, cored and chopped
- 1 cup low-fat Greek yogurt
- 1/2 teaspoon ground cinnamon
- 1 tablespoon ground flaxseed
- 1/4 cup walnuts, chopped (optional)

NUTRITION PER SERVING:
- **Total Calories**: 190 kcal
- **Total Carbohydrates**: 25 g
  - Dietary Fiber: 4 g
  - Sugars: 16 g
- **Protein**: 12 g
- **Total Fat**: 6 g
  - Saturated Fat: 1 g
  - Unsaturated Fat: 4 g
- **Sodium**: 40 mg

INSTRUCTIONS:
1. **Layer the Parfait**: In two serving glasses, start with a layer of Greek yogurt at the bottom. Add a layer of chopped apples over the yogurt.
2. **Add Spices and Nuts**: Sprinkle cinnamon and flaxseed over the apples. If using, add a layer of chopped walnuts for added texture and healthy fats.
3. **Repeat Layers**: Repeat the layering process until all ingredients are used up, finishing with a sprinkle of cinnamon on top.
4. **Chill and Serve**: Chill the parfait in the refrigerator for about 30 minutes before serving to allow the flavors to meld.

INGREDIENT SUBSTITUTIONS:
- **Apple Alternative**: Pears can be used instead of apples for a similar texture and sweetness with a slight flavor variation.
- **Yogurt Substitute**: For a dairy-free alternative, use coconut or almond-based yogurt.
- **Nut Free**: Skip the walnuts and use pumpkin seeds for crunch without the nuts.

Blueberry Almond Smoothie

SERVINGS: 2
PREPARATION TIME: 5 minutes
COOKING TIME: No cooking required
INGREDIENTS:
- 1 cup fresh blueberries
- 1 cup unsweetened almond milk
- 1/2 cup Greek yogurt, plain
- 2 tablespoons almond butter
- 1 tablespoon chia seeds
- Ice cubes (optional, for thicker smoothie)

NUTRITION PER SERVING:
- **Total Calories**: 235 kcal
- **Total Carbohydrates**: 18 g
  - Dietary Fiber: 5 g
  - Sugars: 10 g
- **Protein**: 10 g
- **Total Fat**: 15 g
  - Saturated Fat: 1 g
  - Unsaturated Fat: 12 g
- **Sodium**: 95 mg

INSTRUCTIONS:
1. **Blend Ingredients**: In a blender, combine blueberries, almond milk, Greek yogurt, almond butter, and chia seeds. Add ice cubes if a thicker consistency is desired.
2. **Process Until Smooth**: Blend on high speed until smooth and creamy.
3. **Serve Immediately**: Pour the smoothie into two glasses and serve immediately for the freshest taste.

INGREDIENT SUBSTITUTIONS:
- **Berry Variation**: Substitute blueberries with strawberries or raspberries for a different berry flavor while maintaining similar nutritional benefits.
- **Nut Butter Swap**: If allergic to almonds, use sunflower seed butter to keep the creamy texture and enrich the flavor.
- **Dairy-Free Option**: Replace Greek yogurt with a non-dairy yogurt such as coconut yogurt to make this smoothie completely dairy-free.

Kiwi Spinach Smoothie

SERVINGS: 2
PREPARATION TIME: 5 minutes
COOKING TIME: No cooking required
INGREDIENTS:
- 2 ripe kiwis, peeled and sliced
- 1 cup fresh spinach leaves
- 1/2 cucumber, peeled and chopped
- 1 cup unsweetened almond milk
- 1 tablespoon flaxseed meal
- Ice cubes (optional, for thicker smoothie)

NUTRITION PER SERVING:
- **Total Calories**: 120 kcal
- **Total Carbohydrates**: 18 g
  - Dietary Fiber: 5 g
  - Sugars: 10 g
- **Protein**: 3 g
- **Total Fat**: 4 g
  - Saturated Fat: 0 g
  - Unsaturated Fat: 3 g
- **Sodium**: 55 mg

INSTRUCTIONS:
1. **Combine Ingredients**: In a blender, add kiwis, spinach, cucumber, almond milk, and flaxseed meal. If a thicker consistency is preferred, add some ice cubes.
2. **Blend Smoothly**: Blend on high until all components are thoroughly mixed and the smoothie reaches a creamy consistency.
3. **Ready to Serve**: Pour into two glasses and serve fresh.

INGREDIENT SUBSTITUTIONS:
- **Fruit Swap**: Replace kiwi with green apple or pear for a different yet subtle tartness while keeping the nutritional profile similar.
- **Greens Change**: Use kale instead of spinach for an earthier flavor and additional nutritional benefits, such as more vitamins K and C.
- **Seed Variation**: Substitute flaxseed meal with chia seeds to vary the texture and slightly adjust the omega-3 fatty acid content, still keeping the health benefits aligned with a diabetic-friendly diet.

Raspberry Lime Yogurt

SERVINGS: 2
PREPARATION TIME: 5 minutes
COOKING TIME: No cooking required
INGREDIENTS:

- 1 cup low-fat Greek yogurt
- 1/2 cup fresh raspberries
- Zest of 1 lime
- 1 tablespoon lime juice
- 1 teaspoon honey (optional, depending on your dietary needs)

NUTRITION PER SERVING:

- **Total Calories**: 120 kcal
- **Total Carbohydrates**: 15 g
  - Dietary Fiber: 2 g
  - Sugars: 12 g
- **Protein**: 9 g
- **Total Fat**: 2 g
  - Saturated Fat: 1 g
  - Unsaturated Fat: 1 g
- **Sodium**: 45 mg

INSTRUCTIONS:

1. **Mix Ingredients**: In a medium bowl, combine the Greek yogurt, raspberries, lime zest, and lime juice. If using, drizzle with honey.
2. **Blend Lightly**: Gently fold the ingredients together until well mixed. For a smoother texture, lightly mash the raspberries as you mix.
3. **Chill and Serve**: Divide the yogurt mixture into two servings and refrigerate for at least 30 minutes before serving to enhance the flavors.

INGREDIENT SUBSTITUTIONS:

- **Berry Variation**: Substitute raspberries with blackberries or strawberries to alter the taste while maintaining similar levels of antioxidants and fiber.
- **Sweetener Option**: Instead of honey, you can use a small amount of stevia or monk fruit sweetener for a lower glycemic index.
- **Citrus Twist**: Replace lime with lemon for a different citrus note that still complements the raspberries effectively.

Cherry Vanilla Smoothie

SERVINGS: 2
PREPARATION TIME: 5 minutes
COOKING TIME: No cooking required
INGREDIENTS:

- 1 cup unsweetened almond milk
- 1/2 cup frozen cherries
- 1/4 cup Greek yogurt, plain
- 1 teaspoon vanilla extract
- Ice cubes (optional, depending on desired thickness)

NUTRITION PER SERVING:

- **Total Calories**: 95 kcal
- **Total Carbohydrates**: 13 g
  - Dietary Fiber: 2 g
  - Sugars: 9 g
- **Protein**: 4 g
- **Total Fat**: 3 g
  - Saturated Fat: 0.5 g
  - Unsaturated Fat: 2.5 g
- **Sodium**: 55 mg

INSTRUCTIONS:

1. **Combine Ingredients**: In a blender, combine the unsweetened almond milk, frozen cherries, Greek yogurt, and vanilla extract. Add ice cubes if a thicker consistency is desired.
2. **Blend**: Blend on high until smooth and creamy.
3. **Serve**: Pour the smoothie into two glasses and serve immediately for the freshest taste.

INGREDIENT SUBSTITUTIONS:

- **Fruit Swap**: Replace cherries with frozen strawberries or raspberries to change the flavor while keeping the antioxidant benefits and maintaining a similar carbohydrate content.
- **Milk Alternative**: Use coconut milk or oat milk instead of almond milk for a different flavor profile and creamy texture, adjusting the carbohydrate and fat content accordingly.
- **Protein Boost**: Add a scoop of vanilla protein powder for an extra protein punch, which will help in managing hunger and blood sugar levels.

Banana Nut Yogurt

SERVINGS: 2
PREPARATION TIME: 5 minutes
COOKING TIME: No cooking required
INGREDIENTS:

- 1 cup low-fat Greek yogurt
- 1 small banana, sliced
- 2 tablespoons chopped walnuts
- 1/4 teaspoon cinnamon

NUTRITION PER SERVING:

- **Total Calories**: 190 kcal
- **Total Carbohydrates**: 24 g
    - Dietary Fiber: 3 g
    - Sugars: 15 g
- **Protein**: 12 g
- **Total Fat**: 8 g
    - Saturated Fat: 1 g
    - Unsaturated Fat: 7 g
- **Sodium**: 45 mg

INSTRUCTIONS:

1. **Prepare the Base**: Divide the Greek yogurt between two bowls.
2. **Add Toppings**: Top each bowl of yogurt with sliced banana, chopped walnuts, and a sprinkle of cinnamon.
3. **Serve**: Enjoy immediately for the best texture and freshness.

INGREDIENT SUBSTITUTIONS:

- **Fruit Swap**: Substitute sliced banana with diced pear or apple for a different flavor while keeping a similar texture and sweetness.
- **Nut Alternative**: Use almonds or pecans instead of walnuts to vary the texture and flavor, maintaining a good source of healthy fats.
- **Spice Variation**: Swap cinnamon for nutmeg or pumpkin spice to give a different seasonal flair without significantly altering the nutritional profile.

Green Tea Smoothie

SERVINGS: 2
PREPARATION TIME: 5 minutes
COOKING TIME: No cooking required
INGREDIENTS:

- 1 cup brewed green tea, cooled
- 1/2 cup unsweetened almond milk
- 1 cup spinach leaves
- 1/2 medium avocado
- 1 tablespoon chia seeds
- 1/2 teaspoon vanilla extract
- Ice cubes (optional for thicker consistency)

NUTRITION PER SERVING:

- **Total Calories**: 150 kcal
- **Total Carbohydrates**: 12 g
    - Dietary Fiber: 6 g
    - Sugars: 2 g
- **Protein**: 3 g
- **Total Fat**: 11 g
    - Saturated Fat: 1.5 g
    - Unsaturated Fat: 8.5 g
- **Sodium**: 30 mg

INSTRUCTIONS:

1. **Blend Ingredients**: In a blender, combine the brewed green tea, almond milk, spinach, avocado, chia seeds, vanilla extract, and ice cubes. Blend until smooth.
2. **Serve Immediately**: Pour the smoothie into two glasses and serve immediately to maintain the freshness and nutrient content.

INGREDIENT SUBSTITUTIONS:

- **Milk Alternative**: Substitute almond milk with coconut milk or soy milk for a different flavor and creaminess while keeping the carbohydrate content similar.
- **Add Sweetness**: If a sweeter taste is desired, add a small amount of stevia or a few drops of monk fruit extract, which do not significantly alter the sugar content.
- **Flavor Twist**: Instead of vanilla, try adding a pinch of cinnamon or matcha powder for an extra boost of flavor and antioxidants.

Caprese Skewers

SERVINGS: 2 (6 skewers each)
PREPARATION TIME: 10 minutes
COOKING TIME: No cooking required
INGREDIENTS:

- 12 cherry tomatoes
- 12 small balls of fresh mozzarella cheese
- 12 fresh basil leaves
- 2 tablespoons extra virgin olive oil
- 1 tablespoon balsamic vinegar
- Salt and pepper to taste

NUTRITION PER SERVING:

- **Total Calories:** 250
- **Total Carbohydrates:** 5 g
    - Dietary Fiber: 1 g
    - Sugars: 3 g
- **Protein:** 14 g
- **Total Fat:** 20 g
    - Saturated Fat: 8 g
    - Unsaturated Fat: 10 g
- **Sodium:** 200 mg

PREPARATION:

1. **Assemble Skewers**: Thread a cherry tomato, a basil leaf, and a mozzarella ball onto a small skewer or toothpick. Repeat this process until all ingredients are used.
2. **Dress Skewers**: Drizzle olive oil and balsamic vinegar over the assembled skewers. Season with salt and pepper to taste.
3. **Chill and Serve**: Place the skewers in the refrigerator to chill for about 15-20 minutes before serving to allow the flavors to meld.

INGREDIENT SUBSTITUTIONS:

- **Mozzarella Cheese**: Substitute with low-fat mozzarella to reduce fat content while maintaining the creamy texture.
- **Olive Oil**: Use avocado oil for a different source of healthy fats with a milder taste.
- **Balsamic Vinegar**: Try apple cider vinegar for a slightly sweeter and fruitier acidity, adjusting the sweetness level accordingly.

Desserts Recipes

Sugar-Free Chocolate Mousse

PREPARATION TIME: 15 minutes
COOKING TIME: 0 minutes (plus chilling time)
SERVINGS: 4
INGREDIENTS

- 1 cup heavy cream
- 3 tablespoons unsweetened cocoa powder
- 2 tablespoons powdered erythritol (or preferred sugar substitute)
- 1 teaspoon vanilla extract
- A pinch of salt
- Dark chocolate shavings or cocoa nibs for garnish (optional)

NUTRITION PER SERVING

- **Total Calories:** 170 kcal
- **Total Carbs:** 3 g
  - Dietary Fiber: 1 g
  - Sugars: 1 g
- **Protein:** 2 g
- **Total Fat:** 17 g
  - Saturated Fats: 11 g
  - Unsaturated Fats: 5 g
- **Sodium:** 30 mg

PREPARATION

1. **Chill the Bowl:** Place a mixing bowl and beaters in the freezer for about 10 minutes to chill.
2. **Whip the Cream:** Remove the bowl from the freezer. Pour the heavy cream into the chilled bowl. Using an electric mixer, whip the cream on medium-high speed until it begins to thicken.
3. **Add Ingredients:** Add the unsweetened cocoa powder, powdered erythritol, vanilla extract, and a pinch of salt to the whipped cream.
4. **Continue Whipping:** Continue to whip the mixture until stiff peaks form. Be careful not to over-whip, as this can cause the cream to become grainy.
5. **Serve and Chill:** Spoon the mousse into four serving dishes. Refrigerate for at least 1 hour to allow the mousse to set.
6. **Garnish and Enjoy:** Before serving, garnish with dark chocolate shavings or cocoa nibs, if desired. Enjoy your sugar-free chocolate mousse!

Low-Carb Berry Cheesecake

PREPARATION TIME: 20 minutes
COOKING TIME: 45 minutes
CHILLING TIME: 4 hours
TOTAL TIME: 5 hours and 5 minutes
SERVINGS: 12

INGREDIENTS

For the Crust:
- 1 1/2 cups almond flour
- 1/4 cup powdered erythritol (or preferred sugar substitute)
- 1/4 cup melted butter
- 1 teaspoon vanilla extract

For the Filling:
- 24 ounces cream cheese, softened
- 3/4 cup powdered erythritol (or preferred sugar substitute)
- 3 large eggs
- 1 teaspoon vanilla extract
- 1/4 cup sour cream
- 1/4 cup heavy cream

For the Topping:
- 1 cup mixed berries (strawberries, blueberries, raspberries)
- 2 tablespoons powdered erythritol (or preferred sugar substitute)

NUTRITION PER SERVING
- **Total Calories:** 280 kcal
- **Total Carbs:** 7 g
  - Dietary Fiber: 2 g
  - Sugars: 3 g
- **Protein:** 6 g
- **Total Fat:** 26 g
  - Saturated Fats: 14 g
  - Unsaturated Fats: 10 g
- **Sodium:** 150 mg

PREPARATION

Prepare the Crust:
1. **Preheat Oven:** Preheat your oven to 325°F (160°C).
2. **Mix Ingredients:** In a medium bowl, mix together the almond flour, powdered erythritol, melted butter, and vanilla extract until well combined.
3. **Form the Crust:** Press the mixture firmly into the bottom of a 9-inch springform pan to form an even layer.
4. **Bake:** Bake the crust for 10 minutes, then remove from the oven and let it cool while you prepare the filling.

Prepare the Filling:
1. **Mix Cream Cheese and Sweetener:** In a large mixing bowl, beat the softened cream cheese and powdered erythritol together until smooth and creamy.
2. **Add Eggs:** Add the eggs one at a time, beating well after each addition.
3. **Add Remaining Ingredients:** Beat in the vanilla extract, sour cream, and heavy cream until the mixture is smooth and well combined.
4. **Pour Filling:** Pour the filling over the cooled crust, spreading it out evenly.

Bake the Cheesecake:
1. **Bake:** Bake the cheesecake in the preheated oven for 45 minutes, or until the center is set but still slightly jiggly. The edges should be lightly browned.
2. **Cool:** Turn off the oven and leave the cheesecake inside with the door slightly open for 1 hour to cool gradually.
3. **Chill:** Transfer the cheesecake to the refrigerator and chill for at least 4 hours, or overnight.

Prepare the Topping:
1. **Mix Berries and Sweetener:** In a small bowl, mix the mixed berries with the powdered erythritol.
2. **Top the Cheesecake:** Before serving, spread the berry mixture over the chilled cheesecake.

Almond Flour Cookies

PREPARATION TIME: 10 minutes
COOKING TIME: 15 minutes
SERVINGS: 12 cookies
INGREDIENTS

- 2 cups almond flour
- 1/4 cup powdered erythritol (or preferred sugar substitute)
- 1/4 teaspoon salt
- 1/4 teaspoon baking soda
- 1/4 cup melted coconut oil or butter
- 1 large egg
- 1 teaspoon vanilla extract
- Optional: 1/4 cup sugar-free chocolate chips or chopped nuts

NUTRITION PER SERVING (PER COOKIE)

- **Total Calories:** 140 kcal
- **Total Carbs:** 5 g
  - Dietary Fiber: 2 g; Sugars: 1 g
- **Protein:** 4 g
- **Total Fat:** 12 g
  - Saturated Fats: 4 g
  - Unsaturated Fats: 7 g
- **Sodium:** 40 mg

PREPARATION

1. **Preheat Oven:** Preheat your oven to 350°F (175°C). Line a baking sheet with parchment paper or a silicone baking mat.
2. **Mix Dry Ingredients:** In a medium bowl, whisk together the almond flour, powdered erythritol, salt, and baking soda until well combined.
3. **Add Wet Ingredients:** In another bowl, whisk together the melted coconut oil or butter, egg, and vanilla extract.
4. **Combine Ingredients:** Pour the wet ingredients into the dry ingredients and mix until a dough forms. If using, fold in the sugar-free chocolate chips or chopped nuts.
5. **Form Cookies:** Scoop tablespoons of dough onto the prepared baking sheet, spacing them about 2 inches apart. Gently flatten each dough ball with your fingers or a fork.
6. **Bake:** Bake in the preheated oven for 12-15 minutes, or until the edges are golden brown.
7. **Cool:** Remove from the oven and let the cookies cool on the baking sheet for a few minutes before transferring them to a wire rack to cool completely.

Keto Brownies

PREPARATION TIME: 10 minutes
COOKING TIME: 25 minutes
SERVINGS: 16 brownies
INGREDIENTS

- 1/2 cup butter, melted
- 1/2 cup powdered erythritol (or preferred keto-friendly sweetener)
- 1 teaspoon vanilla extract
- 3 large eggs
- 1/2 cup almond flour
- 1/4 cup unsweetened cocoa powder
- 1/4 teaspoon salt
- 1/2 teaspoon baking powder
- 1/4 cup sugar-free chocolate chips (optional)

NUTRITION PER SERVING (PER BROWNIE)

- **Total Calories:** 120 kcal
- **Total Carbs:** 5 g
  - Dietary Fiber: 2 g
  - Sugars: 1 g
- **Protein:** 3g
- **Total Fat:** 11 g
  - Saturated Fats: 5 g
  - Unsaturated Fats: 5 g
- **Sodium:** 70 mg

PREPARATION

1. **Preheat Oven:** Preheat your oven to 350°F (175°C). Line an 8x8-inch baking pan with parchment paper or grease it lightly.
2. **Mix Wet Ingredients:** In a large bowl, combine the melted butter, powdered erythritol, and vanilla extract. Mix until well combined. Add the eggs, one at a time, beating well after each addition.
3. **Combine Dry Ingredients:** In a separate bowl, whisk together the almond flour, unsweetened cocoa powder, salt, and baking powder until well mixed.
4. **Combine Wet and Dry Ingredients:** Gradually add the dry ingredients to the wet ingredients, stirring until just combined. If using, fold in the sugar-free chocolate chips.
5. **Pour Batter into Pan:** Pour the brownie batter into the prepared baking pan, spreading it out evenly.
6. **Bake:** Bake in the preheated oven for 20-25 minutes, or until a toothpick inserted into the center comes out mostly clean with a few moist crumbs.
7. **Cool and Serve:** Remove the brownies from the oven and let them cool in the pan for about 15 minutes. Then, transfer the brownies to a wire rack to cool completely before cutting into 16 squares.

Coconut Macaroons

PREPARATION TIME: 10 minutes
COOKING TIME: 20 minutes
SERVINGS: 18 macaroons
INGREDIENTS

- 3 cups unsweetened shredded coconut
- 1/2 cup powdered erythritol (or preferred sugar substitute)
- 1/4 cup almond flour
- 1/4 teaspoon salt
- 3 large egg whites
- 1 teaspoon vanilla extract
- Optional: 1/4 cup sugar-free dark chocolate chips, melted (for drizzling)

NUTRITION PER SERVING (PER MACAROON)

- **Total Calories**: 80 kcal
- **Total Carbs:** 5 g
  - Dietary Fiber: 3 g
  - Sugars: 1 g
- **Protein:** 2 g
- **Total Fat:** 7 g
  - Saturated Fats: 6 g
  - Unsaturated Fats: 1 g
- **Sodium:** 40 mg

PREPARATION

1. **Preheat Oven:** Preheat your oven to 350°F (175°C). Line a baking sheet with parchment paper or a silicone baking mat.
2. **Mix Dry Ingredients:** In a large bowl, combine the shredded coconut, powdered erythritol, almond flour, and salt. Mix until well combined.
3. **Whip Egg Whites:** In a separate bowl, beat the egg whites until stiff peaks form. This can be done using a hand mixer or a stand mixer.
4. **Combine Ingredients:** Gently fold the beaten egg whites and vanilla extract into the coconut mixture. Mix until all ingredients are well combined and the mixture holds together.
5. **Form Macaroons:** Using a tablespoon or a small cookie scoop, scoop the mixture and place mounds onto the prepared baking sheet, spacing them about 1 inch apart.
6. **Bake:** Bake in the preheated oven for 15-20 minutes, or until the macaroons are golden brown around the edges and set in the center.
7. **Cool and Optional Drizzle:** Remove from the oven and let the macaroons cool on the baking sheet for a few minutes before transferring them to a wire rack to cool completely. If desired, drizzle with melted sugar-free dark chocolate for an extra touch of sweetness.

Lemon Ricotta Cake

PREPARATION TIME: 15 minutes
COOKING TIME: 45 minutes
SERVINGS: 12
INGREDIENTS

- 1 1/2 cups almond flour
- 1/2 cup powdered erythritol
- 1 teaspoon baking powder
- 1/4 teaspoon salt
- 3 large eggs
- 1 cup ricotta cheese
- 1/4 cup unsweetened almond milk
- 1/4 cup melted butter or coconut oil
- 1 tablespoon lemon zest
- 1/4 cup fresh lemon juice
- 1 teaspoon vanilla extract

NUTRITION PER SERVING (PER SLICE)

- **Total Calories:** 180 kcal
- **Total Carbs:** 6 g
  - Dietary Fiber: 2 g; Sugars: 1 g
- **Protein:** 7 g
- **Total Fat:** 15 g
  - Saturated Fats: 6 g;Unsaturated Fats: 8 g
- **Sodium:** 130 mg

PREPARATION

1. **Preheat Oven:** Preheat your oven to 350°F (175°C). Grease a 9-inch round cake pan and line the bottom with parchment paper.
2. **Mix Dry Ingredients:** In a medium bowl, whisk together the almond flour, powdered erythritol, baking powder, and salt until well combined.
3. **Mix Wet Ingredients:** In a large bowl, beat the eggs until frothy. Add the ricotta cheese, almond milk, melted butter or coconut oil, lemon zest, lemon juice, and vanilla extract. Mix until smooth.
4. **Combine Ingredients:** Gradually add the dry ingredients to the wet ingredients, mixing until just combined. Do not overmix.
5. **Pour Batter into Pan:** Pour the batter into the prepared cake pan and spread it out evenly.
6. **Bake:** Bake in the preheated oven for 40-45 minutes, or until the top is golden brown and a toothpick inserted into the center comes out clean.
7. **Cool and Serve:** Allow the cake to cool in the pan for 10 minutes, then transfer to a wire rack to cool completely. Once cooled, slice into 12 servings and enjoy.

Pumpkin Spice Muffins

PREPARATION TIME: 15 minutes
COOKING TIME: 25 minutes
SERVINGS: 12 muffins
INGREDIENTS

- 1 1/2 cups almond flour
- 1/2 cup coconut flour
- 1/2 cup powdered erythritol (or preferred sugar substitute)
- 1 teaspoon baking soda
- 1/4 teaspoon salt
- 2 teaspoons pumpkin pie spice
- 1 teaspoon ground cinnamon
- 3 large eggs
- 1 cup pumpkin puree (unsweetened)
- 1/2 cup unsweetened almond milk
- 1/4 cup melted coconut oil or butter
- 1 teaspoon vanilla extract

NUTRITION PER SERVING (PER MUFFIN)

- **Total Calories:** 130 kcal
- **Total Carbs:** 8 g
  - Dietary Fiber: 4 g; Sugars: 2 g
- **Protein:** 4 g
- **Total Fat:** 10 g
  - Saturated Fats: 4 g; Unsaturated Fats: 5 g
- **Sodium:** 100 mg

PREPARATION

1. **Preheat Oven:** Preheat your oven to 350°F (175°C). Line a 12-cup muffin tin with paper liners or grease it lightly.
2. **Mix Dry Ingredients:** In a large bowl, whisk together the almond flour, coconut flour, powdered erythritol, baking soda, salt, pumpkin pie spice, and ground cinnamon until well combined.
3. **Mix Wet Ingredients:** In another bowl, beat the eggs and then add the pumpkin puree, unsweetened almond milk, melted coconut oil or butter, and vanilla extract. Mix until smooth.
4. **Combine Ingredients:** Gradually add the wet ingredients to the dry ingredients, mixing until just combined. Be careful not to overmix.
5. **Fill Muffin Tin:** Divide the batter evenly among the 12 muffin cups, filling each about 3/4 full.
6. **Bake:** Bake in the preheated oven for 20-25 minutes, or until a toothpick inserted into the center of a muffin comes out clean.
7. **Cool and Serve:** Allow the muffins to cool in the tin for about 10 minutes, then transfer them to a wire rack to cool completely. Enjoy your diabetic-friendly pumpkin spice muffins!

Strawberry Basil Sorbet

PREPARATION TIME: 15 minutes
FREEZING TIME: 2-3 hours
SERVINGS: 6
INGREDIENTS

- 4 cups fresh strawberries, hulled and halved
- 1/2 cup water
- 1/4 cup powdered erythritol (or preferred sugar substitute)
- 2 tablespoons fresh lemon juice
- 1 tablespoon chopped fresh basil leaves
- Optional: additional basil leaves for garnish

NUTRITION PER SERVING (PER 1/2 CUP SERVING)

- **Total Calories:** 30 kcal
- **Total Carbs:** 8 g
  - Dietary Fiber: 2 g
  - Sugars: 4 g
- **Protein:** 0.5 g
- **Total Fat:** 0.2 g
  - Saturated Fats: 0 g
  - Unsaturated Fats: 0.2 g
- **Sodium:** 2 mg

PREPARATION

1. **Prepare Strawberries:** Place the strawberries in a food processor or blender and blend until smooth. If desired, strain the strawberry puree through a fine mesh sieve to remove the seeds for a smoother texture.
2. **Make Syrup:** In a small saucepan, combine the water and powdered erythritol. Heat over medium heat, stirring until the erythritol is completely dissolved. Remove from heat and let it cool to room temperature.
3. **Combine Ingredients:** In a large bowl, mix the strawberry puree, cooled erythritol syrup, fresh lemon juice, and chopped basil leaves. Stir until well combined.
4. **Freeze Mixture:** Pour the mixture into a shallow, freezer-safe container. Place in the freezer and let it freeze for about 2-3 hours, stirring with a fork every 30 minutes to break up any ice crystals and ensure a smooth texture.
5. **Serve:** Once the sorbet has reached the desired consistency, scoop it into serving bowls. Garnish with additional basil leaves if desired and serve immediately.

Chocolate Peanut Butter Fat Bombs

PREPARATION TIME: 10 minutes
FREEZING TIME: 1 hour
SERVINGS: 12 fat bombs
INGREDIENTS

- 1/2 cup natural peanut butter (unsweetened, no added sugar)
- 1/4 cup coconut oil, melted
- 1/4 cup cocoa powder (unsweetened)
- 2 tablespoons powdered erythritol (or preferred keto-friendly sweetener)
- 1 teaspoon vanilla extract
- A pinch of salt

NUTRITION PER SERVING (PER FAT BOMB)

- **Total Calories:** 100 kcal
- **Total Carbs:** 3 g
  - Dietary Fiber: 1 g
  - Sugars: 0.5 g
- **Protein:** 2 g
- **Total Fat:** 9 g
  - Saturated Fats: 5 g
  - Unsaturated Fats: 4 g
- **Sodium:** 30 mg

PREPARATION

1. **Mix Ingredients:** In a medium bowl, combine the peanut butter, melted coconut oil, cocoa powder, powdered erythritol, vanilla extract, and a pinch of salt. Stir until the mixture is smooth and well combined.
2. **Pour into Molds:** Pour the mixture into a silicone mold or an ice cube tray, filling each compartment about three-quarters full.
3. **Freeze:** Place the mold or tray in the freezer for about 1 hour, or until the fat bombs are solid.
4. **Serve:** Once solid, remove the fat bombs from the mold or tray. Store them in an airtight container in the freezer. Serve directly from the freezer for the best texture.

Cinnamon Apple Slices

PREPARATION TIME: 10 minutes
COOKING TIME: 15 minutes
SERVINGS: 4
INGREDIENTS

- 2 large apples (such as Granny Smith or Fuji)
- 1 tablespoon melted coconut oil or butter
- 1 teaspoon ground cinnamon
- 1 tablespoon powdered erythritol (or preferred sugar substitute)
- 1 teaspoon vanilla extract
- A pinch of salt
- Optional: a squeeze of fresh lemon juice

NUTRITION PER SERVING

- **Total Calories:** 80 kcal
- **Total Carbs:** 16 g
  - Dietary Fiber: 3 g
  - Sugars: 10 g
- **Protein:** 0.5 g
- **Total Fat:** 2 g
  - Saturated Fats: 1.5 g
  - Unsaturated Fats: 0.5 g
- **Sodium:** 10 mg

PREPARATION

1. **Preheat Oven:** Preheat your oven to 375°F (190°C). Line a baking sheet with parchment paper or a silicone baking mat.
2. **Prepare Apples:** Wash and core the apples. Slice them into even, thin slices, about 1/4 inch thick. If desired, drizzle with a bit of lemon juice to prevent browning.
3. **Mix Seasoning:** In a large bowl, combine the melted coconut oil or butter, ground cinnamon, powdered erythritol, vanilla extract, and a pinch of salt. Mix until well combined.
4. **Coat Apple Slices:** Add the apple slices to the bowl and toss them until they are evenly coated with the cinnamon mixture.
5. **Arrange on Baking Sheet:** Spread the apple slices in a single layer on the prepared baking sheet.
6. **Bake:** Bake in the preheated oven for 12-15 minutes, or until the apples are tender and slightly caramelized. Be careful not to overbake, as the apples can become mushy.
7. **Serve:** Remove from the oven and let the apple slices cool slightly before serving. Enjoy them warm or at room temperature.

Blueberry Almond Crumble

PREPARATION TIME: 15 minutes
COOKING TIME: 30 minutes
SERVINGS: 8
INGREDIENTS
For the Filling:

- 4 cups fresh or frozen blueberries
- 1 tablespoon fresh lemon juice
- 1/4 cup powdered erythritol (or preferred sugar substitute)
- 2 tablespoons almond flour
- 1 teaspoon vanilla extract

For the Crumble Topping:

- 1 cup almond flour
- 1/2 cup sliced almonds
- 1/4 cup powdered erythritol (or preferred sugar substitute)
- 1/4 cup melted coconut oil or butter
- 1 teaspoon ground cinnamon
- A pinch of salt

NUTRITION PER SERVING

- **Total Calories:** 140 kcal
- **Total Carbs:** 12 g
  - Dietary Fiber: 4 g;
  - Sugars: 6 g
- **Protein:** 3 g
- **Total Fat:** 11 g
  - Saturated Fats: 4 g;
  - Unsaturated Fats: 7 g
- **Sodium:** 30 mg

PREPARATION

1. **Preheat Oven:** Preheat your oven to 350°F (175°C). Lightly grease an 8x8-inch baking dish or similar-sized ovenproof dish.
2. **Prepare the Filling:** In a large bowl, combine the blueberries, lemon juice, powdered erythritol, almond flour, and vanilla extract. Mix gently until the blueberries are evenly coated. Pour the mixture into the prepared baking dish and spread it out evenly.
3. **Make the Crumble Topping:** In a medium bowl, combine the almond flour, sliced almonds, powdered erythritol, melted coconut oil or butter, ground cinnamon, and a pinch of salt. Mix until the ingredients are well combined and form a crumbly texture.
4. **Top the Blueberries:** Sprinkle the crumble topping evenly over the blueberry filling.
5. **Bake:** Bake in the preheated oven for 25-30 minutes, or until the topping is golden brown and the blueberry filling is bubbling around the edges.
6. **Cool and Serve:** Remove the crumble from the oven and let it cool for about 10 minutes before serving. Enjoy warm or at room temperature.

Vanilla Bean Panna Cotta

PREPARATION TIME: 20 minutes
CHILLING TIME: 4 hours
SERVINGS: 6
INGREDIENTS

- 2 cups heavy cream
- 1 cup unsweetened almond milk
- 1/4 cup powdered erythritol (or preferred sugar substitute)
- 1 vanilla bean (or 2 teaspoons vanilla extract)
- 2 teaspoons unflavored gelatin
- 3 tablespoons cold water

NUTRITION PER SERVING (PER PANNA COTTA)

- **Total Calories:** 220 kcal
- **Total Carbs:** 5 g
  - Dietary Fiber: 0 g
  - Sugars: 2 g
- **Protein:** 3 g
- **Total Fat:** 21 g
  - Saturated Fats: 13 g
  - Unsaturated Fats: 7 g
- **Sodium:** 25 mg

PREPARATION

1. **Prepare the Vanilla:** If using a vanilla bean, slice it lengthwise and scrape out the seeds. Set both the seeds and the pod aside. If using vanilla extract, you will add it later.
2. **Bloom the Gelatin:** In a small bowl, sprinkle the unflavored gelatin over the cold water. Let it sit for about 5 minutes to soften and "bloom."
3. **Heat the Cream Mixture:** In a medium saucepan, combine the heavy cream, unsweetened almond milk, powdered erythritol, vanilla bean seeds and pod (or vanilla extract if using), and a pinch of salt. Heat the mixture over medium heat until it is hot but not boiling, stirring occasionally. Remove from heat.
4. **Dissolve the Gelatin:** Remove the vanilla bean pod from the cream mixture. Add the bloomed gelatin to the hot cream mixture and whisk until the gelatin is completely dissolved.
5. **Strain and Pour:** Pour the mixture through a fine mesh sieve into a large measuring cup or bowl to remove any lumps or remaining vanilla bean pod bits.
6. **Chill:** Pour the panna cotta mixture into six ramekins or dessert glasses. Allow to cool to room temperature, then cover with plastic wrap and refrigerate for at least 4 hours, or until set.
7. **Serve:** Once set, the panna cotta can be served directly in the ramekins or glasses. Optionally, you can unmold the panna cotta onto plates by running a thin knife around the edges and gently inverting them onto the plates.

Raspberry Chia Jam Bars

PREPARATION TIME: 20 minutes
COOKING TIME: 30 minutes
CHILLING TIME: 1 hour
SERVINGS: 16 bars
INGREDIENTS
For the Raspberry Chia Jam:
- 2 cups fresh or frozen raspberries
- 2 tablespoons chia seeds
- 2 tablespoons powdered erythritol (or preferred sugar substitute)
- 1 teaspoon vanilla extract

For the Crust and Crumble Topping:
- 2 cups almond flour
- 1/2 cup unsweetened shredded coconut
- 1/4 cup powdered erythritol (or preferred sugar substitute)
- 1/2 teaspoon baking powder
- 1/4 teaspoon salt
- 1/2 cup melted coconut oil or butter
- 1 teaspoon vanilla extract

NUTRITION PER SERVING (PER BAR)
- **Total Calories:** 160 kcal
- **Total Carbs:** 10 g
  - Dietary Fiber: 4 g
  - Sugars: 2 g
- **Protein:** 3 g
- **Total Fat:** 14 g
  - Saturated Fats: 7 g
  - Unsaturated Fats: 6 g
- **Sodium:** 40 mg

PREPARATION

1. **Prepare the Raspberry Chia Jam:** In a small saucepan, combine the raspberries and powdered erythritol. Cook over medium heat, stirring occasionally, until the raspberries break down and release their juices, about 5-7 minutes. Remove from heat and stir in the chia seeds and vanilla extract. Let the mixture sit for about 10 minutes to thicken, stirring occasionally.

2. **Preheat Oven:** Preheat your oven to 350°F (175°C). Line an 8x8-inch baking dish with parchment paper, leaving some overhang for easy removal.

3. **Prepare the Crust and Topping:** In a large bowl, combine the almond flour, unsweetened shredded coconut, powdered erythritol, baking powder, and salt. Stir in the melted coconut oil or butter and vanilla extract until the mixture is well combined and crumbly.

4. **Form the Crust:** Press about two-thirds of the crust mixture firmly into the bottom of the prepared baking dish to form an even layer.

5. **Add the Jam Layer:** Spread the raspberry chia jam evenly over the crust layer.

6. **Add the Crumble Topping:** Sprinkle the remaining crust mixture over the jam layer, gently pressing it down to adhere.

7. **Bake:** Bake in the preheated oven for 25-30 minutes, or until the top is golden brown.

8. **Cool and Chill:** Remove from the oven and let cool to room temperature. Once cooled, transfer to the refrigerator and chill for at least 1 hour before cutting into bars.

9. **Serve:** Using the parchment paper overhang, lift the bars out of the baking dish and place on a cutting board. Cut into 16 squares and serve.

Carrot Cake Bites

PREPARATION TIME: 20 minutes
COOKING TIME: 0 minutes (no bake)
CHILLING TIME: 1 hour
SERVINGS: 12 bites
INGREDIENTS

- 1 cup grated carrots
- 1 cup almond flour
- 1/2 cup unsweetened shredded coconut
- 1/4 cup powdered erythritol
- 1/4 cup chopped walnuts or pecans
- 1/4 cup almond butter or peanut butter (unsweetened)
- 1 teaspoon vanilla extract
- 1 teaspoon ground cinnamon
- 1/4 teaspoon ground nutmeg
- 1/4 teaspoon ground ginger
- A pinch of salt

NUTRITION PER SERVING (PER BITE)

- **Total Calories:** 80 kcal
- **Total Carbs:** 6 g
  - Dietary Fiber: 2 g; Sugars: 1 g
- **Protein:** 2 g
- **Total Fat:** 6 g
  - Saturated Fats: 2 g; Unsaturated Fats: 4 g
- **Sodium:** 20 mg

Coconut Lime Energy Balls

PREPARATION TIME: 15 minutes
CHILLING TIME: 30 minutes
SERVINGS: 12 energy balls
INGREDIENTS

- 1 cup unsweetened shredded coconut
- 1/2 cup almond flour
- 1/4 cup powdered erythritol (or preferred sugar substitute)
- 2 tablespoons chia seeds
- 2 tablespoons coconut oil, melted
- 2 tablespoons fresh lime juice
- 1 tablespoon lime zest
- 1 teaspoon vanilla extract
- A pinch of salt

NUTRITION PER SERVING (PER ENERGY BALL)

- **Total Calories:** 90 kcal
- **Total Carbs:** 4 g
  - Dietary Fiber: 2 g; Sugars: 1 g
- **Protein:** 2 g
- **Total Fat:** 8 g
  - Saturated Fats: 6 g; Unsaturated Fats: 2 g
- **Sodium:** 10 mg

PREPARATION

1. **Prepare Carrots:** Grate the carrots using a fine grater and set them aside.
2. **Mix Dry Ingredients:** In a large bowl, combine the almond flour, unsweetened shredded coconut, powdered erythritol, chopped walnuts or pecans, ground cinnamon, ground nutmeg, ground ginger, and a pinch of salt. Mix until well combined.
3. **Combine Wet Ingredients:** In a small bowl, mix together the grated carrots, almond butter or peanut butter, and vanilla extract until well combined.
4. **Combine All Ingredients:** Add the wet ingredients to the dry ingredients and mix thoroughly until a dough forms. If the mixture is too dry, you can add a little more almond butter or a splash of water.
5. **Form Bites:** Using a tablespoon or small cookie scoop, scoop out portions of the dough and roll them into balls. Place the balls on a baking sheet lined with parchment paper.
6. **Chill:** Refrigerate the carrot cake bites for at least 1 hour to firm up.
7. **Serve:** Once chilled, the bites are ready to be served. Store any leftovers in an airtight container in the refrigerator.

PREPARATION

1. **Mix Dry Ingredients:** In a large bowl, combine the unsweetened shredded coconut, almond flour, powdered erythritol, and chia seeds. Mix until well combined.
2. **Add Wet Ingredients:** Add the melted coconut oil, fresh lime juice, lime zest, and vanilla extract to the dry ingredients. Mix thoroughly until the mixture holds together. If the mixture is too dry, add a little more lime juice or water, a teaspoon at a time.
3. **Form Energy Balls:** Using a tablespoon or small cookie scoop, scoop out portions of the mixture and roll them into balls. Place the balls on a baking sheet lined with parchment paper.
4. **Chill:** Refrigerate the energy balls for at least 30 minutes to firm up.
5. **Serve:** Once chilled, the energy balls are ready to be served. Store any leftovers in an airtight container in the refrigerator.

365-Day Diabetic Meal Plan

Diabetes management involves comprehensive lifestyle changes, particularly in diet, which is why the implementation of a structured meal plan is crucial. This 365-Day Diabetic Meal Plan is meticulously designed to stabilize blood sugar levels and ensure a balanced, nutritious diet that accommodates the needs of individuals with diabetes.

The primary objective of this meal plan is to stabilize blood glucose levels. Fluctuations in blood sugar can lead to both short-term discomfort and long-term health complications, making dietary consistency and balance critical. This plan emphasizes the inclusion of low glycemic index foods, balanced macronutrients, and dietary fiber, which help in slow glucose absorption and provide a steady energy release. This approach not only aids in maintaining optimal blood glucose levels but also supports overall metabolic health, which is beneficial for preventing diabetes-related complications.

DESIGN OF THE MEAL PLAN

This meal plan is specifically designed for the average woman who aims to lose weight, with a daily caloric intake ranging between 1200-1300 calories. This caloric target is aligned with common dietary recommendations for healthy and sustainable weight loss. It is crucial to note that while this plan provides a structured approach to meal distribution and caloric intake, individual needs may vary. Factors such as age, activity level, and overall health should be considered when adapting this plan. Users are encouraged to adjust portions and snack options to better fit their specific caloric requirements and nutritional needs to ensure both effectiveness and personal dietary satisfaction.

In an earlier chapter, "Setting Up Your Diabetic Diet", methods for calculating individual caloric needs are detailed. Once these needs are established, adjustments to the meal plan should be made accordingly. For instance, if your calculated daily caloric requirement is 2000 calories, and a meal is designed to provide 400 calories but you need 500 calories, you should increase the ingredients by a scale factor— in this case, by 25%. This method ensures that each meal's energy contribution fits your tailored dietary needs while maintaining nutritional balance.

FLEXIBILITY IN CALORIC INTAKE

While precision in tracking caloric intake can be important, it's equally crucial not to become overly fixated on exact daily caloric counts. Striving for an overly rigid approach to nutrition can actually be counterproductive, as it may lead to stress and an unhealthy relationship with food. Nutritional plans should be flexible and adaptable to fit the natural ebb and flow of daily life.

It is completely normal for daily caloric intake to vary—a person might consume 2200 calories one day and 1800 the next, depending on factors like activity level, social engagements, and even fluctuating appetite. What is more important than any single day's intake is the average consumption over a longer period, such as a week. Ensuring that this average aligns with your calculated caloric needs is what truly matters in maintaining effective nutritional balance.

This approach to dieting allows for greater flexibility and makes it easier to handle social meals, special occasions, and the natural variations in daily appetite without falling into a cycle of guilt or restriction. By embracing a more adaptable dietary plan, individuals can ensure that their approach to eating is sustainable over the long term, promoting better overall health and well-being without causing undue stress or unnecessary restrictions. This balanced perspective on calorie counting supports not just physical health, but mental and emotional health as well, making it a more holistic approach to nutrition.

365-DAY MEAL PLAN

Here is the first set of the meal plan for days 1 to 15. You can use this pattern and repeat it for the subsequent 15-day blocks, adjusting as necessary based on any feedback or additional recipes you might want to incorporate later.

DAY	BREAKFAST	SNACK	LUNCH	SNACK	DINNER
1	Berry Protein Smoothie (79)	Mango Coconut Yogurt (127)	Grilled Chicken Salad (92)	Avocado and Radish Toast (126)	Zucchini Lasagna (106)
2	Green Goddess Smoothie (80)	Almond Butter and Pear Toast (125)	Turkey and Avocado Wrap (93)	Raspberry Lime Yogurt (132)	Stuffed Bell Peppers (107)
3	Chia & Flaxseed Smoothie (80)	Strawberry Basil Yogurt (129)	Vegetable Stir-Fry with Tofu (93)	Tuna and Olive Tapenade on Crispbread (126)	Spinach and Mushroom Stuffed Chicken Breast (107)
4	Almond Butter & Banana Smoothie (81)	Cottage Cheese and Tomato Toast (125)	Beef and Broccoli (94)	Cherry Vanilla Smoothie (132)	Cauliflower Mac and Cheese (108)
5	Egg Spinach and Feta Wrap (91)	Peach Ginger Smoothie (127)	Shrimp and Arugula Salad (94)	Hummus and Veggie Pita Pocket (122)	Garlic Lemon Butter Salmon (109)
6	Vegetable Omelet (82)	Kiwi Spinach Smoothie (131)	Lentil and Barley Soup (95)	Ricotta and Roasted Pepper Toast (124)	Korean Beef Bowl with Vegetables (117)
7	Spinach & Feta Egg Muffins (82)	Apple Cinnamon Yogurt Parfait (130)	Chickpea and Farro Soup (96)	Caprese Skewers (134)	Grilled Tuna Steaks with Olive Tapenade (110)
8	Turkish Menemen (83)	Cherry Vanilla Smoothie (132)	White Bean and Quinoa Soup (96)	Banana Nut Yogurt (133)	Cod in Parchment with Asparagus (110)
9	Kale and Cheddar Scramble (83)	Almond Butter and Pear Toast (125)	Mediterranean Vegetable and Bulgur Soup (97)	Strawberry Basil Yogurt (129)	Seafood Paella with Brown Rice (111)
10	Avocado Baked Eggs (84)	Raspberry Lime Yogurt (132)	Split Pea and Rice Soup (97)	Cottage Cheese and Tomato Toast (125)	Chickpea Vegetable Curry (112)
11	Steel-Cut Oats with Apple and Cinnamon (84)	Kiwi Spinach Smoothie (131)	Chickpea Curry with Brown Rice (98)	Chicken Salad Lettuce Wraps (123)	Tofu Stir-Fry with Broccoli and Bell Pepper (112)
12	Overnight Chia Oat Pudding (85)	Apple Cinnamon Yogurt Parfait (130)	Mexican Chicken Salad (99)	Mango Coconut Yogurt (127)	Butternut Squash Risotto (113)
13	Savory Quinoa Porridge (85)	Blueberry Almond Smoothie (131)	Greek Salad with Grilled Salmon (99)	Ricotta and Roasted Pepper Toast (124)	Portobello Mushroom Pizzas (114)
14	Buckwheat Porridge with Hazelnuts (86)	Pineapple Coconut Smoothie (130)	Japanese Soba Noodle Bowl (100)	Avocado and Radish Toast (126)	Lentil Tacos with Homemade Salsa (114)
15	Barley Porridge with Blueberries (86)	Cherry Vanilla Smoothie (132)	Mediterranean Tuna Salad (100)	Chicken Salad Lettuce Wraps (123)	Thai Basil Chicken (115)

365-DAY MEAL PLAN EXPLANATION

This 365-day meal plan, meticulously designed for individuals with diabetes, is crafted to ensure variety and nutritional balance, making it suitable for long-term adherence. It starts with a well-structured 15-day cycle that includes five daily meals: breakfast, a morning snack, lunch, an afternoon snack, and dinner. Each meal is composed to offer a balanced intake of carbohydrates, proteins, and fats, which are crucial for managing blood sugar levels effectively and maintaining overall health.

To keep the meal plan exciting and responsive to personal tastes and seasonal availability, each recipe in the "Diabetic Food Bible" includes suggestions for ingredient substitutions. This allows for a high degree of customization and helps ensure that the meals remain appealing and suitable under various circumstances. After completing the initial 15-day cycle, you can start again, this time swapping ingredients according to the suggestions provided. This not only injects variety into your diet but also empowers you to tailor the meals more closely to your dietary needs and taste preferences.

Expanding on the basic structure, these ingredient swap suggestions allow the meal plan to be extended dramatically. By utilizing the various replacement options outlined for each recipe, it's possible to adapt the meal plan for up to 2,000 days. This vast range ensures that you can enjoy a diverse array of meals over an extended period, avoiding dietary boredom and enhancing your ability to manage diabetes effectively. The suggested swaps are carefully designed to maintain nutritional balance, making it easy to adapt the meals throughout different seasons. This takes advantage of seasonal produce, which can enhance the freshness and cost-effectiveness of your meals.

Ultimately, this flexibility transforms the 365-day meal plan from a mere dietary guideline to a comprehensive, adaptable framework that you can use year-round. Whether you're seeking variety, need to adapt to different seasonal ingredients, or have any other specific dietary requirements, the "Diabetic Food Bible" provides a dynamic and practical approach to dietary management. This plan not only supports your health goals but also accommodates your evolving dietary preferences in a way that is both sustainable and enjoyable.

Managing Diabetes with Exercise

Exercise is a cornerstone of diabetes management, offering a myriad of benefits that extend beyond merely controlling blood sugar levels. For individuals living with diabetes, incorporating regular physical activity into their daily routine is not just beneficial; it's essential. This chapter delves into the importance of exercise in diabetes management and explores the profound impacts it can have on overall health and well-being.

THE IMPORTANCE OF EXERCISE IN DIABETES MANAGEMENT

Managing diabetes involves a delicate balance of medication, diet, and lifestyle choices. Among these, exercise stands out as a powerful tool in maintaining optimal health. Regular physical activity helps improve the body's sensitivity to insulin, allowing cells to use available insulin more effectively to take up glucose during and after exercise. This process not only aids in lowering blood sugar levels but also helps to stabilize them over time, reducing the risk of dangerous spikes and drops.

Exercise also plays a critical role in weight management, which is particularly important for individuals with type 2 diabetes. Excess body fat, especially around the abdomen, can increase the body's resistance to insulin. By engaging in consistent physical activity, individuals can reduce body fat and improve their body's ability to manage insulin and glucose levels.

Moreover, exercise contributes to cardiovascular health, which is a significant concern for diabetics, who are at a higher risk for heart disease and stroke. Regular physical activity strengthens the heart and improves circulation, thereby lowering blood pressure and cholesterol levels.

BENEFITS OF REGULAR PHYSICAL ACTIVITY FOR DIABETICS

The benefits of exercise for diabetics are extensive and well-documented. Here are some of the key advantages:

- **Improved Blood Sugar Control**: Exercise helps muscles use glucose for energy, reducing blood sugar levels. Regular physical activity can lead to more stable blood sugar levels and reduce the need for medication in some cases.

- **Enhanced Insulin Sensitivity**: Physical activity increases the body's sensitivity to insulin, which means that cells can absorb glucose more efficiently. This improvement can help lower blood sugar levels and enhance overall glucose metabolism.

- **Weight Management**: Exercise, combined with a balanced diet, is effective in managing weight. Maintaining a healthy weight can improve insulin sensitivity and blood sugar control, and reduce the risk of complications associated with diabetes.

- **Cardiovascular Health**: Regular exercise strengthens the heart and improves blood circulation, reducing the risk of heart disease, which is a common complication of diabetes. It also helps in lowering blood pressure and bad cholesterol levels while raising good cholesterol levels.

- **Reduced Risk of Complications**: Engaging in regular physical activity can lower the risk of diabetes-related complications such as neuropathy (nerve damage), nephropathy (kidney damage), and retinopathy (eye damage).

- **Improved Mood and Mental Health**: Exercise releases endorphins, the body's natural mood lifters, which can help combat stress, anxiety, and depression. For diabetics, managing mental health is as crucial as managing physical health.

- **Increased Energy Levels**: Regular physical activity can help increase overall energy levels, reduce fatigue, and improve physical endurance. This can enhance daily functioning and quality of life for individuals with diabetes.

- **Better Sleep**: Exercise can improve sleep patterns and quality of sleep, which is vital for overall health and well-being. Good sleep hygiene is particularly important for diabetics, as poor sleep can negatively affect blood sugar levels.

Incorporating exercise into daily routines doesn't have to be daunting. Simple activities like walking, cycling, swimming, or even engaging in household chores can make a significant difference. The key is consistency and finding enjoyable forms of physical activity that can be sustained over the long term.

Understanding the Relationship Between Exercise and Blood Sugar

Exercise plays a pivotal role in managing diabetes by directly influencing blood glucose levels. When you engage in physical activity, your muscles require more energy, which they obtain by utilizing glucose from the bloodstream. This increased glucose uptake by muscle cells helps lower blood sugar levels during and after exercise. Moreover, physical activity enhances the body's sensitivity to insulin, meaning that cells are more efficient at absorbing glucose even when insulin levels are low. This dual action of immediate glucose consumption and improved insulin sensitivity contributes significantly to better blood sugar control.

During exercise, the body initiates several processes that influence glucose levels. Initially, muscles tap into stored glycogen for energy. As these glycogen stores deplete, the liver releases glucose into the bloodstream to meet the energy demands. This natural regulation ensures a steady supply of glucose, preventing drastic fluctuations in blood sugar levels. Furthermore, the hormonal changes induced by physical activity, such as increased levels of adrenaline and glucagon, also facilitate the mobilization of glucose from storage sites in the liver and muscles.

However, while exercise is beneficial, it is crucial to be aware of the potential risks and understand how to mitigate them effectively. One common risk associated with exercise is hypoglycemia, or low blood sugar. This condition can occur during or after physical activity, especially if you use insulin or certain oral diabetes medications that increase insulin production. Symptoms of hypoglycemia include dizziness, shaking, sweating, hunger, irritability, and confusion. To prevent hypoglycemia, it is important to monitor blood sugar levels before, during, and after exercise. Consuming a small, carbohydrate-rich snack before engaging in prolonged or intense physical activity can help maintain stable glucose levels. Additionally, always carry a fast-acting source of glucose, such as glucose tablets or juice, to quickly address any signs of low blood sugar.

Another risk is hyperglycemia, or high blood sugar, which can occur if you exercise when your blood sugar levels are already elevated, particularly if ketones are present. Exercising under these conditions can cause blood sugar levels to rise further. To mitigate this risk, check your blood sugar levels before starting your workout. If your levels are above 250 mg/dL and ketones are present in your urine, it is advisable to avoid exercise and consult your healthcare provider for guidance.

It is also essential to consider individual health conditions when planning an exercise routine. For instance, those with diabetic neuropathy should choose low-impact activities to avoid foot injuries, while individuals with cardiovascular issues may need a tailored exercise plan approved by their doctor. Staying hydrated, wearing appropriate footwear, and gradually increasing the intensity and duration of exercise can further reduce the risk of complications.

Types of Exercises for Diabetics

Exercise is a cornerstone of effective diabetes management, offering numerous benefits from improved blood sugar control to enhanced overall health. Engaging in a variety of physical activities can optimize these benefits, ensuring a comprehensive approach to fitness. Here, we explore the different types of exercises that are particularly beneficial for diabetics, including aerobic exercises, strength training, and flexibility and balance exercises.

AEROBIC EXERCISES

Aerobic exercises, also known as cardiovascular or endurance exercises, are activities that increase your heart rate and breathing. They are particularly effective in lowering blood glucose levels by improving the efficiency of insulin in your body and increasing glucose uptake by muscles. Here are some popular forms of aerobic exercises:

- **Walking**: Walking is a simple yet highly effective aerobic exercise. It requires no special equipment and can be done almost anywhere. Even a brisk 30-minute walk daily can significantly improve cardiovascular health and assist in maintaining stable blood sugar levels.

- **Running**: For those who prefer a more vigorous workout, running can be an excellent option. It burns more calories in a shorter period compared to walking and offers substantial cardiovascular benefits. However, it's important to build up gradually to avoid injuries, especially for those new to running.

- **Cycling**: Whether done on a stationary bike or outdoors, cycling is a low-impact exercise that is gentle on the joints. It strengthens the heart and improves lung capacity while helping to regulate blood sugar levels.

- **Swimming**: Swimming and water aerobics are superb exercises for diabetics, particularly for those with joint issues or mobility challenges. The buoyancy of water reduces stress on the joints while providing resistance that enhances muscle strength and cardiovascular fitness.

STRENGTH TRAINING

Strength training, also known as resistance training, involves exercises designed to improve muscle strength and endurance. This form of exercise is crucial for diabetics as it increases muscle mass, which in turn enhances glucose utilization and insulin sensitivity.

- **Weight Lifting**: Using free weights, weight machines, or resistance bands can effectively build muscle strength. Incorporating weight lifting into your routine can help manage blood sugar levels by promoting glucose uptake into muscles during and after exercise.

- **Bodyweight Exercises**: Exercises such as push-ups, squats, and lunges use your body weight as resistance. These exercises are convenient and can be done anywhere, making them an excellent option for building strength without the need for special equipment. They also improve balance and coordination, which is beneficial for overall mobility and injury prevention.

FLEXIBILITY AND BALANCE EXERCISES

Flexibility and balance exercises are essential for maintaining joint health, preventing injuries, and improving overall physical function. They are particularly beneficial for diabetics as they enhance movement efficiency and reduce the risk of falls.

- **Yoga**: Yoga combines physical postures, breathing exercises, and meditation. It enhances flexibility, balance, and strength while promoting relaxation and stress reduction. Regular yoga practice can help lower blood sugar levels, improve insulin sensitivity, and support mental well-being.

- **Pilates**: Pilates focuses on core strength, flexibility, and overall body conditioning. It involves a series of controlled movements that enhance muscle strength and stability, which can improve balance and posture.

- **Tai Chi**: This ancient Chinese practice involves slow, deliberate movements and deep breathing. Tai Chi improves flexibility, balance, and muscle strength, making it particularly suitable for older adults or those with joint issues. It also helps reduce stress, which can positively impact blood sugar levels.

STARTING FROM A SEDENTARY STATE

For those starting from a sedentary state, it's crucial not to fixate on achieving high levels of physical activity immediately. Instead, focus on gradually incorporating exercise into your routine. Beginning with just one hour of physical activity twice a week can be sufficient, provided that the effort is consistent and serious. This approach helps build a sustainable habit without overwhelming yourself. As your fitness improves, you can gradually increase the frequency and duration of your workouts.

Creating an Exercise Plan

Creating an effective exercise plan is crucial for managing diabetes and improving overall health. A well-structured plan should include setting realistic goals and personalizing activities based on individual needs and preferences. This ensures that the exercise regimen is not only effective but also sustainable and enjoyable.

SETTING REALISTIC GOALS

Setting realistic goals is the foundation of any successful exercise plan. Begin by assessing your current fitness level and health status. For many, starting small and gradually increasing the intensity and duration of exercise is key.

Realistic goals are specific, measurable, achievable, relevant, and time-bound (SMART). For example, instead of setting a vague goal like "I want to exercise more," a SMART goal would be "I will walk for 30 minutes, three times a week, for the next month." This approach makes goals clear and attainable, providing a sense of accomplishment and motivation to continue.

PERSONALIZING THE EXERCISE PLAN

Personalizing your exercise plan involves tailoring activities to fit your individual needs, preferences, and lifestyle. This customization ensures that the exercise regimen is enjoyable and sustainable, increasing the likelihood of long-term adherence.

1. **Assess Your Health and Fitness Level**: Start with a baseline assessment, considering factors such as your age, weight, current fitness level, and any existing health conditions. Consult your healthcare provider to identify any limitations or special considerations.

2. **Identify Your Preferences**: Choose activities you enjoy, as this increases the likelihood of sticking with the program. Whether it's walking, swimming, cycling, or yoga, selecting enjoyable exercises makes the routine feel less like a chore.

3. **Consider Your Schedule**: Integrate exercise into your daily routine in a way that fits your lifestyle. If you have a busy schedule, short, frequent sessions might be more manageable than longer workouts.

4. **Set Incremental Milestones**: Break down your main goal into smaller, manageable milestones. This allows you to track progress and make adjustments as needed.

5. **Plan for Variety**: Incorporate different types of exercises to work various muscle groups and prevent boredom. Combining aerobic exercises, strength training, and flexibility exercises ensures a well-rounded fitness routine.

EXAMPLE: PERSONALIZING AN EXERCISE PLAN

Let's consider an example of Jane, a 45-year-old woman with type 2 diabetes who wants to start incorporating physical activity into her routine. Jane has been mostly sedentary, but she's motivated to improve her health.

1. **Assess Health and Fitness Level**: Jane consults her doctor, who advises her to start with low-impact exercises due to her knee arthritis. Her doctor recommends starting slowly and gradually increasing intensity.

2. **Identify Preferences**: Jane enjoys being outdoors and finds walking relaxing. She also likes the idea of trying yoga for flexibility and stress relief.

3. **Consider Schedule**: Jane works full-time and has a busy family life. She decides that early mornings are the best time for her to exercise without interruptions.

4. **Set Incremental Milestones**: Jane sets a SMART goal to walk for 20 minutes every morning, five days a week, for the first month. She also plans to attend a beginner's yoga class once a week.

5. **Plan for Variety**: To keep things interesting, Jane decides to explore different walking routes in her neighborhood and park. After the first month, she plans to add a 10-minute strength training session twice a week using bodyweight exercises like squats and push-ups.

Jane's personalized exercise plan might look like this:

- **Weeks 1-4**:

  - Walk for 20 minutes every morning, Monday to Friday.

  - Attend a 1-hour beginner's yoga class on Saturday mornings.

- **Weeks 5-8**:

  - Increase walking to 30 minutes every morning, Monday to Friday.

  - Continue the 1-hour yoga class on Saturdays.

  - Add a 10-minute bodyweight strength training session on Tuesdays and Thursdays.

By setting realistic goals and personalizing her exercise plan, Jane can gradually build her fitness level, improve her blood sugar control, and enhance her overall well-being. This approach ensures that her exercise routine is enjoyable, manageable, and sustainable, leading to long-term health benefits.

Special Bonus: Your Custom Shopping List

Dear Reader,

As a valuable addition to your journey through "Diabetic Food Bible", I've prepared an exclusive shopping list tailored to complement the meal plans found within these pages. This carefully curated list aims to simplify your grocery shopping experience, ensuring you have all the right ingredients to prepare diabetic-friendly meals that are both nutritious and delicious.

How to Access Your Shopping List

You can easily access your personalized shopping list by scanning the QR code below with your smartphone. Alternatively, if you prefer, you can visit https://jgreenwayauthor.com/shopping-list to download the list directly to your device.

By using this shopping list, you'll save time at the grocery store and ensure that your kitchen is stocked with the right foods to support your dietary needs.

Thank you for trusting the "Diabetic Food Bible" as your guide. Here's to a healthier, happier you!

Warm regards,

Julia Greenway

Kitchen Conversion Table (US to Metric)

DRY MEASUREMENTS

TSP	TBSP	Cup	Fluid Oz	Grams/Pound
3 tsp	1 tbsp	1/16 C	1/2 oz	14 g
6 tsp	2 tbsp	1/8 C	1 oz	28 g
12 tsp	4 tbsp	1/4 C	2 oz	57 g
16 tsp	5tbsp + 1 tsp	1/3 C	2 2/3 oz	76 g
24 tsp	8 tbsp	1/2 C	4 oz	113 g
32 tsp	10 tbsp + 2 tsp	2/3 C	5 1/3 oz	151 g
36 tsp	12 tbsp	3/4 C	6 oz	170 g
48 tsp	16 tbsp	1 C	8 oz	227 g

LIQUID MEASUREMENTS

Measure	Fluid Oz	TBSP	TSP	Liters/Milliliters
1 gal	4 quarts	256 tbsp	768 tsp	3.8 liters
4 cups	1 quart	64 tbsp	192 tsp	0.95 liters
2 cups	1 pint	32 tbsp	96 tsp	473 ml
1 cup	8 oz	16 tbsp	48 tsp	237 ml
3/4 cup	6 oz	12 tbsp	36 tsp	177 ml
2/3 cup	5 1/3 oz	10 tbsp + 2 tsp	32 tsp	158 ml
1/2 cup	4 oz	8 tbsp	24 tsp	118 ml
1/3 cup	2 2/3 oz	5 tbsp + 1 tsp	16 tsp	79 ml
1/4 cup	2 oz	4 tbsp	12 tsp	59 ml
1/8 cup	1 oz	2 tbsp	6 tsp	30 ml
1/16 cup	½ oz	1 tbsp	3 tsp	15 ml

WEIGHT MEASUREMENT

Grams	Ounces
14 g	1/2 oz
28 g	1 oz
57 g	2 oz
85 g	3 oz
113 g	4 oz
141 g	5 oz
170 g	6 oz
198 g	7 oz
227 g	8 oz
255 g	9 oz
283 g	10 oz
312 g	11 oz
340 g	12 oz
369 g	13 oz
397 g	14 oz
425 g	15 oz
454 g	1 lb

Glossary of Terms

Antioxidants	Compounds that help neutralize free radicals in the body, potentially reducing the risk of chronic diseases.
Anti-Inflammatory Foods	Foods that reduce inflammation levels in the body, which can help mitigate insulin resistance.
Beta Cells	Cells in the pancreas that produce insulin.
Blood Glucose Monitoring	The regular testing of blood sugar levels to manage diabetes.
Carbohydrates	Macronutrients that are the primary source of energy for the body; categorized into simple and complex forms.
Cardiovascular Disease	A common complication of diabetes, involving the heart and blood vessels.
Cellular Insulin Sensitivity	The efficiency with which cells respond to insulin.
Chronic Inflammation	Long-term inflammation that can contribute to the development of diabetes.
Complex Carbohydrates	Carbohydrates that are broken down slowly by the body, helping to manage blood sugar levels.
Diabetes Management	Ongoing treatment and lifestyle adjustments to control diabetes symptoms and progression.
Dietary Fiber	A type of carbohydrate that aids in digestion and blood sugar control.
Fasting	Refraining from eating for a specified period, significant for metabolic health tests.
Fatty Acids	Components of fats essential for various body functions, including omega-3 and omega-6.
Folate	A B vitamin important for cell function and tissue growth, found in various foods including grains.
Gestational Diabetes	A type of diabetes that develops during pregnancy.
Glycemic Index (GI)	A scale that ranks carbohydrate-containing foods by their impact on blood glucose levels.
Glycemic Load (GL	A metric that considers the glycemic index in conjunction with the carbohydrate content per serving of food.
Glucose	A simple sugar that is an essential energy source for the body's cells.
Glucose Transporter Type 4 (GLUT4)	A protein that facilitates the transport of glucose across cell membranes.
Heart Disease	Diseases and conditions affecting the heart, often exacerbated by diabetes.
Hyperglycemia	Elevated blood sugar levels, commonly associated with diabetes.
Hypoglycemia	Low blood sugar levels, which can occur in people with diabetes.
Insulin	A hormone produced by the pancreas that regulates blood sugar levels.

Insulin Resistance	A condition where the body's cells do not respond properly to insulin.
Insulin Sensitivity	How sensitive the body's cells are to insulin, affecting how effectively the body can use glucose for energy.
Insulin Therapy	The use of insulin injections to control blood sugar levels in people with diabetes.
Ketoacidosis	A serious diabetes complication where the body produces excess blood acids (ketones).
Lean Proteins	High-quality proteins that contain relatively low amounts of fat.
Macronutrients	The nutrients required in large amounts that provide energy: carbohydrates, proteins, and fats.
Manganese	A trace mineral important for many bodily functions, including the metabolism of amino acids, cholesterol, glucose, and carbohydrates.
Magnesium	A mineral essential for many body processes, including regulating muscle and nerve function, blood sugar levels, and blood pressure.
Metabolic Health	The state of physical and chemical processes used by the body to convert or use energy.
Micronutrients	Essential vitamins and minerals needed in small amounts for proper body functioning.
Monounsaturated Fats (MUFAs)	A type of healthy fat found in various oils and foods that helps improve blood lipid profiles.
Nutritional Profile	The breakdown of nutrients (like vitamins, minerals, and macronutrients) in a food item.
Obesity	Excessive body fat accumulation, which significantly increases the risk of developing type 2 diabetes.
Omega-3 Fatty Acids	Essential fats the body can't make on its own; beneficial for heart health and found in high amounts in flaxseeds, walnuts, and fish.
Pancreas	An organ that produces insulin and other important enzymes and hormones for digestion.
Phosphorus	A mineral that plays an essential role in the formation of bones and teeth and helps the body make protein for the growth, maintenance, and repair of cells and tissues.
Polyunsaturated Fats (PUFAs)	Essential fats found in plant and fish oils that are necessary for cellular function and heart health.
Prediabetes	A condition where blood sugar levels are high, but not high enough to be classified as diabetes.
Proteins	Macronutrients that are essential for the growth and repair of body tissues.
Saturated Fats	Fats that can raise the level of cholesterol in the blood and increase the risk of heart disease.
Type 1 Diabetes	A form of diabetes where the body's immune system destroys insulin-producing cells.

Type 2 Diabetes   A prevalent form of diabetes characterized by insulin resistance and insulin production issues.

Unsaturated Fats   Fats that can help reduce the risk of heart disease and lower cholesterol levels.

Vegetable Intake   The consumption of vegetables, which is important for providing essential nutrients and fiber.

Visceral Fat   Body fat that is stored within the abdominal cavity and is associated with numerous health risks.

Vitamins and Minerals   Essential nutrients that perform hundreds of roles in the body, including healing wounds and bolstering your immune system.

Whole Grains   Grains that contain all essential parts of the seed; can help manage blood sugar levels and provide fiber.

Zinc   A mineral that helps the immune system fight off bacteria and viruses, also important for making proteins and DNA.

Index

Y

Z